HD
8066
F74

Fried, Albert
EXCEPT TO WALK FREE

DATE DUE

APR 23 1976			
APR 23 1976			
MAY 16 1978			
JUN 7 1978			
MAR 23 1984			
JUL 30 RCD			

SACRAMENTO CITY COLLEGE
3835 Freeport Blvd.
Sacramento, California 95822

DEMCO FRESNO

ALBERT FRIED is Professor of Political Science at Sarah Lawrence College. He is the editor of *Socialism in America: From the Shakers to the Third International—A Documentary History*; and co-editor, with Ronald Sanders, of *Socialist Thought: A Documentary History*.

Except to Walk Free

DOCUMENTS AND NOTES IN THE HISTORY
OF AMERICAN LABOR

Edited by Albert Fried

ANCHOR BOOKS
Anchor Press/Doubleday
Garden City, New York
1974

This anthology has been prepared especially for Anchor Books and has never before appeared in book form.

Library of Congress Cataloging in Publication Data
Fried, Albert, comp.
Except to walk free.
Bibliography: p. 321
1. Labor and laboring classes—United States—
History—Sources. 2. Trade-unions—United States—
History—Sources. I. Title.
HD8066.F74   331′.0973
ISBN 0-385-02947-0
LIBRARY OF CONGRESS CATALOG CARD NUMBER 73-13105

COPYRIGHT © 1974 BY ALBERT FRIED
ALL RIGHTS RESERVED
PRINTED IN THE UNITED STATES OF AMERICA
FIRST EDITION

To Walter Reuther
In Memoriam

What do you suppose will satisfy the soul,
except to walk free and own no superior?
                WALT WHITMAN, *Leaves of Grass*

Contents

INTRODUCTION Labor and Democracy   1

CHAPTER I Preindustrial America, 1829–64   15

1. WORKING MEN AND POLITICS, 1829   22
   New York *Free Enquirer*, October 7, 1829 (John R. Commons and others, *A Documentary History of American Industrial Society* [hereafter referred to as Commons], vol. V, pp. 93–94)

2. WORKING MEN AND AGRARIANISM, 1829   24
   Working Man's Advocate, October 31, 1829 (Commons, vol. V, pp. 149–51, 153)

3. WORKING MEN AND THE PUBLIC SCHOOLS, 1830   28
   Mechanics' Free Press, August 21, 1830 (Commons, vol. V, pp. 61–63)

4. FRANCES WRIGHT, 1830   30
   New York *Free Enquirer*, November 27, 1830 (Commons, vol. V, pp. 180–81)

5. GARRISON AND THE WORKING MEN, 1831   32
   (from the *Liberator*)

6. WORKING MEN AND WOMEN, 1834   38
   The Man, September 17, 1834 (Commons, vol. VI, pp. 217–19)

7. THE NATIONAL TRADES' UNION: 1, 1835   41
   National Trades' Union, October 10, 1835 (Commons, vol. VI, p. 259)

Contents

8. THE NATIONAL TRADES' UNIONS 2, 1836   43
   National Laborer, November 26, 1836 (Commons, vol. VI, pp. 294–97)

9. CONSPIRACY CASES, 1836   47
   New York *Courier and Enquirer*, May 31, 1836 (Commons, vol. IV, pp. 315–19)

10. COMMONWEALTH V. HUNT, 1842   52
    Mass. Reports, 4 Metcalf 45

11. COMMUNITARIANISM AND WORKING
    MEN: 1, 1843   55
    The Phalanx, November 4, 1843

12. COMMUNITARIANISM AND WORKING
    MEN: 2, 1845   57
    Working Man's Advocate, January 11, 1845 (Commons, vol. VIII, pp. 263–65)

13. VOTE YOURSELF A FARM, 1846   60
    True Workingman, January 24, 1846 (Commons, vol. VII, pp. 305–7)

14. FREDERICK DOUGLASS, 1853   63
    Frederick Douglass' Paper, March 4, 1853

15. SLAVEHOLDERS AND THE WORKING
    MEN, 1858   67
    Congressional Globe, U. S. Senate, 1858, p. 968

16. THE FIRST INTERNATIONAL ON THE
    CIVIL WAR, 1864   69
    (Letter drafted by Karl Marx, on behalf of the International Workingmen's Association, to President Lincoln)

CHAPTER II   Transition, 1864–86   73

1. WILLIAM H. SYLVIS, 1864   86
   J. C. Sylvis, ed., *The Life, Speeches, Labor, and*

Contents

Essays of William H. Sylvis (New York, 1872), pp. 99–102, 112–14, 116–17

2. THE NATIONAL LABOR UNION, 1867   92
Commons, vol. IX, pp. 173–77, 179–82

3. THE NEGRO NATIONAL LABOR UNION, 1869   97
The New Era, January 13, 1870

4. THE KNIGHTS OF LABOR: 1, 1869   99
Commons, vol. X, pp. 21–24

5. THE INTERNATIONAL WORKINGMEN'S ASSOCIATION, 1871   104
Commons, vol. IX, pp. 357–59

6. WENDELL PHILLIPS, 1872   107
Wendell Phillips, *Speeches, Lectures, and Letters* (Boston, 1892), pp. 169–70, 172–76

7. THE GREAT UPRISING, 1877   111
Joseph A. Dacus, *Annals of the Great Strikes of the United States*, pp. 88–90, 205–9, 214–16

8. THE KNIGHTS OF LABOR: 2, 1878   119
Terence V. Powderly, *Thirty Years of Labor* (Columbus, Ohio, 1889), pp. 243–44

9. THE ANARCHOCOMMUNISTS, 1883   122
Richard T. Ely, *The Labor Movement in America* (New York, 1886), pp. 360–63

10. HENRY GEORGE, 1885   127
Henry George, *Our Land and Land Policy* (New York, 1901), pp. 204–5, 215–16, 218

11. THE KNIGHTS OF LABOR: 3, 1886   131
Proceedings of the General Assembly of the Knights of Labor (Cleveland, 1886), p. 12

12. THE KNIGHTS OF LABOR: 4, 1886   133

Contents

Proceedings of the General Assembly of the Knights of Labor (Cleveland, 1886), p. 13

CHAPTER III   The A.F. of L., 1883–1929   137

1. THE A.F. OF L.: 1, 1883   150
   U. S. Senate Committee on Education and Labor, *Relations Between Labor and Capital*, 48th Congress, 1885, vol. I, pp. 374–75

2. THE A.F. OF L.: 2, 1886   153
   Report of Proceedings of the First Annual Convention of the American Federation of Labor (Columbus, Ohio, 1886), pp. 3–4

3. THE PULLMAN STRIKE: 1, 1894   157
   United States Strike Commission, *Report on the Chicago Strike of June–July, 1894* (Washington, 1895), pp. 87–88

4. THE PULLMAN STRIKE: 2, 1894   160
   United States Strike Commission, *Report on the Chicago Strike of June–July, 1894* (Washington, 1895), pp. 142–44

5. DANIEL DE LEON, 1896   163
   Daniel De Leon, *Reform or Revolution* (New York, 1896)

6. THE A.F. OF L. AND THE BLACKS, 1898   168
   American Federationist, vol. IV, pp. 269–71

7. GOMPERS AND THE SOCIALISTS: 1, 1924   171
   (From *American Federation of Labor History, Encyclopedia, Reference Book* [Washington, 1919–24])

8. EUGENE V. DEBS, 1910   174
   (From "Working Class Politics," *International Socialist Review*, November 1910)

Contents

9. GOMPERS AND THE SOCIALISTS: 2, 1914   178
   (From *The Double Edge of Labor's Sword* (New York, 1914), pp. 45–46, 50, 130–32)
10. THE I.W.W., 1915   184
    Commission on Industrial Relations, 64th Congress, 1st Session, Senate Document 415 (Washington, 1916), vol. XI, pp. 10575, 10582–83
11. THE LUDLOW MASSACRE, 1915   189
    Commission on Industrial Relations, 64th Congress, 1st Session, Senate Document 415 (Washington, 1916), vol. VIII, pp. 8004–6
12. THE YELLOW-DOG CONTRACT, 1916   194
    Hitchman Coal and Coke Co. v. Mitchell, 245 U.S. 240, 250
13. W. E. B. DUBOIS ON THE A.F. OF L., 1918   196
    The Crisis, March 1918
14. THE STEEL STRIKE, 1919   199
    Mary Heaton Vorse, *Men and Steel* (London, 1922), pp. 48–51, 60–61, 99–100, 152–53

CHAPTER IV   The C.I.O., 1935–41   209

1. THE WAGNER ACT: 1, 1935   220
   The National Labor Relations Act, 1935, 49 Stat. 449–50
2. THE C.I.O. INSURGENTS, 1935   222
   Report of Proceedings of the Fifty-fifth Annual Convention of the American Federation of Labor (Washington, 1935), pp. 523–24
3. THE CRAFT-UNION PRINCIPLE, 1935   225
   Report of Proceedings of the Fifty-fifth Annual Convention of the American Federation of Labor (Washington, 1935), pp. 553–56

Contents

4. AKRON: THE FIRST SIT-DOWN, 1936   229
   Ruth McKenney, *Industrial Valley* (New York, 1939), pp. 248–51, 257–58, 262–63, 267–68

5. THE GENERAL MOTORS SIT-DOWN: 1, 1937   239
   "Statement by General Motors Corporation," *N.A.M. Labor Relations Bulletin* (January 22, 1937), p. 8

6. THE GENERAL MOTORS SIT-DOWN: 2, 1937   241
   Mary Heaton Vorse, "New Life Begins for Auto Workers," *United Automobile Worker*, February 13, 1937

7. THE WAGNER ACT: 2, 1937   245
   National Labor Relations Board v. Jones and Laughlin Steel Corporation, 301 U.S. 1 (1937)

8. THE WAGNER ACT: 3, 1937   248
   Franklin D. Roosevelt, *Public Papers and Addresses* (New York, 1941), vol. VI, pp. 153–54

9. VIOLENCE AGAINST LABOR: 1, 1937–39   250
   U. S. Senate Committee on Education and Labor, *Violations of Free Speech and the Rights of Labor*, 75th Congress, 2nd Session, 1938, Senate Report 46, Part 3

10. VIOLENCE AGAINST LABOR: 2, 1937–39   252
    U. S. Senate Committee on Education and Labor, *Oppressive Labor Practices Act*, 76th Congress, 1st Session, Hearings, pp. 14, 16, 18, 26

11. A. PHILIP RANDOLPH'S CALL FOR A MARCH, 1941   257
    The Black Worker, May 1941

CHAPTER V   The New World of Labor, 1947–74   263

1. THE TAFT-HARTLEY ACT, 1947   276
   Public Law 101, 80th Congress

Contents

2. EXPULSION OF THE COMMUNISTS, 1949   279
   Congress of Industrial Organizations, Proceedings, Eleventh Constitutional Convention (Cleveland, 1949), pp. 240, 262–63, 267, 273, 304–6, 325

3. A.F.L.-C.I.O. CONSTITUTION, 1955   288
   Report of the First Constitutional Convention of the A.F.L.-C.I.O.

4. UNION RACKETEERING: 1, 1957   291
   Report of Proceedings of the Sixteenth Constitutional Convention of the United Automobile, Aircraft and Agricultural Implement Workers of America (Atlantic City, 1957), pp. 4–5

5. UNION RACKETEERING: 2, 1962   294
   U. S. Senate Committee on Government Operations, 87th Congress, 2nd Session, 1962, Report No. 1784, pp. 37–39

6. THE A.F.L.-C.I.O. AND BLACKS, 1962   298
   United States House Committee on Education and Labor, 87th Congress, 2nd Session, Part 2, *Equal Employment Opportunity*, pp. 850–51, 853–55

7. WALTER REUTHER VS. THE A.F.L.-C.I.O., 1967   302
   (From a letter to U.A.W. locals dated February 8, 1967, from Walter Reuther)

8. GRIGGS V. DUKE POWER, 1971
   401 U.S. 424   308

9. WORK IN AMERICA, 1972   311
   Report of a special task force to the Secretary of Health, Education and Welfare, pp. 13, 14, 28–29, 31, 32, 37, 92–93, 147

BIBLIOGRAPHY   321

INDEX   331

Preface

Several years ago, while teaching a course to a group of ironworkers, I looked in vain for an easily accessible, one-volume documented history of American labor. The few such histories that were available to us (see Bibliography) I thought too limited in scope and range. I wanted something more comprehensive, something that would do justice to the whole subject, beginning with the age of Jacksonian democracy, when American labor first announced itself to the world. I also decided that if I had the time and inclination I might even put together my own collection of documents and notes.

That tenuous decision, hardening into resolve, has at last eventuated in the book I am presenting here. In it I have attempted to bring to life the successive labor movements in America from the 1820s to the present—movements that mostly failed, but that, in failing, contributed to the emergence of trade unions as permanent institutions. The organization of workers, the establishment of unions—that is the dominant theme of the book.

Now, I realize full well that I could have done another kind of book, that I could have taken a different approach: I could have emphasized, say, the evolution of work habits from agriculture to handicrafts to industry,

Preface

thereby tracing the history of alienation; or I could have emphasized the problems—cultural and psychological as well as economic—that black and female and ethnic workers have suffered down through the years. These, I grant, are all valid enough and should be pursued in depth. But they should be grounded in what I assume is more fundamental understanding of working-class experience.

For regardless of what one may discover in the personal, sexual, and cultural lives of workers, the fact is that they freed themselves from the worst caprices of power only by organizing themselves—by uniting their separate wills and acting together as brothers and sisters. And to this day that fact has lost none of its force. The working poor, who continue to subsist on the edge of penury, will break the desperate cycle of their lives when they too have been unionized.

The union movement, whatever we think of it now, whatever our disappointments with it, has been the durable bond of solidarity between past and present, the essential datum in the history of American labor.

Many people have helped me, and for once I will forbear to mention their names. All, that is, but two whom I am privileged to call friends: Herbert Hill, whose long struggle in behalf of the insulted and injured is itself part of the history of our time; and B. J. Widick, who has fought for social justice for more than forty years and from whom I (like many others) have learned about labor and so much else besides.

Except to Walk Free

INTRODUCTION
Labor and Democracy

Labor and democracy: inseparable fates, inseparable histories. And nowhere have they been yoked together more closely than in the United States.

In the early-nineteenth century, American "working men"—the mechanics and artisans of the cities—stood in the forefront of the nascent democratic movement. Working men, above all others, insisted that democracy fulfill its promise of equality. In the 1820s and '30s they formed political parties and trade unions for the express purpose of claiming rights that belonged to them as citizens: the right to public schools for their children, the right to leisure and dignity and freedom from fear (the ten-hour day, the abolition of imprisonment for debt), the right to vote and participate actively in public affairs (even hold office), the right to associate freely and go out on strike. In securing these rights, working men significantly enlarged the possibilities of democracy.

Democracy was a broad-based movement affecting different people in different ways. The entrepreneurial class, for instance, fought the old aristocracy and its structure of privileges as fiercely as working men did. Entrepreneurs wanted to enlarge *their* possibilities—their right to enjoy the blessings of an open, competitive market, where talent, energy, virtue, and good luck counted most in the race for life. Inevitably, a conflict arose between those sometime allies. For it was in the interest of the entrepreneurial class to bring working men into the open market, where their labor could be bought competitively, subject to the same economic imperatives that governed all other commodities. But working men had a contrary interest: to preserve their autonomy as skilled craftsmen, their status as free-born Americans. They were determined not to join those who were compelled to obey the pitiless commands of the marketplace: the women and children of the New England factories, the destitute immigrants from Ireland, the "free" blacks condemned to unceasing poverty and degradation.

The entrepreneurial class, of course, proved triumphant. The burgeoning market economy, with its accompanying cycle of prosperity and depression, brushed aside every obstacle that working men could throw in its path. Parties, trade unions, co-operatives, agrarian and socialist nostrums —none of these enabled them to maintain the autonomy they had assumed was their birthright in the new democracy. The distance between the earlier promise of equality and the condition of their lives had grown irreparable.

The Civil War, though it destroyed the slavocracy in the name of free labor, also hastened the defeat of the working men. By stimulating industrialism, the war helped raise the entrepreneurial class to absolute supremacy. In the era of factories and mines and railroads, skilled craftsmen tried desperately to hold on to their vocation, their one lever of independence. To avoid the swelling ranks of the wage-earning proletariat, they again formed unions and political parties and co-operatives and sought easy credit or cheap land or restrictions on immigration. And once again every organization or movement they supported went under, every proposal they advanced (except the exclusion of Chinese) came to nought.

And so the filaments that bound labor to democracy began to disintegrate. Industrial violence became endemic after the depression of 1873. Strikes and lockouts and, often enough, pitched battles between workers and authorities became an integral part of the American way of life for decades—until well into the twentieth century. For most workers, in fact, industrial relations amounted to a continuous state of war in the Hobbesian sense of the term, peace being simply the absence of overt strife, the silent obedience to force.

It was in the tumultuous 1870s that American labor first encountered a revolutionary critique of the system. Marxists and anarchists, arriving with the new wave of German immigrants, preached that democracy in America was a delusion, a cover behind which capitalism reduced workers to wage slaves, and that their only recourse was to mobilize their collective strength as a class and prepare to seize power the moment the system broke down, as ineluctably it must.

But the revolutionary alternative drew scant support, even from the ranks of the unskilled, the chief victims of industrial capitalism. All but a few American workers still believed that they might redress their grievances by political means, still clung to the hope of personal independence outside the industrial machine, still thought that the issue was a moral one: the demonic forces of greed violating the natural harmony that obtained between the workers and farmers and small tradesmen who exploited no one's labor but their own.

That is why the American Federation of Labor, inauspiciously launched in 1886, turned out to be such a momentous event in the history of American democracy.

Except to Walk Free

The A.F. of L. established a basis, a strategy, under which workers could acquire a measure of freedom *within* the world that industrial capitalism had fashioned.

The important feature of the A.F. of L. was the attitude that underlay it. Its members implicitly acknowledged their class status. They assumed no natural or primordial harmony among independent producers, but a relentless struggle for available goods between those who owned their labor and skills and those who owned the means of production. The A.F. of L., in other words, bore witness to the validity of the revolutionary critique of capitalism, its leaders (who had grown up under Marxist tutelage) having transformed class consciousness into trade-union consciousness.

This meant that the class struggle had to be carried out on a more modest, more manageable scale. Whatever the future of society, whatever might happen to capitalism given its inherent contradictions, the workers of a particular trade—so the A.F. of L. announced at the outset—must organize unions for the sole purpose of gaining minimal advantages for themselves here and now: better pay and working conditions, shorter hours, seniority, and the like. Such unions, furthermore, must stay clear of political entanglements, their policy toward the state to be determined pragmatically, by whether it aids or injures their interests. The A.F. of L. professed only one ideology: to advance the material well-being of its members.

This it did with incredible success. In the thirty-seven years that Samuel Gompers was its president (1886–1924) the A.F. of L.'s membership rose from under two hundred thousand to about four million. This spectacular increase reflected its ability to make good its promise of securing more money and leisure and prestige for its rank and file. It also reflected something more fundamental. The col-

Labor and Democracy

lective-bargaining agreements that A.F. of L. unions won freed their members from the tyrannical power, the arbitrary will, of their employers; for the first time, due process, or the rule of law, was applied to the workplace. The A.F. of L. had brought about a visible extension of democracy.

But it was still a democracy for the few, the extension of a restricted privilege. The A.F. of L., after all, embraced a tight little aristocracy of the highly skilled, the better educated, the more reputable ethnic pedigrees (preponderantly German, Irish, and native-born). Unlike the artisans and craftsmen who had fought a losing campaign against industry in times past, these workers possessed skills—as machinists, carpenters, construction workers, teamsters, *et al.*—that industry required, and they prospered and grew as industry prospered and grew, as America became by the 1890s the pre-eminent economic power in the world.

The extraordinary success of the A.F. of L. had the effect of sharply dividing the working class; the A.F. of L. was a class within a class—or, rather, above it. Unskilled and semiskilled workers, many of them recently arrived from eastern and southern Europe, found themselves completely at the mercy of large industry, mere hands or commodities, as dispensable as the goods they produced. Organizing such a disparate mass into unions would have been a prodigious task under any circumstances. The presence of the A.F. of L. made it that much more difficult. For to bring the factory workers en masse into A.F. of L. unions would have created jurisdictional problems, jeopardizing the hard-won gains made by the crafts and their established leadership. There were, moreover, ethnic and racial grounds for not broadening the union base: the A.F. of L. rank and file scarcely relished the prospect of

Except to Walk Free

fraternizing with Poles, Jews, Italians, blacks, and other such alien or pariah groups. The A.F. of L., then, was more than indifferent to the unionization of industrial workers; it went out of its way to oppose it.

Spokesmen for the unskilled and unorganized attacked the A.F. of L. for betraying not only the working class as a whole but even its particular constituency, even the crafts it represented. Small, elite unions, each separate and distinct, they argued, could not in the long run stand up to huge, trustified industries, to enormous concentrations of economic power. Only industrial unions, encompassing every trade or craft within their purview, could hope to do so.

But it was little more than a hope. Business enterprise, aided by the government, easily put down the major strikes of the 1890s—strikes from which the A.F. of L. remained conspicuously aloof. These unhappy experiences led the apostles of industrial unionism (typified by Eugene V. Debs) to conclude that workers must also organize to take over the government, that only through politics could industrial unionism succeed. This was what the socialists had been saying all along. Thus the two movements, industrial unionism and socialism, were by the turn of the century united in common antipathy to the capitalist system and the A.F. of L.

But there were different socialisms corresponding to different conceptions of industrial unionism. Moderate socialists, represented by the fast-rising Socialist Party of America, believed that the assault against capitalism should be conducted on two fronts simultaneously: by recruiting workers into the Socialist Party, getting them to vote for its local and national candidates (chief among them Debs, who between 1900 and 1920 ran for the presidency in every election but one), and by building up the socialist-led unions *within* the A.F. of L. Eventually—such was the Socialist Party strategy—the workers' armies on both fronts would converge in a grand march of victory.

Revolutionary socialists denied that anyone truly favoring industrial unionism could operate within the system, least of all within the reactionary A.F. of L. Here, however, the revolutionists parted ways: One small group, the Industrial Workers of the World, advocated industrial unionism pure and simple, the unions themselves replacing the state and the legal structure; the other small group, the Socialist Labor Party, also advocated a government of, by, and for industrial unions, but only *after* the Party had captured the state and established the co-operative commonwealth. To an outsider, the distinctions between the I.W.W. and the S.L.P. might seem trivial; they were serious enough to make the I.W.W. and the S.L.P. bitter rivals.

The ferment of conflict before World War I gave American workers—whatever their condition, status, or ideology—reason to hope that their fortunes would change for the better. For if the A.F. of L. was burgeoning, so, on the other hand, were the Socialist Party and the socialist unions. The I.W.W., though minuscule, was causing a stir and quickening the spirit of radicals wherever it appeared. And even the progressive movement, middle class though it was in constituency and aims, was professing keen sympathy for labor and crystallizing that sympathy into reform legislation across the country. America was shifting perceptibly to the left.

This period of ferment and hope suddenly came to a close. The First World War and the Bolshevik Revolution conspired to devastate the American left. By the early 1920s little remained of the once flourishing socialist movement—only a band of hostile sects. The A.F. of L., meanwhile, was more prosperous and conservative than ever. Samuel Gompers had prevailed over his long-time adversaries.

But by the time Gompers died, in 1924, the A.F. of L. had begun its own precipitous decline—this in the face of an extraordinary economic upturn. The main beneficiaries of the boom were those new industries—auto, rubber, electrical, chemical, telephone, etc.—which sedulously maintained "open shops": i.e., excluded unions. Even the few industrial unions within the A.F. of L. (coal mining and the garment trades) shrank to a vestige of their former selves. So that what had started out as a defeat for the left had turned into a rout of labor in general.

This pointed up a lesson often repeated in the past, namely that trade unionism is historically borne along by —conversely, that it tends to stagnate in the absence of— broad movements of social reform. There is no more convincing example of this lesson than the A.F. of L. itself. It owed everything, its birth, its development, its respectability, to the various radicalisms of its time.

Not that the important A.F. of L. unions of the 1920s were especially concerned about the wreckage all around them. They at least were secure in their rights and prerogatives. They had no quarrel with the system. In fact, they never felt so conciliatory toward it, so inclined to uphold it against its critics on the left.

For labor in general, however, the prospects were grim. Industry was expanding in mighty leaps, adding immeasurably to the power of the new, determinedly anti-union corporate elites. The middle class was embracing the gospel of wealth as though its salvation depended on it. Not since the days of the robber barons (when there were far fewer workers, when America was still a land of farmers)

Labor and Democracy

was the country and its politics so conservative in outlook. It seemed that only an upheaval of seismic magnitude —a miracle—could rescue the working class from its malaise.

That upheaval did come, of course, in the form of the Great Depression, which overnight forced the economic machine to a halt, leaving some 16 million workers jobless and destitute. But the Great Depression was able to achieve—so enormous was its impact on the country—what all the radical agitation and parties and strikes of decades past could not: It brought industrial unionism to the United States.

The proposition might be worded another way: *Only* an upheaval of such magnitude could have brought it to America. How else could a pro-labor government such as the New Deal (compared, that is, to previous governments) have taken power and put across legislation that was indispensable to the creation of unions? How else could the left have suddenly sprung to life, *ab ovo*, sending thousands of young proselytizers of every faith—Communist, socialist, Trotskyist, *et al.*—into the field to help organize the unorganized and provide the cadres of the new unions? How else would the workers themselves have found the confidence and energy to engage in such a sustained battle, such a multitude of strikes, among them the most ferocious ever fought in this country? How else would giant industry have yielded to something it had hitherto anathematized as irremediably evil, a lethal threat to the free-enterprise system and all its works? The upheaval had wrought a revolution.

And like most revolutions it was accomplished in a few swift strokes. Within two years, between 1935 and 1937, the Committee for Industrial Organization (later Congress of Industrial Organizations) had organized the

Except to Walk Free

major mass-production industries or had laid the groundwork for their future organization. And by the end of the decade, the C.I.O., now five million strong, had planted its roots deep in the soil of American life.

It was also a revolution full of ironies. The man most responsible for carrying it off, John L. Lewis, head of the United Mine Workers, was the man farthest removed from the radical or revolutionary traditions of industrial unionism. Few leaders of the A.F. of L. were more conservative in economic and political philosophy than he. Yet he became the guiding force behind the C.I.O., throwing into the struggle against big business and the A.F. of L. the resources of his powerful union and his own remarkable talents as a public figure and negotiator. Setting aside ancient animosities, Lewis welcomed into the fold anyone, regardless of ideology, who cared to join up for the duration. Revolutionaries accepted Lewis's warm embrace in the belief that they would use him for their ends. But the C.I.O. was built to his specifications, not theirs. Industrial unionism came to America under conservative auspices.

The final irony was the C.I.O.'s effect on the size and character of the A.F. of L. The success of the industrial-union campaign, the appearance on the landscape of very large and militant labor organizations, made the A.F. of L. all at once seem not unattractive to businessmen. For the choice was no longer between open and union shops, but between the A.F. of L. and the C.I.O., and unless workers could be brought into the former they would certainly join the latter. So the late 1930s, and especially the war years, witnessed a spectacular increase in the A.F. of L., a doubling of its membership (from three and a half million to seven), a reassertion of its hegemony over organized labor. And this expansion—adding to the irony—tended to

Labor and Democracy

bring more and more disparate trades into one big union (e.g., the teamsters) thus introducing, through the back door, the industrial principle into the citadel of the craft empire. The A.F. of L., however, assimilated this principle to its needs as effortlessly as it had every other.

Since World War II, a new epoch has opened up in the history of American labor. Trade unionism has come into its own. It has taken its place as an impregnable institution, growing steadily, reaping considerable benefits for its members in a society of proliferating affluence, a society more or less free of the cyclical hazards that once bedeviled it.[1] And despite the transformation of the economy from one based overwhelmingly on the production of goods to one based increasingly—if not predominantly—on the production of services, organized labor now represents a quarter of the total work force, some 21 million people out of 85 million. This has been no minor accomplishment.

Nor has the trade-union movement ever been so powerful as today. No labor leader has been so eagerly sought out by Presidents as George Meany, head of the A.F.L.-C.I.O. since its founding, in 1955. Even conservative politicians and retrograde capitalists have ceased to call into question the legitimacy of unions. That question has been settled.

According to the conventional view, unions form an essential component in the American pluralistic system. They constitute an interest group able now to countervail the power of big business, thereby restoring or keeping faith with the traditional separation of powers on

[1] There have been a handful of downturns since the War: 1946–47, 1953–54, 1955–56, 1958–59, 1970–71, 1973–74. But these have been notably brief and mild (unemployment never rising above 7½ per cent) compared to the traumas of the past.

Except to Walk Free

which American liberty ultimately rests. Unions, in short, have broken the stranglehold that the trusts and the oligopolies had once held in the United States. Democracy owes them a profound debt of gratitude. Their triumph has been the nation's.

This conventional view—the standard "pluralistic model" that social scientists are fond of invoking—is valid enough as far as it goes. The trouble with it is that it defines labor's role in neutral or even negative terms. All it expects of unions is that they survive as institutions so that they may limit the excesses of other institutions (their excesses being limited in turn). The pluralistic model celebrates stability and equilibrium—i.e., the status quo—and does not concern itself with either the internal structure of the unions or their social values.

The pluralistic model, in other words, conforms closely to organized labor's image of itself. To persevere as an institution appears to be the abiding purpose of the A.F.L.-C.I.O. and its affiliate unions; most of them, at any rate. Unions have become more and more bureaucratic, the better to deal with their counterparts in big business and government, the better also to deal with the complexities of their own organization. And with bureaucracy has come hierarchy, the perpetuation of oligarchic rule—the absence, in a word, of democratic procedures. It is the old A.F. of L. redivivus.

Organized labor asks little of the world at large beyond the satisfaction of its own demands, narrowly conceived. Unions in general have been content to play the neutral or negative role that the pluralistic model assigns them. Their major spokesmen, beginning with venerable George Meany, have opposed the various insurgencies of recent times: civil rights (as it relates to jobs, seniority, etc.),

Labor and Democracy

women's rights,[2] environmentalism, the mass uprising against the Vietnam holocaust. The truth is, no institution other than the Pentagon itself has waged the Cold War more implacably, has justified the ways of the military-industrial complex more dutifully, than the A.F.L.-C.I.O. under George Meany.

Not all of organized labor has been this ossified. The second-largest union in the country, the United Auto Workers, has come to represent an alternative. Despite its mammoth size (nearly a million and a half members), the U.A.W. has practiced a relatively high degree of democracy in the selection of its officers, in the opportunities it provides its rank and file for active involvement in union affairs. It has attempted to enlarge the social horizons of its members, to raise their consciousness, as it were. It has retained a minimal sense of solidarity with the poor and disenfranchised of America. It has kept alive the spirit of its own insurgent youth.

The point here is not to idealize any particular union (there being much to criticize even in the best of them). It is to discern possibilities beyond those exhausted by the conventional view, by indexes that register membership growth, pay raises, and the like, important as they are. Is organized labor only a neutral or negative part of American democracy? At most a countervailing power, one among several competing interest groups? Or is it capable of assuming another role, one that calls forth more exalted, more creative and far-reaching affirmations of democracy?

To the extent that the United States remains a coun-

[2] For years the A.F.L.-C.I.O. assiduously lobbied against the Equal Rights Amendment, which promises to guarantee equal protection of the laws to women. In its 1973 convention, however, the A.F.L.-C.I.O. made a *volte-face* and now supports ratification.

try where defense expenditures can amount to a third of the federal budget, over 80 billion dollars a year; where stupendous wealth and power coexists with abysmal poverty and despair (which is not to minimize the size and strength of the middle class); where impersonal bureaucracies grow more remote and alexandrian and dysfunctional; where institutions persist in excluding racial and ethnic minorities and women, this in the teeth of all the laws that have been passed, the administrative agencies that have been created, the court decisions that have been handed down; where unceasing rapacity, pillage, waste, and neglect have rendered much of the environment uninhabitable; where workers, white collar as well as blue, feel more and more discontented with the mindless and dehumanizing labor they are required to perform—to the extent that the United States remains such a country, the future of its democracy is gravely problematic.

What should organized labor do? It would be foolish and arrogant to prescribe a solution here. One can at least hope that labor will bestir itself and join—perhaps lead— a sweeping social-reform movement; that it will identify with the weak, the disinherited, the unorganized; that it will deal with the malaise in its own ranks, with its own departure from democratic standards; that it will strive (as B. J. Widick and Irving Howe once suggested) to unite the traditional polarities of American trade unionism: the idealism that the I.W.W. embodied—the idealism that binds together all who live by their labor—and the realism, the will to endure, that the A.F. of L. always exemplified. Can they ever be united? The health of American democracy will depend on it.

I
Preindustrial America
1829-64

In May 1830 a Newark, New Jersey, newspaper wrote: "From Maine to Georgia, within a few months past, we discern symptoms of a revolution which will be second to none save that of '76."

The paper was referring to the sudden emergence ("a few months past" being only a slight exaggeration) of self-styled "Working Men's" parties in cities and towns across the country. Nothing like it had ever happened before in the United States. Here were working people organizing as a political bloc, drawing up manifestoes and lists of demands, voting for—and in some instances electing—their own candidates for state and local offices. As far back as early colonial days there had been workers' organizations, even strikes, but these had been sporadic, isolated, strictly limited in purpose. The working men's parties of 1829-30 constituted a movement, an organized force, capable of producing, for some at any rate, "symptoms of a revolution."

In fact, the working men's parties were seeking only to extend and deepen a revolution that was already well under way. During the previous decade Americans had risen up in militant affirmation of their equal rights and had deposed the established elites—the well-born, the privi-

Except to Walk Free

leged few—from their seats of power at every level of government. The cataract of reform unloosed by political democracy had swept everything before it.

For working people, however, political democracy in itself was insufficient. What good, after all, was the right to vote or the opportunity to hold office or the rhetoric of democracy if one still had to work from dawn to dusk six days a week? if one could be imprisoned indefinitely for incurring the slightest debt or failing to show up for militia duty? if one could not afford to send his children to school, thereby condemning them to a life of drudgery and servitude? if banks served only the rich or favored only insiders? if one had no redress when employers or contractors defaulted on payment for work performed? How, working men wanted to know, could they be active, virtuous citizens of a democracy unless they enjoyed minimal economic freedoms, including the leisure to reflect on, and participate in, public affairs?

Hence their insistent demands for a ten-hour day, abolition of imprisonment for debt and of mandatory militia service, free universal education, dissolution of banking (and other) monopolies, and a "mechanics' lien" law. Hence their spontaneous upsurge across the political landscape of America.

From their inception, the working men's parties attracted the support of radicals—the intellectual movers and shakers of the time—who regarded the cause of working people as the cause of democracy itself, who defined justice in broadly egalitarian terms, no social system being just, in their view, that deprived men of any part of the fruit of their labor and kept them enthralled in ignorance and superstition. And marching in the advance guard of these radicals was the New York City Working Men's Party, its ranks filled with such heretics as Frances

Preindustrial America

("Fanny") Wright and Robert Dale Owen (son of Robert Owen), who had been closely connected with New Harmony and other communitarian experiments and who now advocated the creation of state-financed, community-run public schools; also the likes of Robert Skidmore and George Evans, leaders of the extreme agrarian faction, uncompromising apostles of Jefferson and Paine and Godwin, who argued that since the earth belonged "in usufruct to the living" the state should expropriate and redistribute the land in precisely equal lots every generation or so. The New York City Working Men's Party carried the logic of democracy to its furthest possibility.

But democracy also demonstrated that it could devour even its most radical offspring. Any group with a following, whatever its ideology, found itself eagerly courted by politicians on the make. Democrats and Whigs (i.e., Jacksonians and anti-Jacksonians) rapidly assimilated the working men's parties and adopted, in turn, most of the reforms they had been plumping for. By 1832, within three years of their emergence, they had disappeared entirely from view.

The working men's *movement*, however, did not disappear. It only assumed a different persona. No longer did working men join their own local parties. They formed associations or unions in their particular trades. These unions amounted to closed shops, for they alone decided who could or could not work and what kind of collective action should be taken in the event of opposition from the merchants or master craftsmen who employed them. Within a remarkably short period, between 1833 and 1837, the major trades—scores of them, from biscuit making to weaving—were everywhere organized. And they were organized into more and more comprehensive units. There grew up overnight an elaborate network of "city centrals" and regional federations of such unions and, at the summit, a "National Trades' Union," which claimed to embrace some three hundred thousand workers, an astonishingly large number (even allowing for exaggeration), given the fact that fewer than a million Americans were engaged in non-agricultural production at the time.

It was fear of the entrepreneurial class—the merchant capitalists and the shop masters—that brought about the spectacular rise of trade unions in the 1830s. Entrepreneurs were men who bought and sold goods in an expanding, competitive market or money economy. Their interest, if not their survival, compelled them to seek out the cheapest possible sources of labor; in other words, to make skilled craftsmen as subject to the imperatives of the open market as they were. Skilled craftsmen saw this as an attempt to reduce them to the staus of mere laborers, like the women and children who toiled in the factories of New England. The establishment of unions was their way of preserving their autonomy, their vested rights.

It was a struggle the working men were bound to lose. They were fighting a rear-guard action (though neither they nor the entrepreneurs were aware of it then). The power of the market was, of course, irresistible. Every turnpike and canal and railroad that was laid, every new machine that was introduced, every new factory that was built (though these were still pretty much confined to a handful of places in Massachusetts and Rhode Island), every turn in the cycle of boom and bust, strengthened the hand of the entrepreneurial class—those among it who survived the grueling competitive race. The history of these working men in the first half of the nineteenth century is a melancholy one; less melancholy, to be sure, than the history of unskilled labor—largely women and

Preindustrial America

children and blacks. But American democracy was never intended to benefit *them*.

Entrepreneurs struck back at the unions by invoking the conspiracy laws against them. These laws, which had come down from medieval England hoary with age and creaking with disuse, were as vague and ill-defined as the term conspiracy itself. According to custom it was unnecessary to prove the illegality of the *object* that men "conspired" to accomplish; it was only necessary to prove that they had come together—presumably to act in restraint of trade or overthrow the government. A trade union was, therefore, a conspiracy by definition. And it was a dangerous one if it *behaved* as a union; that is, if its members dared go out on strike. To strike was to run the risk of going to jail or paying a heavy fine.[1]

What effect, if any, the numerous conspiracy trials had on the union movement will never be known, because the movement went under in the great economic collapse of 1837, leaving hardly a trace behind. The city centrals, the regional federations, the National Trades' Union—all were completely devastated. For the first time, Americans had to confront significant unemployment and urban poverty, hitherto thought to be exclusively European phenomena, quite alien to these shores. The working men, once proud and defiant, were laid low, humbled, content to hire themselves out at any price to whoever would buy their labor power.

Nor did the working men's movement ever fully recover from the shock, even after economic conditions improved in the 1840s. Trade unions returned, but they were much fewer in number and far less assertive than before.

---

[1] But thanks in part to the celebrated *Commonwealth* v. *Hunt* decision of 1842, unions ceased eventually to be regarded as conspiracies. See Document 10 below.

Except to Walk Free

The entrepreneurial class was able more and more to bypass the established trades and recruit its own labor—a task made all the simpler by the enormous influx of immigrants during the 1840s and '50s, most of them Irish, nearly all of them destitute and unskilled.[2] The failure of working men to unionize corresponded to the steady decline in their living standards. One example will suffice: In 1837, iron-boilers (who were highly skilled mechanics) made seven dollars a ton; in 1858, with no change in the rate of productivity, and in the face of higher costs, they were making three to four dollars a ton. The condition of the iron-boilers may help explain why the term "wage slavery" entered the vocabulary of the time.

And the unhappy condition of working men in general may also explain why so many of them got caught up in one or another of the reform ideologies—utopianism, agrarianism ("Vote Yourself a Farm"), co-operativism, religious revivalism, etc.—that sprouted so luxuriantly in the hothouse climate of the 1840s. These working men had concluded that only the reconstruction of society at large could guarantee what they sought above all: their autonomy as craftsmen and their freedom from the vicissitudes of the market, the rapacity of entrepreneurs, the invincible laws of "progress." They wanted to return to the older, more settled life habits of their forebears, to the day when—so it seemed in the glow of retrospect—the satanic forces of greed and selfishness were strictly circumscribed and harshly dealt with.

By the 1850s, at any rate, the reform impulse had given way to the overwhelming issue of slavery. And on this issue working men scarcely distinguished themselves. It would be safe to say that working men tended to dislike

[2] Between 1841 and 1861 the immigrant population increased about sixfold over the previous twenty years.

abolitionists at least as much as they did the southern slaveholders. Working men had never felt comfortable with the abolitionists, who, they maintained, were more concerned about the chattel slaves in the distant South than the wage slaves suffering under their very noses. And while working men abhorred slavery they feared the consequences of emancipation. They feared the competition that might arise from the presence of large numbers of free blacks in their midst—these on top of the Irish who were streaming in by the boatload.

These fears were acute not simply because blacks represented a lower economic class. Working men perceived blacks as the symbols of the degradation and oppression that, perhaps, awaited them too—as bearers of a permanent, irremediable taint of inferiority. White working men may not have been more racist than other whites. But, fearing their own inferiority and homelessness, they invested their racism with a particular edge, a particular vehemence.

Hence their resentment, equally, of the South, which was seeking to spread slavery across the continent, and of the abolitionists, who were seeking to destroy it and, implicitly, bring about the diffusion of the black population. Working men would have preferred to keep slavery intact within its borders while abominating it as a moral and legal wrong. But this position, after all, was also Lincoln's and the Republican Party's from 1854 to 1861, when the Civil War swept slavery away in a sea of blood.

1. WORKING MEN AND POLITICS*

1829

> Philadelphia working men chose delegates in
> 1829 to determine which candidates for the state
> legislature they should support in the upcoming
> election. Below is the letter the delegates sent
> each of the candidates.

Sir: The Delegates of the Working Men for the city, having placed your name in the list of fourteen, (from which seven will be chosen) as a candidate for the State Legislature; they are desirous (through the medium of the undersigned committee) to obtain your views in relation to the following subjects:

First. An equal and general system of Education.

Second. The banking system, and all other exclusive monopolies, considered with regard to the good or ill effects produced upon the productive classes by their operations.

Third. Lotteries, whether a total abolishment of them is not essential to the moral as well as pecuniary interest of society. Upon the important subject of Education we wish most distinctly to understand whether you do, or do not consider it essential to the welfare of the rising generation, "That an open school and competent teachers for every child in the state, from the lowest branch of an infant school to the lecture rooms of practical science,

---

* New York *Free Enquirer*, October 7, 1829 (John R. Commons and others, *A Documentary History of American Industrial Society* [hereafter referred to as Commons], vol. V, pp. 93–94).

should be established, and those who superintend them to be chosen by the people."

Our object in soliciting your views, sir, upon these several important points, is to enable us in the discharge of our duty, as delegates, to select such men for the Legislature, as are willing as well as competent, to legislate upon subjects which the Working Men of the city consider of the greatest importance, not only to themselves but the community at large. If your views should be in accordance with the interests of those we have the honor to represent, we request you to allow us to place your name on our Ticket.

2. WORKING MEN AND AGRARIANISM*

1829

The "Committee of Fifty" constituted the agrarian wing of the New York City Working Men's Party. The statement and resolutions it drew up closely followed the scheme presented by its leader, Thomas Skidmore, in his tract The Rights of Man to Property.

... Your committee, therefore, feel that all human society, our own as well as every other, is constructed radically wrong; that in the first foundation of government in this state the division of the soil should have been equal, at least, among families; and that provision should have been made (if property must descend in a family line) that it should descend in an equal manner, instead of having been placed at the disposal of the caprice of testators. They even go farther, and say, as their opinion, that inasmuch as the people resident on the soil, at the first formation of our government, had equal right thereto, as individuals, not as members of families, so also had their immediate successors the same right. But this has never been accorded to them; nay, even the families themselves of the first settlers, as we have seen, had nothing of equality existing between them; and, as a certain and natural result, we see thousands of our people of the present day in deep distress and poverty, dependent for their daily subsistence upon a few among us whom

* *Working Man's Advocate*, October 31, 1829 (Commons, vol. V, pp. 149-51, 153).

the unnatural operation of our own free and republican institutions, as we are pleased to call them, has thus arbitrarily and barbarously made enormously rich.

But though, as your committee believe, it is to this unnatural and unequal organization of society that we are to look for the prime source of all our oppressions; of that which places over us task masters, with power to require unreasonable toil; with power to withhold an adequate recompense; with power to deny employment altogether; and thus inflict upon us untold suffering; still your committee are sensible that this fountain of your distresses is not to be dried up but by a revolution; a civil revolution, it is true, since three hundred thousand freemen in this state have the power, through their votes at the ballot boxes, to bring it about, without resorting, as most other countries must do, to the use of the bayonet.

But although your committee are sensible that, until a revolution take place, such as shall leave behind it no trace of that government which has denied to every human being an equal amount of property on arriving at the age of maturity, and previous thereto, equal food, clothing, and instruction at the public expense, nothing can save the great mass of the community from the evils under which they now suffer; still they are also sensible, approaching as we are the eve of one of our annual elections, that there is an opportunity offered us of abating, of assuaging, of preventing the aggravation of our calamities, by resorting to the polls, and there electing, if we can, men who, from their own sufferings, know how to feel for ours, and who, from consanguinity of feeling, will be disposed to do all they can to afford a remedy. . . .

Resolved, that hereditary transmission of wealth on the one hand, and poverty on the other, has brought down to the present generation all the evils of the feudal system,

Except to Walk Free

and that this, in our opinion, is the prime source of all our calamities.

RESOLVED, that these calamities have been greatly aggravated and increased by a legislation which has employed all its energy to create and sustain exclusive privileges; and that among the objects of such privileges, banking institutions stand most conspicuous.

RESOLVED, that these institutions, as it regards our own state, stand constantly indebted to the public, according to the best of our information, in the sum of thirty or thirty-five millions of dollars.

RESOLVED, if they are to be suffered to remain among us, that they ought no less to pay interest on the debt they owe to the community, than that the community itself should pay interest on any debt it may owe them. . . .

RESOLVED, that, so far as it goes, it is a connection of church with state; since the principle which would remit to a priest the taxes on his property, thus making a gift to him from the public treasury of that amount, might with equal propriety be extended to the payment of his annual salary.

RESOLVED, in the opinion of this meeting, that not less than three or four hundred thousand dollars, are annually plundered from the useful and industrious classes of our citizens, for the want of a lien law on buildings; and that this is a full and sufficient reason why it ought to be granted.

RESOLVED, as an insurmountable reason in favor of a lien law, if there were no other, that it ought to be passed; as with it, the poor and industrious mechanic and laborer can have no power to injure the rich; but without it, the rich may, as they do, plunder the poor of their earnings without restraint.

Preindustrial America

RESOLVED, that past experience teaches, that we have nothing to hope from the aristocratic orders of society; and that our only course to pursue is, to send men of our own description, if we can, to the legislature at Albany.

3. WORKING MEN AND THE PUBLIC SCHOOLS*

1830

> The reason working men everywhere gave for demanding a free public school system is set forth in this statement by a group of Philadelphia "operatives."

In looking over one of your late numbers, I was rejoiced to find that some friend has noticed the sufferings of people employed in our manufactories; particularly in that of cotton. It is a well known fact, that the principal part of the helps in cotton factories consist of boys and girls, we may safely say from six to seventeen years of age, and are confined to steady employment during the longest days in the year, from daylight until dark, allowing, at the outside, one hour and a half per day. In consequence of this close confinement, it renders it entirely impossible for the parents of such children to obtain for them any education or knowledge, save that of working that machine, which they are compelled to work, and that too with a small sum, that is hardly sufficient to support nature, while they on the other hand are rolling in wealth, of[f] the vitals of these poor children every day. We noticed the observation of our Pawtucket friend in your number of June 19th, 1830, lamenting the grievances of the children employed in those factories. We think his

* *Mechanics' Free Press*, August 21, 1830 (Commons, vol. V, pp. 61–63).

Preindustrial America

observations very correct, with regard to their being brought up as ignorant as Arabs of the Desert; for we are confident that not more than one-sixth of the boys and girls employed in such factories are capable of reading or writing their own name. We have known many instances where parents who are capable of giving their children a trifling education one at a time, deprived of that opportunity by their employer's threats, that if they did take one child from their employ, (a short time for school,) such family must leave the employment—and we have even known these threats put in execution. Now as our friend observes, we may establish schools and academies, and devise every means for the instruction of youth in vain, unless we also give time for application; we have heard it remarked to some employers, that it would be commendable to congress to shorten the hours of labour in factories; the reply was: it would be an infringement on the rights of the people. We know the average number of hands employed by one manufacturer to be, at the lowest estimate, fifty men, women and children. Now the query is: whether this individual, or this number employed by him, is the people.

It is not our intention at present, to undertake, a thorough discussion of this interesting subject, but rather to give some hints on the subject, which, we hope, may attract the notice of your readers, and be the means of arousing some abler pen to write on the matter; for we think it is high time the public should begin to notice the evil that it begets. We see the evil that follows the system of long labor much better than we can express it; but we hope our weak endeavors may not prove ineffectual. We must acknowledge our inability prevents us from expressing our sentiment fluently, at present, but we hope to appear again in a more correct manner.

4. FRANCES WRIGHT*

1830

Frances Wright had been an outspoken advocate of human rights since her youth in England. She had been friendly with philosophical radicals such as Bentham and James Mill and liberal statesmen such as LaFayette (whom she accompanied on a tour of the United States). In 1826 she fell in with Robert Owen's New Harmony experiment. Then she launched one of her own, in Nashoba, Tennessee, dedicated to the emancipation of slaves. Nashoba, like New Harmony, failed, and she came to New York, where (with Robert Dale Owen) she led one of the factions of the Working Men's Party. She was an electrifying speaker and writer, and a string of epithets (e.g., the "High Priestess of Beelzebub") were attached to her name. Following is part of an article she wrote, "The People at War," for a working men's newspaper in 1830.

What distinguishes the present from every other struggle in which the human race has been engaged, is, that the present is, evidently, openly and acknowledgedly, a war of class, and that this war is universal. It is no longer nation pitched against nation for the good pleasure and sport of Kings and great Captains, nor sect cutting the throats and roasting the carcasses of sect for the glory of God and satisfaction of priests, nor is it one army butchering an-

* New York *Free Enquirer*, November 27, 1830 (Commons, vol. V, pp. 180–81).

Preindustrial America

other to promote the fortunes of their leaders—to pass from a James to a George or a Charles to a Louis Philip the privilege of coining laws, money and peers, and dividing the good things of the land among his followers. No; it is now every where the oppressed millions who are making common cause against oppression; it is the ridden people of the earth who are struggling to throw from their backs the "booted and spurred" riders whose legitimate title to starve as well as to work them to death will no longer pass current; it is labor rising up against idleness, industry against money, justice against law and against privilege. And truly the struggle hath not come too soon. Truly there hath been oppression and outrage enough on the one side, and suffering and endurance enough on the other, to render the millions rather chargeable with excess of patience and other abundance of good nature than with too eager a spirit for the redress of injury, not to speak of recourse to vengeance.

It has been long clear to me that in every country the best feelings and the best sense are found with the laboring and useful classes, and the worst feelings and the worst sense with the idle and the useless. Until all classes shall be merged into one however by gradual but fundamental changes in the whole organization of society, much bad feeling must prevail every where. . . .

5. GARRISON AND THE WORKING MEN

1831

In the very first issue of his Liberator *(which inaugurated the abolitionist crusade) William Lloyd Garrison criticized "the working classes" for the complaints they were making. He returned to the issue on other occasions, and was answered at last by someone who signed his name "W." (probably Robert West), who presented an excellent summary of the working men's argument. All the extracts are from the* Liberator.

January 1, 1831

An attempt has been made—it is still making—we regret to say, with considerable success—to enflame the minds of our working classes against the more opulent, and to persuade men that they are condemned and oppressed by a wealthy aristocracy. That public grievances exist is unquestionably true; but they are not confined to any one class of society. Every profession is interested in their removal—the rich as well as the poor. It is in the highest degree criminal, therefore, to exasperate our mechanics to deeds of violence, or to array them under a party banner; for it is not true that, at any time, they have been the objects of reproach. Labor is not dishonorable. The industrious artisan, in a government like ours, will be held in better estimation than the wealthy idler.

Our limits will not allow us to enlarge on the subject; we may return to it another time. We are the friends of reform; but this is not reform; which in curing one evil threatens to inflict a thousand others.

January 29, 1831

Society, like the ocean, has its mutations. In a republican government especially, where hereditary distinctions are obsolete and the people possess unlimited power; where the avenues to wealth, distinction and supremacy are open to all; it must, in the nature of things, be full of inequalities. But these can exist without an assumption of rights—without even a semblance of oppression. There is a prevalent opinion that wealth and aristocracy are indissolubly allied; and the poor and vulgar are taught to consider the opulent as their natural enemies. Those who inculcate this pernicious doctrine are the worst enemies of the people and, in grain, the real nobility. There is, no doubt, an abuse of wealth as well as of talent, office and emolument; but where is the evidence that our wealthy citizens, as a body, are hostile to the interests of the laboring classes? It is not found in their commercial enterprises, which whiten the ocean with canvas and give employment to a useful and numerous class of men; it is not found in the manufacturing establishments which multiply labor and cheapen the necessities of the poor; it is not found in the luxuries of their tables, or the adornments of their dwellings, for which they must pay in proportion to their extravagance.

It is a miserable characteristic of human nature to look with an envious eye upon those who are more fortunate in their pursuits, or more exalted in their station. In every grade their are unprincipled, avaricious and despotic men; but shall individual cases condemn the whole body? Perhaps it would be nearer the truth to affirm that mechanics are more inimical to the success of each other, more unjust toward each other, than the rich toward them.— Nominate an intelligent mechanic to fill a responsible office; and by whom is he thrust down so quickly as by his own brethren? If our mechanics do not retain their due proportion of power and influence, theirs is the fault.

It is said there are too many priests, too many lawyers, too many doctors, and too many drones. If this be an evil, how shall it be curtailed? We know of no other mode than by living so righteously as to require no spiritual admonitions; so equitably as to need no appeal to the courts; so abstemiously as to avoid all medical prescriptions; so industriously as to make indolence—whether among the rich or the poor—dishonorable. The clergy, the medical faculty, and the members of the bar are certainly not useless to society; but the sooner we render their aid unnecessary, the happier will be our world.

We feel that our remarks are occupying more space than we can well spare, and must defer their conclusion to another paper. It must not be understood that we are opposed to the reformation of public abuses. Wherever they exist let a speedy and judicious remedy be applied.

In giving place to the following communication, we are enabled to say in behalf of the writer that, as a friend, we admire his moral qualities; and, as a citizen, appreciate his republican and active habits. There is nothing to which we object in his exposition of the designs of the working classes; it remains to be seen how far we shall agree in the mode of redress.

To the Editor of the Liberator.

My Dear Sir—Although you do not appear to have perceived it, I think there is a very intimate connection between the interests of the workingmen's party and your own. *You* are striving to excite the attention of your countrymen to the injustice of holding their fellow men in bondage and depriving them of the fruits of their toil. *We* are aiming at a similar object, only in application to another portion of our fellow men. In the history of the origin of slavery is to be found the explanation of those evils we deplore and seek to remove, as well as those you have attacked. The inequalities in the condition of the citizens and families of this republic have originated in the same causes. These causes are:

1. The assumption on the part of a fortunate *few* among our ancestors, in ancient times and countries, of the right to command the labor and services of their fellow countrymen—either as slaves, villeins, vassals, serfs, or operatives; and to remunerate them for their labor only to such an extent as they in their sovereign pleasure saw meet to bestow.

2. The abject ignorance in which these large masses of mankind have been kept by the few who have usurped authority over them, and controlled their condition.

3. The indolence, vice and depravity which such injustice has naturally engendered among the enslaved and oppressed—habits consequent upon the depression of spirits produced by suffering and the deprivation of all the enjoyments of life.

4. The perpetuation of opinions, habits of thinking, deportment and usage toward those working classes which, though nominally *free*, still are in Europe and America to a great extent *dependent* on the power and will of the wealthy, educated and exalted.

5. The vale and the price of labor have been rated not by the *worth of their product*, but by the *power* of those who command its proceeds, or for whom it is performed —*to obtain it* and enjoy its benefits.

Except to Walk Free

And finally—a disposition to regard and treat men who have been degraded by oppression as deficient in intellectual capacity and moral ability to become equal to the fortunate few in those refinements and accomplishments which these esteem as entitled to consideration and respect. And the infliction of punishment in the various forms of neglect, indifference, contumely, or oppression—for a character which has been the inevitable result of the condition in which these laboring classes have been kept and the circumstances by which they have been surrounded.

Now, you propose to remedy these evils by extending to the enslaved the sympathy of the philanthropic; by educating and otherwise fitting them to take care of themselves; and by awakening the moral sense of those who now enjoy the fruit of their labors, to the injustice and wickedness of thus robbing their fellow men of the products of their industry and toil.

We seek to enlighten our brethren in the knowledge of their rights and duties; to excite them to the acquisition of useful knowledge and the practice of virtue; and to cherish that self-respect which they are entitled to feel, who support and sustain all other classes of society. We, too, appeal to the moral sense of the wealthy and powerful, and to their justice and philanthropy, in behalf of those whose labors give value to their estates—income to their capital—ornament and beauty to their dwellings and apartments. We demand of these that they should pay the hard-working farmer and mechanic not only a fair equivalent for his services, but that homage and respect which are due him who braves the inclemency of winter and the intensity of summer; who toils early and late to raise up into life a virtuous family. We insist that where reason and argument will not avail it is a duty owed by the workingmen to themselves and the world to exert their power through the ballot box—and, by ameliorating our system of laws, to eradicate those evils which operate so extensively and so unjustly.

W.

6. WORKING MEN AND WOMEN*

1834

> The condition of women in New England factories was among the burning subjects raised in the first meeting of the National Trades' Union.

Mr. Douglass said he rose to suggest to the members of this Convention, the propriety, and the duty, of taking into consideration the condition and prospects of the females engaged in manufacturing establishments in this country. For himself, he considered it one of the most important subjects which could occupy their attention—a subject in which our future welfare was deeply concerned.

He observed, that in the single village of Lowell, there were about 4000 females of various ages, now dragging out a life of slavery and wretchedness. It is enough to make one's heart ache, said he, to behold these degraded females, as they pass out of the factory—to mark their wan countenances—their woe-stricken appearance. These establishments are the present abode of wretchedness, disease and misery; and are inevitably calculated to perpetuate them—if not to destroy liberty itself! . . .

We talk, said Mr. D., of the rising generation! What must that generation be, coming from such a stock of disease and deformity? What a race, in comparison to our hardy forefathers, whose iron nerves could second their resolute souls to meet any emergency! It is of little use for us to legislate here, said Mr. D., while this factory system is undoing more than our united exertions can

* *The Man*, September 17, 1834 (Commons, vol. VI, pp. 217–19).

possibly build up. It was his confirmed opinion, that this system was laying the foundation of an aristocracy; and is so intended by its projectors. He believed it to be a deliberate plot of the enemies of freedom and equality, to ruin the farmers, to break down that sturdy, independent spirit, so characteristic of the former race, so unpropitious to the future schemes of aristocrats. They can command more money than the farmer, and are applying their "facilities" to draw his sons and daughters from the farm to the factories. For a few years past, the sons of our farmers, as soon as they are of sufficient age, have been induced to hasten off to the factory, where for a few pence more than they could get at home, they are taught to become the willing servants, the servile instruments of their employer's oppression and extortion! The daughters, too, must quit the farm house, the seat of ruddy health and former content, for a confined and baneful workshop, where, to be sure, she earns a little more money, for a short time; but as surely loses health, if not her good character, her happiness! . . .

It is our duty, sir, to look to these establishments; to calculate the consequences of their further spread. We must look after these men of high percentage, bred to that, and who care for nothing else. Who shall reform this system but the working men? This is, indeed, the most important work we have to do. How shall we avert the evil? They resort to piece work, that we may not be able to reach them. But we must devise a remedy; we must appeal to the people to join, to set their faces against this system, as one pregnant with our certain destruction. We must go before our legislatures—must expose these "beings"—not to use a harsher term—who destroy life for gain—who make their enormous percentage at a yearly expense of hundreds of lives! They must be forced

Except to Walk Free

to shut their mills at a regular hour; there must be a certain time over which they shall not work; that all the inmates may have an opportunity to rest their weary limbs, and to enjoy free and wholesome air. . . .

7. THE NATIONAL TRADES' UNION: 1*

1835

> The constitution of the National Trades' Union, a brief document, was adopted at the October 1835 convention, held in New York City.

Constitution. Article I. This Association shall be styled the "National Trades' Union of the United States."

Article II. The object of this Union shall be to recommend such measures to the various Unions and Associations represented herein, as may tend to advance the moral, intellectual, and social condition, and pecuniary interests of the laboring classes; and to promote the establishment of Trade Associations and Trades' Unions in every section of the United States: and also to publish and disseminate such information as may be useful to mechanics and working men generally, and to unite and harmonize the efforts of the productive classes of our country.

Article III. *Section* 1. This Union shall be composed of delegates from the several Trades' Unions in the United States, and from Trade Societies in places where no Unions are established; the number not to exceed one from each Association or Society: to be elected in such manner as the several Unions and Societies may direct—and shall hold office for one year.

Section 2. Each delegate, before taking his seat in the Convention, shall present a certificate of his election,

* *National Trades' Union*, October 10, 1835 (Commons, vol. VI, p. 259).

Except to Walk Free

signed by the President and Secretary of the T. Union to which he belongs, or from the President and Secretary of the Society he may represent, in case no Union exists in the vicinity of such Society. . . .

8. THE NATIONAL TRADES' UNION: 2*

1836

The following report was submitted to the N.T.U.'s 1836 convention (again held in New York). It is a cogent summary of the organization's reason for existing.

The Committee on Trades' Unions, beg leave to report:

That owing to the short space of time allotted to them, they are unable to make as full and elaborate a report as the magnitude of the subject entrusted to them is entitled to; they will, however, endeavor to discharge the duties assigned to them. And, first: The importance of Union and Co-operation is manifest to all reflecting men, and the motto of "United we stand, divided we fall," is no where more applicable than to the interests of the working people; therefore interest, duty, and patriotism, demand that we should pursue with energy every measure calculated to secure for ourselves and our children, for the bereaved widow and her orphan, an adequate reward for their labor. The question naturally arises, how can this be accomplished? We reply by Union, and by Union alone.

Therefore, as a basis, we recommend to the several Unions composing this Convention, an immediate and energetic action in the formation of Trades' Societies and Trades' Unions, in all parts of our country, know-

* *National Laborer*, November 26, 1836 (Commons, vol. VI, pp. 294–97).

Except to Walk Free

ing that the reason why the producers are oppressed and speculated upon, is on account of the divisions and want of union among themselves; to divide and conquer is the policy of the Aristocracy; to unite as one man, is an only hope of success. We would also urge on the Trade Societies in the United States, to open an immediate and extensive correspondence with other societies of the same trade as themselves, in all places where they exist, and where none are formed, to solicit their fellow-workmen to enter into immediate and energetic measures for their formation.

On the resolution referred to your Committee, requiring them to investigate what is the causes of the apathy manifested by the mechanics in the Eastern States, we would trace it first to competition amongst themselves for employment; secondly, a want of confidence in each other, causing petty jealousies and selfishness to predominate over that generous and manly pride, inherent in the human heart; and lastly, a want of proper information touching their own interests, showing them why he who produces all, receives but a fraction of his own labor; while he who riots in indolence, obtains all the luxuries, and enjoys all the pleasures of life.

To remove this, we recommend that proper information concerning the principles, the objects, and the policy of Trades' Unions, with the advantages that have resulted to those societies which compose those already in existence, and the benefits that must accrue to us by sustaining those Unions, be disseminated amongst the workingmen generally, both by pamphlets and by lectures; by precept, and by our own example; this we conceive to be our best, and in fact, our only remedy.

The subject of maintaining a healthful equilibrium of supply and demand, your Committee are convinced is of the most vital importance. In the Atlantic cities, the evils flowing from surplus labor, is perhaps more materially felt than in the interior of the manufacturing states; therefore, any propositions which may tend to equalize, or distribute in judicious proportions, labor throughout the country, must operate beneficially to the whole of those who depend on productive industry for their subsistence. In one or more of the districts which is here represented, it is well known that they are at all times liable to sudden fluctuations in the prices of labor, from the accessions and increase of emigration. Those who thrive from the labor of the producer, incited by their avarice, are always ready to take the advantage of the description of persons above alluded to; the destitute situation of the stranger in our land, is seized upon with avidity by the capitalist, and agents are frequently appointed, whose duty it is to engage the operative at wages far below those established by Trade Societies. Your Committee do not intend to say that agents are generally appointed for this purpose; they merely state that this is one of the schemes resorted to for the express object of depreciating the price of labor.

That undue advantage can at all times be secured to the capitalist from surplus labor in any one place, cannot be doubted; the admission, then, of so serious a fact, should admonish this body to devise some plan whereby a district of country thus afflicted, could be immediately relieved. In order to carry so important an object into execution, the following propositions are submitted.

1st. That a Board of Commissioners, consisting of one from each Union, be appointed by this Convention.

2d. That it shall be one of the specific duties of each member of the Board, to obtain a precise list of the

Except to Walk Free

members belonging to the respective Societies of the Union to which he is attached.

3d. That said Commissioners, through correspondence, shall keep the different Unions constantly advised of the number of members, and likewise to give such information as they may possess with regard to the demand for labor in their respective vicinities.

4th. That a portion of the National Fund be set apart to supply members with means for the purpose of enabling them to remove to such places as are not overstocked with numbers, at the same time making members drawing on this fund liable to refund the amount which they may have received, through the operation of the Society or Union of their separate locations. All of which is respectfully submitted.

9. CONSPIRACY CASES*

1836

People v. *Faulkner* was typical of the conspiracy cases tried in 1836. Faulkner was one of twenty journeymen tailors in New York City arrested and indicted for the crime of organizing a strike.

COURT OF OYER AND TERMINER. Before his honor Judge Edwards, and Aldermen Benson, Banks, Randall, and Ingraham.

The People *vs.* Henry Faulkner, Wm. Livingston, James Noe, Alexander Hume, Peter Moss, Joshua Bussey, George Smith, John Welsh, Daniel J. Gray, Thomas Keating, Thos. Renton, Howell Vail, John Bromberger, Stephen Norris, Jas. Magee, Alexander Douglass, John Dillon, James Skillig, Daniel Rose, and Thomas Douglass —(20).

The accused, who are journeymen tailors and members of the Union Society of Journeymen Tailors, were indicted for a conspiracy to injure trade and commerce, and for riot, and assault and battery, &c.

From the mass of evidence adduced, it appeared that in the month of October last, the journeymen tailors belonging to the Society struck, as it is termed, for higher wages, and refused to work until their demands for higher rates were complied with. That this object attained, they resumed their labors, and continued to operate until some time in January last, when they again struck, and ceased

* New York *Courier and Enquirer*, May 31, 1836 (Commons, vol. IV, pp. 315–19).

Except to Walk Free

to labor for those who had employed them. This strike was characterized by some features that had never before been presented to employers. One of these was, that the master workmen were each to keep a slate, and enter on it the names of their journeymen as they successively took out their jobs; no one was to take a job out of his turn, and no one to have a second job until all had been supplied, &c. The journeymen, in the event of this proposition not being acceded to, were to refuse to work for those employers; who, on their parts, finding such an arrangement exceedingly troublesome and injurious, refused compliance, and their hands immediately left. In consequence of this non-conformance with these regulations, and others proposed, the parent Society adopted resolutions to carry out their purposes of coercion, and to compel the employers into a subserviency to their views.

Committees were appointed by them, consisting of eight or ten each in number, whose business it was made, under a penalty, to watch the shops of the master tailors; to see who went in and out with jobs; and to induce or persuade all journeymen working at the shops under the prohibition to abstain from working and join the Society; and in case of their refusal, to denounce them as unworthy of their friendship, to proscribe them in such a manner, that they could not get employment in regular shops, here or any where else, where there were Unions; to refuse even to work with them, or to work in any shop where they should be employed; and literally to hunt them from all tailors' society. This purpose, in January, was carried into full effect. All the regular shops were watched by squads of from 8 to 15, called committees, who paraded before the doors and windows from early in the morning to about 9 o'clock at night, often

Preindustrial America

spreading their cloaks and coats before the windows to darken them, insulting, villifying, and applying the most oprobrious epithets to the journeymen who continued in employ; dignifying them with the name "dungs," following and intercepting their movements when they went away with jobs, and threatening them with violence unless they struck, quit work and joined them. These acts of outrage and insult continued for nearly or quite 3 months before they were suspended, to the great annoyance of journeymen at work; the great loss and detriment of employers, the frequent disturbance of the peace, the collection of tumultuous assemblages, the alarm of many who were timid, and to the injury of the free and untrammelled operations of trade and commerce. To counteract these hostile measures, (which emanated from the Trades Union Societies, and the actors in which were supported in part by stipends from those societies) the master tailors in January associated for purposes of defense as a society of master tailors, and adopted a tariff of prices which was proposed to the journeymen and rejected.

The long continuance of the annoyances and interruptions to trade, ultimately brought matters to a focus, and the master tailors preferred complaints, and caused defendants, and five others, who were the principal actors in the conspiracy to be arrested—all of whom were indicted by the Grand Jury at the Sessions, and the cause handed over to this court for trial. The acts of which they stood charged were clearly and unequivocally established by irrefutable evidence, four days being occupied in the receipt of it; and after the cause was summed up with great ability, on both sides, by Messrs. J. R. Whiting and H. M. Western for the defence, and by Messrs. N. B. Blunt and R. H. Morris for the people, Judge Edwards

Except to Walk Free

charged the jury yesterday evening in a clear and cogent manner, against all such lawless combinations, as violations of law, destructive of the rights of employers, and others not associated, who were employed; detrimental to the public interests generally, and injurious to trade and commerce. He rested his opinion of the legal guilt of the accused, principally on the opinion delivered by Judge Savage, of the Supreme Court, in an analogous case; and also, on the revised statutes; and read a portion of the former case, as decided by the Supreme Court, on an appeal from a decision of the Court of Sessions of Ontario County, where the journeymen shoemakers had met, and ordained, that none of them should work under certain prices, established by themselves. Judge E. laid great stress upon this decision, and hoped that the Jury would not by their verdict, subvert a law which had been rendered valid, by the decision of the highest tribunal in the State.

He also quoted the following section from the Revised Statutes, vol. 2d, page 621.

"No agreement to commit a felony except a burglary, or arson, can be considered as a conspiracy, unless some object be effected by one or more of the parties having formed the agreement." This the Judge remarked was all the law necessary upon the case, and he considered the charges as laid in the indictment fully sustained by the evidence. He spoke in very strong terms against all combinations, which if suffered to go on, none could say, where they would terminate. He considered all the defendants guilty.

The Judge then gave the case to the jury, and they, after being absent about 30 minutes, returned a verdict of Guilty; but as it was the first case, they recommended the defendants to the clemency of the court.

The Counsel for the accused excepted to the Judge's charges, and wished ten days to prepare a formal bill for his signature, which he denied.

(Judge Edwards stated that he would sentence the defendants on Monday next, and the Court was adjourned until Wednesday at 10 o'clock, when Shannon will be put upon his trial for arson.)

10. COMMONWEALTH V. HUNT*

1842

In 1840, members of the Bootmakers' Society of Boston were tried for engaging in a "criminal conspiracy" (they had forced an employer to fire a working man who had refused to join their union) and found guilty. The verdict was foregone, the judge having raised the specter of insurrection, anarchy, and despotism. The case came before the Supreme Judicial Court of the Commonwealth of Massachusetts, presided over by the redoubtable Chief Justice Lemuel Shaw (who also happened to be Herman Melville's father-in-law). Shaw threw out the conviction in his landmark decision. In doing so he rendered the conspiracy laws a dead letter. The distinction he drew between a legitimate combination and an illegitimate one validated the principle of trade unionism in the United States.

Shaw, C.J. . . . The general rule of the common law is, that it is a criminal and indictable offense, for two or more to confederate and combine together, by concerted means, to do that which is unlawful or criminal, to the injury of the public, or portions or classes of the community, or even to the rights of an individual. This rule of law may be equally in force as a rule of the common law, in England and in this Commonwealth. . . .

Stripped then of these introductory recitals and alleged

* Mass. Reports, 4 Metcalf 45.

Preindustrial America

injurious consequences, and of the qualifying epithets attached to the facts, the averment is this; that the defendants and others formed themselves into a society, and agreed not to work for any person who should employ any journeyman or other person, not a member of such society, after notice given him to discharge such workman. The manifest intent of the association is, to induce all those engaged in the same occupation to become members of it. Such a purpose is not unlawful. It would give them a power which might be exerted for useful and honorable purposes, or for dangerous and pernicious ones. If the latter were the real and actual object, and susceptible of proof, it should have been specially charged. Such an association might be useful to afford each other assistance in times of poverty, sickness and distress; or to raise their intellectual, moral and social condition; or to make improvement in their art; or for other proper purposes. Or the association might be designed for purposes of oppression and injustice. . . .

Nor can we perceive that the objects of this association, whatever they may have been, were to be attained by criminal means. The means which they proposed to employ, as averred in this court, and which, as we are now to presume, were established by the proof, were, that they would not work for a person, who, after due notice, should employ a journeyman not a member of this society. Supposing the object of the association to be laudable and lawful, or at least not unlawful, are these means criminal? The case supposes that these persons are not bound by contract, but free to work for whom they please, or not to work, if they so prefer. In this state of things, we cannot perceive that it is criminal for men to agree together to exercise their own acknowledged rights in such manner as best to subserve their own

Except to Walk Free

interests. . . . [I]t seems to us that as the object would be lawful, and the means not unlawful, such an agreement could not be pronounced a criminal conspiracy. . . .

We think, therefore, that associations may be entered into, the object of which is to adopt measures that may have a tendency to impoverish another, that is, to diminish his gains and profits, and yet so far from being criminal or unlawful, the object may be meritorious and public spirited. The legality of such an association will, therefore, depend upon the means to be used for its accomplishment. . . .

11. COMMUNITARIANISM AND WORKING MEN: 1[*]

1843

> The Fourierist, or associationist, movement got under way in the early 1840s and found its main body of adherents among the Brahmins and intellectuals who were seeking to live transcendentally, according to an ethic of love rather than greed. Their attitude toward unions and strikes may be gathered from this passage excerpted from *The Phalanx*, one of the movement's leading publications.

There has been a very general "turn-out" in all the Atlantic cities among the working classes. In every trade almost there has been a strike for higher wages, and generally the demands of the workmen have been complied with by the "masters." The reaction in the commercial world has stimulated business a little, which has increased slightly the demand for labor, and as the population of this country has not yet become dense and excessive, the working classes by the subversive means of counter-coalitions to those which exist under our present false system of Industry and Commerce—leagues of wealth and industrial monopoly—are enabled to obtain a small advance of wages. But how trifling and pitiful an amount of benefit, after all, they receive, by such means, even when and for the time they do succeed; and how

[*] *The Phalanx*, November 4, 1843.

Except to Walk Free

miserably inadequate to meet their wants and satisfy their rights, are such beggarly additions to their wages. Will not the working classes, the intelligent producers of this country, see what a miserable shift and expedient to better their condition is a "strike for wages?" Will they not see how uncertain the tenure by which they hold the little advantage they gain by it? Will they not see how degrading the position which forces them to appeal to and beg concessions of employers? Will they not see this and a thousand other evils connected with a false system of industry, and learn that the only remedy is a union among themselves to produce for themselves, to associate, and combine, and owning the land on which they live and the tools and machinery with which they work, enjoy the products of their own labor? We hope so, and then all such "civilized" false association, will be unnecessary. . . .

12. COMMUNITARIANISM AND WORKING MEN: 2*

1845

A number of unions were sufficiently influenced by the communitarian ethic to start up their own producer co-operatives. One such co-operative was formed by the Boston Mechanics' and Laborers' Association in 1845. Following is a statement drafted by a special committee of the Association.

It is our belief that the same causes of evil and suffering are operative in this country, that, in the Old World, are developed to giant magnitude, and are crushing the producers of wealth to the very dust, and that unless a speedy change can be effected in our social condition the time is not far distant when the laborers of the United States will be as dependent, as oppressed, and as wretched, as are their brethren in Europe. Here, as there, the soil, motive power and machinery are monopolized by the idle few; all the sources of wealth, all the instrumentalities of life, and even the right and privilege of industry are taken away from the people. Monopoly has laid its ruthless hands upon labor itself, and forced the sale of the muscles and skill of the toiling many, and under the specious name of "wages" is robbing them

---

* *Working Man's Advocate*, January 11, 1845 (Commons, vol. VIII, pp. 263–65).

Except to Walk Free

of the fruits of their industry. Universal monopoly is the bane of labor not less in America than in Europe. . . .

The remedy lies in a radical change of principle and policy. Our isolated position and interests, and our antisocial habits, must be abandoned. The Money-power must be superseded by the Man-power. Universal Monopoly must give place to Societary ownership, occupancy, and use. The right of every human being to the soil whereon, and the tools and machinery wherewith to labor must be established; the right of every man to the productions of his hands must be acknowledged, and the law of God universally applied, "If a man will not work neither shall he eat."

It is the belief of your Committee, that these objects can only be gained by Industrial Association, or union among the laboring classes. The direction and profits of industry must be kept in the hands of the producers. Laborers must own their own shops and factories; work their own stock, sell their own merchandise, and enjoy the fruits of their own toil. Our Lowells must be owned by the artizans who build them, and the operatives who run the machinery and do all the work. And the dividend, instead of being given to the idle parasites of a distant city, should be shared among those who perform the labor. Our Lynns must give the fortunes made by the dealer and employer, to those who use the awl and work the material. Our Cape Anns must exchange their own oil, combine the vast benefits of commerce with their poorly paid navigation, and not pay the rents of so many city stores, nor support in luxury so many city merchants. In other words, all interests must be united, all trades combined, and all branches of usefulness be equally paid. The farmer, manufacturer, the mechanic, and the merchant, must belong to the same

Preindustrial America

Firm, and share the proceeds proportionally to the labor each has contributed. The country's wealth belongs to, and must be given to the country's labor.

As the means of applying this remedy, your committee recommend, that an Industrial Firm of this description shall be immediately established in the city of Boston, and that an effort be put forth by this Association, to induce the industrial classes to combine their skill, and capital, and labor in this undertaking, as the only hope that is now left, of ameliorating their condition, and remedying the evils to which they are exposed. . . .

13. VOTE YOURSELF A FARM*

1846

This is the famous appeal by the agrarian leader George H. Evans to the working men of the United States. Hundreds of thousands of copies were distributed as handbills. "Vote Yourself a Farm" had an enormous influence, its central tenet being incorporated into the Free Soil and later the Republican Party platforms. It became law with the passage of the Homestead Act of 1862.

Are you an American citizen? Then you are a joint-owner of the public lands. Why not take enough of your property to provide yourself a home? Why not vote yourself a farm?

Remember poor Richard's saying: "Now I have a sheep and a cow, every one bids me 'good morrow.'" If a man have a house and a home of his own, though it be a thousand miles off, he is well received in other people's houses; while the homeless wretch is turned away. The bare right to a farm, though you should never go near it, would save you from many an insult. Therefore, Vote yourself a farm.

Are you a party follower? Then you have long enough employed your vote to benefit scheming office-seekers; use it for once to benefit yourself—Vote yourself a farm.

Are you tired of slavery—of drudging for others—of

* *True Workingman,* January 24, 1846 (Commons, vol. VII, pp. 305-7).

poverty and its attendant miseries? Then, Vote yourself a farm.

Are you endowed with reason? Then you must know that your right to life hereby includes the right to a place to live in—the right to a home. Assert this right, so long denied mankind by feudal robbers and their attorneys. Vote yourself a farm.

Are you a believer in the scriptures? Then assert that the land is the Lord's, because He made it. Resist then the blasphemers who exact money for His work, even as you would resist them should they claim to be worshipped for His holiness. Emancipate the poor from the necessity of encouraging such blasphemy—Vote the freedom of the public lands.

Are you a man? Then assert the sacred rights of man—especially your right to stand upon God's earth, and to till it for your own profit. Vote yourself a farm.

Would you free your country, and the sons of toil everywhere, from the heartless, irresponsible mastery of the aristocracy of avarice? Would you disarm this aristocracy of its chief weapon, the fearful power of banishment from God's earth? Then join with your neighbors to form a true American party, having for its guidance the principles of the American revolution, and whose chief measures shall be—1. To limit the quantity of land that any one man may henceforth monopolize or inherit; and 2. To make the public lands free to actual settlers only, each having the right to sell his improvements to any man not possessed of other land. These great measures once carried, wealth would become a changed social element; it would then consist of the accumulated products of human labor, instead of a hoggish monopoly of the products of God's labor; and the antagonism of capital and labor would forever cease. Capital could no

Except to Walk Free

longer grasp the largest share of the laborer's earnings, as a reward for not doing him all the injury the laws of the feudal aristocracy authorize, viz: the denial of all stock to work upon and all place to live in. To derive any profit from the laborer, it must first give him work; for it could no longer wax fat by levying a dead tax upon his existence. The hairy iniquities of Norman land pirates would cease to pass current as American law. Capital, with its power for good undiminished, would lose the power to oppress; and a new era would dawn upon the earth, and rejoice the souls of a thousand generations. Therefore forget not to Vote yourself a farm.

14. FREDERICK DOUGLASS*

1853

In his writings and speeches before the Civil War, Frederick Douglass, the great leader of the black abolitionist movement, returned time and again to the vexing problem of what to do about the free blacks of the North. Their condition continued to deteriorate, indeed to grow desperate, as a result of racism, the hostility of working men, and competition from the new Irish proletariat.

The old avocations, by which colored men obtained a livelihood, are rapidly, unceasingly and inevitably passing into other hands; every hour sees the black man elbowed out of employment by some newly arrived emigrant, whose hunger and whose color are thought to give him a better title to the place; and so we believe it will continue to be until the last prop is levelled beneath us.

As a black man, we say if we cannot stand up, let us fall down. We desire to be a man among men while we do live; and when we cannot, we wish to die. It is evident, painfully evident to every reflecting mind, that the means of living, for colored men, are becoming more and more precarious and limited. Employments and callings, formerly monopolized by us, are so no longer.

White men are becoming house-servants, cooks and stewards on vessels—at hotels.—They are becoming por-

* *Frederick Douglass' Paper*, March 4, 1853.

Except to Walk Free

ters, stevedores, wood-sawyers, hod-carriers, brick-makers, white-washers and barbers, so that the blacks can scarcely find the means of subsistence—a few years ago, and a *white* barber would have been a curiosity—now their poles stand on every street. Formerly blacks were almost the exclusive coachmen in wealthy families: this is so no longer; white men are now employed, and for aught we see, they fill their servile station with an obsequiousness as profound as that of the blacks. The readiness and ease with which they adapt themselves to these conditions ought not to be lost sight of by the colored people. The meaning is very important, and we should learn it. We are taught our insecurity by it. Without the means of living, life is a curse, and leaves us at the mercy of the oppressor to become his debased slaves. Now, colored men, what do you mean to do, for you must do something? The American Colonization Society tells you to go to Liberia. Mr. Bibbs tells you to go to Canada. Others tell you to go to school. We tell you to go to work; and to work you must go or die. Men are not valued in this country, or in any country, for what they *are*; they are valued for what they can *do*. It is in vain that we talk about being men, if we do not the work of men. We must become valuable to society in other departments of industry than those servile ones from which we are rapidly being excluded. We must show that we can *do* as well as *be*; and to this end we must learn trades. When we can build as well as live in houses; when we can *make* as well as *wear* shoes; when we can produce as well as consume wheat, corn and rye—then we shall become valuable to society. Society is a hard-hearted affair.—With it the helpless may expect no higher dignity than that of paupers. The individual must lay society under obligation to him, or society will honor him only as a stranger and sojourner. *How* shall this be done? In this manner: use every means, strain every nerve to master some important mechanical art. At present, the facilities for doing this are few—institutions of learning are more readily opened to you than the work-shop; but the Lord helps them who will help themselves, and we have no doubt that new facilities will be presented as we press forward.

If the alternative were presented to us of learning a trade or of getting an education, we would learn the trade, for the reason, that with the trade we could get the education, while with the education we could not get the trade. What we, as a people, need most, is the means for our own elevation.—An educated colored man, in the United States, unless he has within him the heart of a hero, and is willing to engage in a lifelong battle for his rights, as a man, finds few inducements to remain in this country. He is isolated in the land of his birth—debarred by his color from congenial association with whites; he is equally cast out by the ignorance of the *blacks*. The remedy for this must comprehend the elevation of the masses; and this can only be done by putting the mechanic arts within the reach of colored men.

We have now stated pretty strongly the case of our colored countrymen; perhaps some will say, *too* strongly; but we know whereof we affirm.

In view of this state of things, we appeal to the abolitionists, What boss anti-slavery mechanic will take a black boy into his wheelwright's shop, his blacksmith's shop, his joiner's shop, his cabinet shop? Here is something *practical*; where are the whites and where are the blacks that will respond to it? Where are the anti-slavery milliners and seamstresses that will take colored girls and teach them trades, by which they can obtain an honorable

Except to Walk Free

living? The fact that we have made good cooks, good waiters, good barbers, and white-washers, induces the belief that we may excel in higher branches of industry. *One thing is certain: we must find new methods of obtaining a livelihood, for the old ones are failing us very fast.*

We, therefore, call upon the intelligent and thinking ones amongst us, to urge upon the colored people within their reach, in all seriousness, the duty and the necessity of giving their children useful and lucrative trades, by which they may commence the battle of life with weapons commensurate with the exigencies of the conflict.

15. SLAVEHOLDERS AND THE WORKING MEN*

1858

Senator James H. Hammond, of South Carolina, was one of the ablest champions of the slavocracy. In speech after speech he would accuse the North of hypocrisy in asserting that its working men were free. He would also threaten to carry his message to northern working men, arousing them to rebellion just as abolitionists were arousing the slaves. The passage below is taken from the Senate debates of March 4, 1858.

The Senator from New York said yesterday that the whole world had abolished slavery. Aye, the *name*, but not the thing; all the powers of the earth cannot abolish it. God only can do it when he repeals the fiat, 'the poor ye always have with you'; for the man who lives by daily labor, and scarcely lives at that, and who has to put out his labor in the market and take the best he can get for it—in short, your whole hireling class of manual laborers and 'operatives,' as you call them, are essentially slaves. The difference between us is, that our slaves are hired for life and well compensated; there is no starvation, no begging, no want of employment among our people, and not too much employment either. Yours are hired by the day, not cared for, and scantily compensated which

* *Congressional Globe*, U. S. Senate, 1858, p. 968.

Except to Walk Free

may be proved in the most painful manner at any hour, in any street, in any of your large towns. Why, you meet more beggars in one day, in any single street of the city of New York, than you would meet in a lifetime in the whole South. We do not think that whites should be slaves, either by law or necessity. Our slaves are black, of another and inferior race. The status in which we have placed them is an elevation. They are elevated from a condition in which God first created them, by being made our slaves. None of that race on the whole face of the globe can be compared with the slaves of the South. They are happy, content, unaspiring, and utterly incapable, from intellectual weakness, ever to give any trouble by their aspirations.

Your slaves are white, of your own race: you are brothers of one blood. They are your equals in natural endowment of intellect, and they feel galled by their degradation. Our slaves do not vote. We give them no political power. Yours do vote; and being the majority, they are the depositaries of all your political power. If they knew the tremendous secret, that the ballot-box is stronger than an army with bayonets, and could combine, where would you be? Your society would be reconstructed, your government overthrown, your property divided, not as they have mistakenly attempted to initiate such proceedings by meetings in parks, with arms in their hands, but by the quiet process of the ballot-box. You have been making war upon us to our very hearthstones. How would you like us to send lecturers or agitators North, to teach these people this, to aid and assist in combining, and to lead them? . . .

16. THE FIRST INTERNATIONAL ON THE CIVIL WAR

1864

In late November 1864 the recently formed International Workingmen's Association congratulated Lincoln on his re-election to the presidency. The letter tells why the European—particularly the British—workers, at considerable cost to themselves (the absence of cotton resulting in the loss of jobs), rallied behind the Union cause. The letter was drafted by Karl Marx.

To Abraham Lincoln,
President of the United States of America.

Sir:—We congratulate the American people upon your re-election by a large majority. If resistance to the Slave Power was the watchword of your first election, the triumphal war-cry of your re-election is Death to Slavery.

From the commencement of the titanic American strife the workingmen of Europe felt distinctively that the Star Spangled Banner carried the destiny of their class. The contest for the territories which opened the *dire epopèe*, was it not to decide whether the virgin soil of immense tracts should be wedded to the labor of the immigrant or be prostituted by the tramp of the slavedriver?

When an oligarchy of 300,000 slaveholders dared to inscribe for the first time in the annals of the world "Slavery" on the banner of armed revolt, when on the very spots where hardly a century ago the idea of one

Except to Walk Free

great Democratic Republic had first sprung up, whence the first declaration of the Rights of Man was issued, and the first impulse given to the European Revolution of the eighteenth century, when on those very spots counter-revolution, with systematic thoroughness, gloried in rescinding "the ideas entertained at the time of the formation of the old constitution" and maintained "slavery to be a beneficial institution," indeed, the only solution of the great problem of the "relation of capital to labor," and cynically proclaimed property in man "the cornerstone of the new edifice,"—then the working classes of Europe understood at once, even before the fanatic partisanship of the upper classes, for the Confederate gentry had given its dismal warning, that the slaveholders' rebellion was to sound the tocsin for a general holy war of property against labor, and that for the men of labor, with their hopes for the future, even their past conquests were at stake in that tremendous conflict on the other side of the Atlantic. Everywhere they bore therefore patiently the hardships imposed upon them by the cotton crisis, opposed enthusiastically the pro-slavery intervention —importunities of their betters—and from most parts of Europe contributed their quota of blood to the good of the cause.

While the working men, the true political power of the North, allowed slavery to defile their own republic, while before the Negro, mastered and sold without his concurrence, they boasted it the highest prerogative of the white-skinned laborer to sell himself and choose his own master, they were unable to attain the true freedom of labor, or to support their European brethren in their struggle for emancipation; but this barrier to progress has been swept off by the red sea of civil war.

The working men of Europe felt sure that, as the

American War of Independence initiated a new era of ascendency for the middle class, so the American Antislavery War will do for the working classes. They consider it an earnest sign of the epoch to come that it fell to the lot of Abraham Lincoln, the single-minded son of the working class, to lead his country through the matchless struggle for the rescue of the enchained race and the reconstruction of a social world.

II

Transition 1864–86

As noted earlier, working men in the pre-Civil War years suffered from what might be called a consciousness lag. They responded to the rise of a market economy and an exploitative class by throwing up various modes of defense, joining parties, unions, and reform movements, all designed to preserve their status as skilled craftsmen, their autonomy as self-sufficient producers. Inevitably, these defenses crumbled before the engine of "progress" —i.e., laissez-faire capitalism—and, by the 1850s, only a handful of the unions established earlier (typographers, stonecutters, cigar makers, iron molders) had survived, and these by the skin of their teeth.

This lag in working men's consciousness widened appreciably in the years following the Civil War. For while industrialism was overnight transforming the United States, building an economy based more and more on unskilled and semi-skilled labor—in a word, the wage system —and otherwise revolutionizing every aspect of society, working men continued to think and act as "working men": as inhabitants of stable small towns and homogeneous communities, their vocations and their independence assured. They came to terms with the trauma of industrialism by retreating into the beleaguered fortresses of the

Except to Walk Free

past, and this was reflected in the kind of organizations they set up.

Perhaps there was no other way they could have fought back. A lag in consciousness, after all, can never be overcome by a mere *leap* of consciousness, a sudden change in one's state of mind. Not unless the leap accompanies a lived experience. The understanding of one's environment, of one's self, is paved with repeated failures. Only then, not sooner, does a new consciousness, one capable of dealing with conditions as they are, get born in the flesh. American working men had to experience the ordeal of successive failures—their period of gestation, as it were—before they could give birth, in the 1880s, to a consciousness that enabled them, at last, to respond effectively.

The Civil War gave a tremendous stimulus to the (northern) economy. And, after a brief postwar slump, the boom continued at an unprecedented pace, marked as it was by a great spurt in railroad building, factory production, and coal mining.

But working men found themselves in a familiar bind. There was a sustained demand for the goods they were producing—goods fashioned in their entirety by their own hands (or in co-operation with partners), and for the goods put out by unskilled labor, by those employed in factories and paid in wages. These two sectors of the economy, handicraft and industrial, independent producers and wage earners, existed side by side, occupants of a dual culture. As long as prosperity lasted, they coexisted in peace, each of them benefiting from the prevailing sellers' market (labor being a commodity, like any other).

The skilled workers sought to maintain as much distance as possible between themselves and the wage sys-

Transition

tem. It was the specific function of the trade union to act as a buffer against the wage system. Through unions, they hoped to control the labor supply, resist the introduction of labor-saving machinery, and fight for cheaper money so that they could borrow capital as easily as the large producers did. In short, they wanted to hold on to the handicraft system at all costs.

And so the number of local trade unions rose egregiously throughout the 1860s. At the start of the Civil War, there were fewer than a hundred locals in the country. When the war was over, the number had grown to over three hundred, and by the end of the 1860s, it stood at well over a thousand. These, furthermore, were confederated into larger collectivities (shades of the 1830s): city centrals, co-operatives, regional associations, and, encompassing all of them, a National Labor Union.

Nothing pointed up the skilled workers' fears of industrialism so emphatically as their unions' attitude toward black workers, now that blacks were liberated and might join the swelling ranks of the labor force. Whites regarded blacks as the human extension of the machine. Under the racist scheme of things, blacks could not be artisans and mechanics, only factory hands, the wage system being in that sense a *black* system. Accordingly, no national union in the 1860s admitted blacks, whatever their skills. They had to form their own unions, all pitifully small and vulnerable, the victims at once of racial animosity and industrial necessity. Everything was conspiring to grind them down to the lowest stratum of the proletariat.[1]

Yet the union movement, then as before, conceived

---

[1] There was one lower: the Chinese. From the 1860s on, the Chinese were the most severely victimized group in American society. They were the special target of organized labor.

Except to Walk Free

itself to be the vanguard of American democracy. Working men believed that they were keeping faith with the sacred tradition of Jefferson and Jackson. Being independent producers, they were exploiting no one's labor but their own, and so were engaged in mortal combat with the banks and monopolies and middlemen, who, unproductive themselves, grew fat and powerful on the labor of others. From its inception, then, the National Labor Union was as dedicated to broad social reform as it was to bread-and-butter economic gains.

Reformers of every stripe came to National Labor Union conventions, where they advanced their special panaceas for regenerating the country and restoring it to the people. Some proposed that free loans for everyone be guaranteed by the government; others that the eight-hour day be instituted at once as a way of stimulating further productivity; still others, apostles of the agrarian creed, that land be distributed to all working men who wanted it, thereby creating a labor shortage; and others yet (among them Susan B. Anthony) that women workers, who had particular reason to groan under the weight of industrial exploitation, be given the same rights as men. The National Labor Union paid due heed to these reforms, and in one convention after another officially stamped its approval on them.

To implement such reforms it was, of course, necessary to get laws passed by the state and federal governments; that is, to win political power. Increasingly, then, the N.L.U. became a political organization, abandoning, in the process, its commitments to trade unionism, to mundane economic goals. Increasingly, the trade unions withdrew from the N.L.U. In 1872 it took the final step, renaming itself the National Reform Party, complete with platform, candidates, etc.

Transition

The National Reform Party's career was very brief. After encountering some difficulty in finding a presidential candidate, it settled on the Democratic nominee, a Tammany boss of no visible distinction. The party managed to draw only about thirty thousand votes in the election and expired soon after, unnoticed and unmourned.

But the fate of the National Labor Union was a trifle compared to what lay immediately in store for American workers. Between 1873 and 1878 the country suffered by far its deepest and longest depression. Most unions, of course, were wiped out; and the sturdy ones that did endure were reduced to a fraction of their strength.

The cities, already overcrowded with immigrant poor, became charnel houses of indigence and squalor. Mass protests broke out everywhere. Riots often followed, accompanied by pitched battles between the police or the militia and the ragtail armies of the poor. An "insurrectionary spirit" hovered constantly over the streets of the larger cities. Armories were hastily built to guard the better neighborhoods and train personnel in techniques for putting down civil disorder.

Even more ominous from the government's point of view was the industrial violence. Here the distinction must again be drawn between the two sectors of the economy: the working men's and the unskilled laborers'. Unskilled laborers might be hired and fired at will, and they had to take the wages that were offered or lump it. But working men, proud and defiant as ever, would not allow themselves to be treated as commodities, would not easily submit to longer hours, reduced payments, the arbitrary will of employers—not without a struggle. Their resistance took the form of strikes, which, on occasion, developed into armed warfare. There was, for example, the six-month-long anthracite-coal strike of 1875, which ended with the execution of ten men alleged to have participated in a conspiracy of terror: members, presumably, of the notorious "Molly Maguires." Above all, there was the great railroad workers' uprising of 1877, which federal troops finally put down, but only after thirty-five people had been killed in fierce combat, millions of dollars of railroad property had been destroyed (no small sum in those days), and whole communities, including militiamen, had gone over to the insurgents.

Workers, skilled and unskilled alike, learned a bitter lesson in the turmoil of the 1870s. They learned that if the massed power of business enterprise could not suppress them, the government—local, state, and federal, separately or in concert—would do the job in the name of "law and order." Fear of worker discontent and urban unrest was the catalyst that brought business and government into close alliance, one that was to continue well into the twentieth century. Workers found themselves caught inescapably between the millstones of economic and political coercion.

Violent struggle was obviously no answer, such struggles having been lost whenever they had been fought. Other answers were not long in coming. The devotees of easy money, or "greenbacks" (i.e., government-issued notes), received a sympathetic hearing. The slump added immeasurably to the debt of independent working men, not to speak of small entrepreneurs and farmers, and cheap credit seemed the only way out. In 1878 the Greenback Labor Party was formed, its program hardly distinguishable from the one advanced ten years before by the National Labor Union. The Greenback Labor Party did well in the 1878 Congressional election (securing over a million votes), but by the time it fielded a candidate in the presidential campaign two years later, prosperity had returned and easy money was no longer in great demand; it had lost its *raison d'être*.

Agrarianism came to life, too, for a season, this time under the tutelage of one of the remarkable men of the day, Henry George. In his great best-selling book *Progress and Poverty* (published in 1879) and in numerous articles and lectures, George contended that the only way to solve the problem of low wages and unemployment was for the government to impose a "single tax" on the "unearned increment" in land values. This, he claimed, would effectively eliminate the landlord class, make even the best land available to the poor, reduce costs to all producers and manufacturers (who would no longer have to pay ground rent), thereby restoring to working men, to all who toiled, their pristine status as free agents. But, like the previous agrarian nostrums, Henry George's harked back to the ideal, or myth, of the yeoman life. It also played into the hands of labor's real adversary, the manufacturing interests. Despite George's own immense popularity, agrarianism was—for those caught in the toils of industrialism—a dying hope.[2]

And, for the first time, a revolutionary socialist movement appeared, in the 1870s, in the form of the North American branch of Marx's International Workingmen's Association (established in London in 1864). The International made some slight headway among foreign-born, mainly German, workers. Its appeal could not be anything but slight. It spoke less to workers' present concerns than those to come, projecting a reality they

---

[2] The agrarianism of the farmers, which gave rise to the Populist movement of the 1890s, was a different matter. George's message was not addressed to them. Those who already owned land had scant cause to favor a single tax.

did not yet comprehend. Echoing Marx, American leaders of the International maintained that since capitalism was fast evolving into a system of giant industries, workers must organize on strictly class lines, the distinction between craft and unskilled being transient and illusory; that political democracy, as practiced, was a sham, the state being only the executive committee of the ruling class; and that workers must, it followed, organize to simultaneously conquer capitalism and overthrow the government. Not that these socialists opposed temporary alliances with radical bourgeois parties; but it must never be at the expense of the ultimate goal—revolutionary change.

Revolutionary socialism went off in two directions in the 1880s. There was, on the one hand, the Marxist-oriented Socialist Labor Party (the International having died in 1874), which engaged in politics, running its own campaigns, or joining third parties (the most successful example: its coalition with other radicals in support of Henry George's candidacy for mayor of New York in 1886, a race that George nearly won), and in general seeking to play a respectable role in society. The Socialist Labor Party, however, was never more than a corporal's guard of German-American intellectuals scattered throughout the various cities of the East and Midwest.

On the other hand, there were the anarchocommunists. Desperation had driven some revolutionists to take up a strategy of direct action. Waiting for the future to unfold was, in their view, a fatal trap, tantamount to submission. Their impatience was consistent with their ideology. Anarchocommunists agreed with the Marxist analysis up to a point. Where Marxists would take state power as the first step toward bringing about a classless society, the state

Transition

disappearing when the classes did, anarchocommunists proposed to destroy the state at once, root and branch, removing the only obstacle to the spontaneous development of the co-operative commonwealth. They combined teaching with deeds, theory with dynamite.

It is customary to dismiss the revolutionary socialists of the time as a congeries of minuscule, foreign-language sects, utterly without influence on American life. In fact, their influence was considerable, though how considerable it would be hard to measure. The leadership of the first durable union movement (as we shall see) owed much to them. So did the Christian Socialists and the Fabians, who made their mark in the 1890s. So did the Socialist Party, which emerged at the turn of the century and rose to some prominence. So did several of the better-known social critics, such as Edward Bellamy, William Dean Howells, Laurence Gronlund, Henry Demarest Lloyd, and others. What they all owed to revolutionary socialism was the realization that there could be no escape from industrial capitalism, that the future lay either with the working class or with the new slavocracy, the owners of industry; that freedom, however defined in personal or moral terms, was possible only through the prior mastery of economic necessity, the "dismal science" being too important to be left to big business and its academic sycophants.

But the ideology (or false consciousness) of American working men as independent, self-reliant producers died hard. And before it gave up the ghost for good it enjoyed one last spectacular fling, one brief moment of high destiny—under the auspices of the Knights of Labor.

The Knights of Labor started out as a conventional organization of artisans. It was founded in 1869 by a Philadelphia garment cutter, Uriah Stephens, whose craft union had recently been wiped out. Stephens reconstituted the tiny union under a new name, the Noble Order of the Knights of Labor, Local Assembly One. The exotic title symbolized the intentions of its members: They would join together in solid fraternity, hidden from their enemies by a cabalistic rite worked out to a fine detail complete with signs, grips, passwords, and elaborate initiation ceremony. In time, other local assemblies (a minimum of ten members in each), representing other trades, sprang up in Philadelphia and elsewhere, these coalescing (in groups of five) to form district assemblies—the equivalent of the city centrals of olden days. There was, in fact, little to distinguish the Noble Order from previous trade unions. All it lacked was a national organization.

A national organization became necessary with the sudden influx of members after the 1877 uprising, the Knights of Labor being the only union movement of any consequence. Only a national body could resolve jurisdictional disputes, lay down policy guidelines, and actively recruit new members. And so, in 1878, the General Assembly of the Knights of Labor was established under a formal constitution. Unlike its predecessors (the National Trades' Union, the National Labor Union), the General Assembly—more accurately, its Executive Board—had considerable power over local bodies: It could dispense or withdraw their franchises at will.

With nationalization and centralization came other far-reaching changes in the character of the organization. It got rid of much of its secretiveness and mumbo-jumbo language. More important, it invited into its ranks every toiler, every wage earner, everyone who lived or profited from his own labor, regardless of race, sex, religion, nationality, ideology, or skill, excluding only those whose moral habits were unsound, who exploited others, or who engaged in parasitic occupations (banking, law, etc.). Its great fraternal motto was "an injury to one is the concern of all."

So that even though it eschewed politics the Knights of Labor became, in effect, the political party of the underclass, the residuary legatee of the old working men's parties, the National Reform Party, and the Greenback Labor Party. And its demands were roughly similar to theirs: a shorter workday (eight hours), easy money, abolition of convict and immigrant labor, the creation of consumer and producer co-operatives, equitable land distribution, and so forth; as was its object: to bring about a harmonious, classless society of autonomous, self-employed people, according to the standard Jeffersonian-Jacksonian ideal. Which is why the Knights officially opposed strikes as disruptive and selfish, the assertion of class over community.

In the early 1880s the forces of protest had nowhere to go but the Knights of Labor. These included unskilled and semiskilled workers, craft unions, socialists, small businessmen, and farmers. And as the discontent grew, so did the Knights. Between October 1881 and July 1885 its numbers increased from 19,000 to 112,000, its local assemblies from less than two hundred to about a thousand. Enlargement, however, also exacerbated the tensions inherent in it: tensions, for example, between skilled and unskilled workers, between workers on the one hand and petty entrepreneurs and farmers on the other, between district assemblies vying for possession of disparate locals. The latitudinarianism that accounted for its popularity also threatened its viability.

But the threat was only a potential one, and the tensions could easily be put off, as long as the Knights con-

Except to Walk Free

tinued to grow and prosper. And grow and prosper it did —with a vengeance. Within a year and a half, to the end of 1886, its membership rose from 112,000 to 700,000, the number of its local assemblies from nine hundred to fifty-nine hundred. The reason was obvious enough: The Knights had won some highly publicized strikes (despite its aversion to them), in the course of which it had humbled the mighty Jay Gould himself. For a time the Knights seemed invincible.

Events soon demonstrated just how vulnerable the Knights really were, how illusory their strength.

In the first place, the trade unions, more fearful than ever of being swallowed up and dispersed among the several district assemblies, among the unskilled, the small businessmen, and others, went into active opposition to the entire Order.

In the second place, conflict broke out between those who favored a policy of striking for higher wages and those who wanted the Knights to remain consistent with its anti-strike principle, already too often honored in the breach. A number of unauthorized strikes were, in fact, held and lost, and unskilled workers departed from the organization en masse, accusing its leadership of betrayal and mendacity.

In the third place, there was the Chicago Haymarket Massacre, the shoot-out on May 4, 1886, between police and a crowd of anarchocommunists.[3] A great fear of

---

[3] The shoot-out was the culmination of a complex train of circumstances. A strike had been going on at the McCormick Harvester plant for some time. During a melee between strikers and scabs the police intervened, killing several people. The anarchocommunists, who had been active in the strike, held a rally at Haymarket Square to protest the outrage. As the meeting, which had been entirely peaceful, was drawing to a close, the police unaccountably advanced on the speakers' platform. A bomb was then thrown (by whom, no

Transition

anarchism seized the country in the months that followed. This fear, or psychosis, was duly exploited by the enemies of labor, whose position can be reduced to a syllogism: Anarchism was wicked; strikes led to anarchism; therefore strikes were wicked; and since labor organizations were chiefly responsible for strikes, labor organizations were wicked too, and in some respects were the most wicked of all. Of course, it was the Knights, the largest and most successful of the labor organizations, that bore the main obloquy of public disapproval. Newspapers played up the fact that the most famous of the anarcho-communists who had been convicted and hanged, Albert Parsons, happened to be a member of the Order.

The Knights of Labor rapidly disintegrated after 1886, its decline being quite as spectacular as its rise. By the end of the decade it was an organization primarily of discontented farmers and tradesmen; its numbers were down to a mere hundred thousand; its depleted assemblies were functioning mostly in small towns. And while it still upheld the rights of labor and still proudly carried the oriflamme of fraternity, hardly any workers were to be found in its ranks.

---

one knows to this day). The square became a battlefield. When the shooting ended, 11 people lay dead, including 7 policemen, and over 70 hurt.

1. WILLIAM H. SYLVIS*

1864

More than anyone else, William H. Sylvis was the moving force behind the National Labor Union. That he was a formidable leader of working men, he had already demonstrated as president of the iron molders' union. That he was an effective spokesman for them may be seen from the excerpt below of a speech he gave at Buffalo in 1864. His death, in 1869, at the age of forty-one was a serious blow to American working men.

To secure these blessings, two things are absolutely necessary. We want more time and more money; fewer hours of toil, and more wages for what we do. These wants we will supply, and these evils we will remedy through the instrumentality of our organizations. We must have a thorough combination of all branches of labor. And then by co-operation we must erect our own workshops, and establish our own stores, and till our own farms, and live in our own houses—in short, we must absolutely control within ourselves the two elements of capital—labor and money. Then we will not only secure a fair standard of wages, but all the profits of our labor. We must erect our own halls wherein we can establish our own libraries, reading- and lecture-rooms, under the control and management of our own men; and we must have time to use them. We must do our own thinking, and infuse into the minds of our people a high tone of

* J. C. Sylvis, ed., *The Life, Speeches, Labor, and Essays of William H. Sylvis* (New York, 1872), pp. 99–102, 112–14, 116–17.

Transition

morals. We must learn to respect ourselves, and be proud of our occupations and positions. We must hold up our heads, and not be ashamed nor afraid to walk upon the fashionable side of the street. . . .

It has ever been the study and purpose of these men, who arrogate to themselves the right to the enjoyment of all the power and wealth of the world, to make labor entirely subservient to their will—to own it and use it as a part of their machinery, with no other expense than that required to furnish the fuel to keep the machine in motion—all the necessary repairs having to be made by the machine itself. And experience teaches us that in every country they have partly succeeded in their diabolical plan, and in those places where they have obtained control of the law-making power, they have succeeded entirely.

If these things be so, and who will contradict them, what becomes of this so much talked-of identity of interests? In denying the existence of an identity of interests between labor and capital, I do not wish to be understood as saying that there is no identity of interests between *labor* and *money*. I deny that there is an identity of interest between *labor* and *capitalists*. The fact that capital denies to labor the right to regulate its own affairs, would take from the working man the right to place a valuation upon his own labor, destroys at once the theory of an identity of interests; if, as is held by them, the interests of the two are identical, and their positions and relations mutual, there would be no interference whatever one with another; the working man would be left free to place his own price upon his labor, as capitalists are to say what interest or profits they shall have upon money invested. This identity of interests amounts to simply this and nothing more. Capitalists employ labor for

Except to Walk Free

the amount of profit realized, and working men labor for the amount of wages received. This is the only relation existing between them; they are two distinct elements, or rather two distinct classes, with interests as widely separated as the poles. We find capitalists ever watchful of their interests—ever ready to make everything bend to their desires. Then why should not laborers be equally watchful of their interests—equally ready to take advantage of every circumstance to secure good wages and social elevation? Were labor left free to control itself, as it should be and must be, instead of there being an identity of interests, a mutual relation between the two classes, there is an antagonism that ever did and ever will exist; a sort of an irrepressible conflict that commenced with the world, and will only end with it.

If workingmen and capitalists are equal co-partners, composing one vast firm by which the industry of the world is carried on and controlled, why do they not share equally in the profits? Why does capital take to itself the whole loaf, while labor is left to gather up the crumbs? Why does capital roll in luxury and wealth, while labor is left to eke out a miserable existence in poverty and want? Are these the evidences of an identity of interests, of mutual relations, of equal partnership? No, sir. On the contrary, they are evidences of an antagonism. This antagonism is the general origin of all "strikes." Labor has always the same complaints to make, and capital always the same oppressive rules to make, and power to employ. Were it not for this antagonism, labor would often escape the penalty of much misery and moral degradation, and capital the disgrace and ruin consequent upon such dangerous collisions. There is not only a never-ending conflict between the two classes, but capital is, in all cases,

Transition

the aggressor. Labor is always found on the defensive, because

1. Capital enjoys individual power, and in the exercise of that is given to encroach upon the rights and privileges of labor.

2. Labor is individually weak, and only becomes powerful when banded together for self-defence.

3. Capital is jealous of control, or even of remonstrance, and will often object to the interference of labor, even when such an interference would be beneficial to its own interests.

4. Capital is selfish and regardless of the fate, feelings, or condition of labor. The physical condition, intellectual development, and moral training of labor are neglected for that inordinate power which accumulated wealth supplies.

5. Capital is haughty, proud, and insolent, and spurns with contempt the remonstrances of the oppressed, the respectful entreaties of the defrauded, and the cries of the poor and abject.

6. Capital seldom forgives; it loses the finer feelings of the human heart, and knows no other commercial principle than that embodied in the famous axiom of the "Free Trade" school, which says, "buy in the cheapest markct and sell in the dearest," but which, if applied to labor means, "keep down the price of labor and starve the working men; so shall thy profits be many, and thy wealth increased." It must follow, from the admission of these premises, that the interests of employer and employee are not identical. That on the one side, employers are interested, because of profit, to keep down the price of labor; while on the other side, the employees are justified, on account of self-interest, to keep up wages. Thus labor and capital are antagonistic. . . .

Except to Walk Free

Yes, here is that land which "Heaven reserved in pity for the poor"; and it depends upon ourselves whether or not we will enjoy the priceless blessing. It is an inheritance bequeathed to us by the great Giver of all good, and we must prepare ourselves for its possession, qualify ourselves for its enjoyment. Again, Mr. Chairman, why should we not occupy a high social and political position? There is no reason why we *should not*, but there are many reasons why we *do not*.

1. We are not sufficiently educated to properly understand the true principles of social and political science, and too apt to listen to the teachings of those whose interest it is to foster prejudices rather than cultivate intelligence.

2. Our labor occupies too large a portion of our time to enable us to read, study, and reflect. A high degree of intelligence is necessary to enable us to discharge all the duties of citizens. If we were sufficiently well paid for from six to eight hours work a day, to furnish ourselves with the means of cultivation, we would do better work and be more useful men.

3. There is not sufficient union and harmony among us to secure the blessings and conditions we so much need and desire. This can only be accomplished by an earnest, united, and properly directed effort by those who see and appreciate the condition and wants of labor, and understand the true way to ameliorate this condition, and supply these wants.

4. Low wages prevent us from exercising that moral influence over our fellow-men which enables men of wealth to control the social and political affairs of a nation. This can only be accomplished by a thorough combination and co-operation among all branches of industry.

Transition

5. The want of a well-regulated apprentice system has filled the land with a vast number of inferior workmen, who, not being masters of their trade, are more or less subject to the whims and caprices of capitalists.

2. THE NATIONAL LABOR UNION[*]

1867

> Below is the constitution (in part) of the National Labor Union, adopted at the Chicago convention of 1867. Included also is the Union's "Declaration of Principles" (a take-off on the Declaration of Independence) and statement of political strategy.

ARTICLE 1, *Section* 1. This organization shall be known as the National Labor Union, and its jurisdiction shall be confined to the United States.

ARTICLE 2, *Section* 1. The National Labor Union shall be composed of such labor organizations as may now, or hereafter exist, having for their object the amelioration of the condition of those who labor for a living.

ARTICLE 2, *Section* 2. Every international or national organization shall be entitled to three representatives; state organizations to two; trades unions and all other organizations to one representative in the National Labor Congress, provided that representatives shall derive their election direct from the organization they claim to represent.

ARTICLE 2, *Section* 3. Ex-representatives, upon presentation of certificate of good standing in their organization, shall be entitled to a voice, without a vote, in the National Labor Congress. . . .

[Committee on political organization:] Your committee to whom was referred the subject of National

[*] Commons, vol. IX, pp. 173–77, 179–82.

Transition

Labor Organization, have had the same under consideration, and beg leave to report that in their judgment, the time has arrived when the industrial classes should cut themselves aloof from party ties and predilections, and organize themselves into a National Labor Party, the object of which shall be to secure by proper legislation the labor reforms necessary to the prosperity of the nation, and that we recommend to the various local organizations of working men, whenever they may deem it expedient, to nominate candidates for the various offices to be filled, and to support them at the ballot box; and we further recommend to every friend of the labor movement to vote for no candidate not unequivocally pledged to support the principles of the labor reform organization.

We beg further to present the following Declaration of Principles:

We hold these truths to be self evident, that all men are created equal, that they are endowed by their Creator with certain inalienable rights; that among them are life, liberty and the pursuit of happiness; that to secure these rights, governments are instituted among men, deriving their just powers from the consent of the governed.

That there are but two pure forms of government, the autocratic and the democratic; under the former the will of the individual sovereign is the supreme law, under the latter the sovereignty is vested in the whole people, all other forms being a modification of the one or the other of these principles, and that ultimately one or other of these forms must prevail throughout all civilized nations, and it is now for the American people to determine which of these principles shall triumph. . . .

That our monetary, financial and revenue laws are in letter and spirit opposed to the principles of freedom and equality upon which our democratic republican institutions are founded, there is in all their provisions manifestly a studied design to shield non-producing capital from its just proportion of the burdens necessary for the support of the government, imposing them mainly on the industrial wealth-producing classes, thereby condemning them to lives of unremunerated toil, depriving them of the ordinary conveniences and comforts of life; of the time and means necessary for social enjoyment, intellectual culture and moral improvement; and ultimately reducing them to a state of practical servitude.

We further hold that while these unrighteous laws of distribution remain in force, laborers cannot, by any system of combination or co-operation, secure their natural rights. That the first and most important step towards the establishment of the rights of labor, is the institution of a system of true co-operation between non-producing capital and labor. That to effect this most desirable object, money, the medium of distribution to capital and labor, must be instituted upon such a wise and just principle that instead of being a power to centralize the wealth in the hands of a few bankers, usurers, middlemen and non-producers generally, it shall be a power that will distribute products to producers in accordance with the labor or service performed in their production—the servant and not the master of labor. This done the natural rights of labor will be secured, and co-operation in production and in the distribution of products, will follow as a natural consequence. . . . We hold that this can be effected by the issue of treasury notes made a legal tender in the payment of all debts public and private, and convertible at the option of the holder into government bonds, bearing a just rate of interest, sufficiently below the rate of increase in the national wealth by natural production, as to make an equitable distribution of the products of labor between non-producing capital and labor, reserving to Congress the right to alter the same when, in their judgment the public interest would be promoted thereby; giving the government creditor the right to take the lawful money or the interest bearing bonds at his election, with the privilege to the holder to reconvert the bonds into money or the money into bonds, at pleasure.

We hold this to be the true American, or people's monetary system, adapted to the genius of our democratic republican institutions, in harmony with the letter and spirit of the constitution and suited to the wants of the government and business interests of the nation; that it would furnish a medium of exchange, having equal powers, a uniform value and fitted for the performance of all the functions of money, co-extensive with the jurisdiction of government. That with a just rate per cent interest on the government bonds, it would effect the equitable distribution of the products of labor between non-producing capital and labor, giving to laborers a fair compensation for their products, and to capital a just reward for its use; remove the necessity for excessive toil and afford the industrial classes the time and means necessary for social and intellectual culture. With the rate of interest at three per cent on the government bonds, the national debt would be liquidated within less than thirty years without the imposition or collection of one farthing of taxes for that purpose. Thus it would dispense with the hungry hoard of assessors, tax-gatherers and government spies that are now harassing the industrial classes and despoiling them of their substance.

We further hold that it is essential to the prosperity and happiness of the people and the stability of our

Except to Walk Free

democratic republican institutions, that the public domain be distributed as widely as possible among the people; a land monopoly being equally as oppressive to the people and dangerous to our institutions, as the present money monopoly. To prevent this the public lands should be sold in reasonable quantities, and to none but actual occupants. . . .

We further hold that intelligence and virtue in the sovereignty are necessary to a wise administration of justice, and that as our institutions are founded upon the theory of sovereignty in the people, in order to their preservation and perpetuity, it is the imperative duty of Congress to make such wise and just regulations as shall afford all the means of acquiring the knowledge requisite to the intelligent exercise of the privileges and duties pertaining to sovereignty, and that Congress should ordain that eight hours labor between the rising and setting of the sun should constitute a day's work in all government works and places where the national government has exclusive jurisdiction, and that it is equally imperative on the several states to make like provision by legal enactment. . . .

3. THE NEGRO NATIONAL LABOR UNION*

1869

> Excluded from the National Labor Union, black workers formed their own organization in 1869. How different its attitudes were on racial and ethnic equality may be judged from this official statement of its beliefs.

In our organization we make no discrimination as to nationality, sex, or color. Any labor movement based upon such discrimination and embracing a small part of the great working masses of the country, while repelling others because of its partial and sectional character, will prove to be of very little value. Indeed, such a movement, narrow and divisional, will be suicidal, for it arrays against the classes represented by it all other laboring classes which ought to be rather allied in the closest union, and avoid these dissensions and divisions which in the past have given wealth the advantage over labor.

We would have "the poor white man" of the South, born to a heritage of poverty and degradation like his black compeer in social life, feel that labor in our organization seeks the elevation of all its sons and daughters; pledges its united strength not to advance the interests of a special class; but in its spirit of reasonableness and generous catholicity would promote the welfare and happiness of all who "earn their bread in the sweat of their brow."

With us, too, numbers count, and we know the maxim, "in union there is strength," has its significance in the

* *The New Era,* January 13, 1870.

Except to Walk Free

affairs of labor no less than in politics. Hence our industrial movement, emancipating itself from every national and partial sentiment, broadens and deepens its foundations so as to rest thereon a superstructure capacious enough to accommodate at the altar of common interest the Irish, the Negro and the German laborer; to which, so far from being excluded, the "poor white" native of the South, struggling out of moral and pecuniary death into life "real and earnest," the white mechanic and laborer of the North, so long ill taught and advised that his true interest is gained by hatred and abuse of the laborer of African descent, as well as the Chinaman, whom designing persons, partially enslaving, would make in the plantation service of the South the rival and competitor of the former slave class of the country, having with us one and the same interest, are all invited, earnestly urged, to join us in our movement, and thus aid in the protection and conservation of their and our interests.

In the cultivation of such spirit of generosity on our part, and the magnanimous conduct which it prompts, we hope, by argument and appeal addressed to the white mechanics, laborers and trades unions of our country, to our legislators and countrymen at large, to overcome the prejudices now existing against us so far as to secure a fair opportunity for the display and remuneration of our industrial capabilities.

We launch our organization, then, in the fullest confidence, knowing that, if wisely and judiciously managed, it must bring to all concerned, strength and advantage, and especially to the colored American as its earliest fruits that power which comes from competence and wealth, education and the ballot, made strong through a union whose fundamental principles are just, impartial and catholic.

4. THE KNIGHTS OF LABOR: 1*

1869

Following is part of the strange rites of initiation drawn up mainly by Uriah S. Stephens. A guide to the meaning of the initials may be helpful to the reader. "M.W." is Master Workman; "U.K." is Unknown Workman; "S.O. and M.A." is Secrecy, Obedience and Mutual Assistance; "W.F." is Worthy Foreman. Asterisks stand for the Noble Order of the Knights of Labor.

U.K. M.W., Mr. ———, has satisfactorily answered all inquiries and now desires to be covered with our shield and admitted to fellowship in this noble and holy Order.

After a short pause, and amid perfect silence, the M.W. says:

M.W. Place him at the centre and administer the vow.

*The U.K. places the candidate and friends at the centre; places their left hands on the sacred Scriptures, fingers over, thumb under; directs the candidate to grasp the * of his friend, the friend that of the U.K., and the U.K. takes that of the candidate, the three forming a triangle over and around the Altar, and all pronounce the Vow. Affirmation, when preferred by the candidate, made in the same way.*

I ——— ———, do truly and solemnly swear (or affirm), that I will never reveal, by word, act, art, or implication, positive or negative, to any person or persons whatsoever the name or object of this Order, the name, or person of

---

* Commons, vol. X, pp. 21–24.

Except to Walk Free

any one a member thereof, its signs, mysteries, arts, privileges or benefits: now or hereafter, given to, or conferred on me, any words spoken, acts done, or objects intended; except in a legal, and authorized manner, or by special permission of the Order granted to me.

I do truly and solemnly promise strictly to obey all laws, regulations, solemn injunctions, and legal summons, that may be sent, said or handed to me.

I do truly and solemnly promise that I will to the best of my ability, defend the life, interest, reputation and family, of all true members of this Order, help and assist all employed, and unemployed, unfortunate, or distressed Brothers to procure employ, secure just remuneration, relieve their distress, and counsel others to aid them, so that they and theirs may receive and enjoy the just fruits of their labor, and exercise of their art.

All this I swear (or affirm), without reservation or evasion, to do and perform until death, or honorable discharge (an accepted resignation), and bind myself under the penalty of the scorn and neglect due to perjury, and violated honor, as one unworthy of trust or assistance. So help me God, and keep me steadfast unto the end. Amen.

All respond Amen.

The M.W. gives one tap to seat the Assembly. The U.K. will, after the Assembly is seated, proceed with the candidate to the Capital, and report to the M.W. . . . .

U.K. M.W., Mr. ——— ———, has taken the solemn vow of S.O. and M.A.

M.W. That act has covered him with the shield of our Brotherhood. Proceed with him to the Base of the Sanctuary, there to receive the instructions of the W.F.

Arrived at the Base the U.K. introduces the candidate to the W.F. thus:

Transition

U.K. W.F., by permission of this Assembly of true *s and the command of the M.W., I present to you Mr. ——— ———, for instruction.

W.F. In the beginning God ordained that man should labor, not as a curse, but as a blessing; not as a punishment, but as a means of development, physically, mentally, morally, and has set thereunto his seal of approval, in the rich increase and reward. By labor is brought forth the kindly fruits of the earth in rich abundance for our sustenance and comfort; by labor, (not exhaustive) is promoted health of body and strength of mind; and labor garners the priceless stores of wisdom and knowledge. It is the "Philosopher's Stone," everything it touches turns to gold. "Labor is noble and holy." To glorify God in its exercise, to defend it from degradation, to divest it of the evils to body, mind and estate, which ignorance and greed have imposed; to rescue the toiler from the grasp of the selfish is a work worthy of the noblest and best of our race. Without your seeking, without even your knowledge, you have been selected from among your fellows, for that exalted purpose. Are you willing to accept the responsibility, and trusting in God and the support of sworn true *s, labor with what ability you possess, for the triumph of these principles among men?

The candidate answers. If affirmatively, the W.F. will say to the candidate and the U.K.:

W.F. We will now proceed with our friend to the M.W.

And accompanying them to the M.W. says:

W.F. M.W., I present Mr. ——— ———, as a fitting and worthy person to receive the honor of fellowship with this noble and holy Order.

The M.W. taking his hand will say:

M.W. On behalf of the toiling millions on earth, I wel-

Except to Walk Free

come you to this Sanctuary, dedicated to the service of God, by serving humanity. Open and public associations having failed, after a struggle of centuries, to protect or advance the interest of labor, we have lawfully constituted this Assembly. Hid from public view, covered by an impenetrable veil of secrecy (not to promote or shield wrong doing) but to shield ourselves and you, from persecution and wrong by men in our own sphere and calling, as well as others out of it, when we endeavor to secure the just reward of our toil. In using this power of organized effort and co-operation, we but imitate the example of capital heretofore set in numberless instances. In all the multifarious branches of trade, capital has its combinations, and whether intended or not, it crushes the manly hopes of labor and tramples poor humanity in the dust. We mean no conflict with legitimate enterprise, no antagonism to necessary capital, but men in their haste and greed, blinded by self interest, overlook the interests of others, and sometimes even violate the rights of those they deem helpless. We mean to uphold the dignity of labor, to affirm the nobility of all who live in accordance with the ordinance of God, "in the sweat of thy brow shalt thou eat bread." We mean to create a healthy public opinion on the subject of labor (the only creator of values or capital), and the justice of its receiving a full, just share of the values or capital it has created. We shall with all our strength, support laws made to harmonize the interests of labor and capital, for labor alone gives life and value to capital, and also those laws which tend to lighten the exhaustiveness of toil. We shall use every lawful and honorable means to procure and retain employ for one another, coupled with just and fair remuneration, and should accident or misfortune befall one of our number, render such aid as lies within our power to give, without inquiring his coun-

Transition

try or his creed; and without approving of general strikes among artisans, yet should it become justly necessary to enjoin an oppressor, we will protect and aid any of our number who thereby may suffer loss, and as opportunity offers, extend a helping hand to all branches of honorable toil. Such is but an epitome of our objects. Your duties and obligations, your privileges and benefits you will learn as you mingle with, and become acquainted in, the noble and holy Order of the *s of *. . . .

5. THE INTERNATIONAL WORKINGMEN'S ASSOCIATION*

1871

The North American Central Committee of the International was formed in May 1871 and met regularly at the Tenth Ward Hotel, in lower Manhattan. The committee consisted of delegates from ten small groups (or sections), seven of them New York City. Following is the appeal it sent out to the workers of the United States.

The I.W.A. has spread over the entire civilized world and is planting its roots among the working classes of all countries, where modern industry reigns (England, Germany, France, Belgium, Austria, Switzerland, Spain, Italy, Russia, Holland, United States, etc.). Its central body or board of administration, the General Council of the I.W.A., is sitting at London and in its last official communication of March 14th distinctly recognizes and acknowledges the organization of the undersigned C.C. and "expresses its satisfaction with our activity." Every Trades Union or Labor Society of this country may affiliate with this Central Committee of the I.W.A. by acknowledging and defending the principles and rules of the I.W.A. and remitting an annual due of two cents per member for the General Council and five cents per member for this Central Committee to the undersigned and also electing a delegate.

* Commons, vol. IX, pp. 357–59.

Transition

The principles of the I.W.A. may be condensed in the following extracts from its rules:

> The emancipation of the working classes must be conquered by the working classes themselves.
>
> The struggle for the emancipation of the working classes means not a struggle for class privileges and monopolies, but for equal rights and duties and the abolition of all class rule.
>
> The economical subjection of the man of labor to the monopolizer of the means of labor, that is the sources of life, lies at the bottom of servitude in all its forms, of all social misery, mental degradation and political dependence;
>
> The economical emancipation of the working classes is therefore the great end to which every political movement ought to be subordinate as a means.
>
> All efforts aiming at that great end have hitherto failed from the want of solidarity between the manifold divisions of labor in each country and from the absence of a fraternal bond of union between the working classes of different countries. The emancipation of labor is neither a local, nor a national, but a social problem embracing all countries, in which modern society exists and depending for its solution on the concurrence, practical and theoretical, of the most advanced countries.

The National Labor Congress at Cincinnati, August, 1870, and the N.Y. State Workingmen's Assembly, January, 1871, both passed resolutions acknowledging and recommending the principles of the I.W.A.

FELLOW-WORKINGMEN! This Central Committee is in duty bound to make every effort for uniting the working classes of this country and to collect everything tending to enlighten them on their own condition. Recognizing this, as you surely will, also as an important duty of yours, you are hereby solicited to enter into communi-

Except to Walk Free

cations with us and to report to us everything at your disposal referring to the condition of your trade and associates as well as in general of working men in your district. We are willing and ready to reciprocate with all due care and dispatch.

A full and clear knowledge of the interests of our class will, we are satisfied, soon influence you in declaring your affiliation to that fraternal union of the laborers of all countries destined to break the yoke, under which the working class languish—the wages—slavery.

Working men of all countries, unite! Fraternal greeting. The North American Central Committee of the International Workingmen's Association.

6. WENDELL PHILLIPS*

1872

Wendell Phillips, the great abolitionist, turned his attention to "the labor question" after the Civil War. He was one of the first to perceive that the only antidote to the power of industrial capital (the equivalent for Phillips of the old slavocracy) was the power of working men organized into unions and parties and as such advocating a co-operative ethic. Here is one of his typical speeches of the time, delivered to the Knights of St. Crispin, a union of shoemakers.

. . . I rejoice at every effort working-men make to organize; I do not care on what basis they do it. Men sometimes say to me, "Are you an Internationalist?" I say, "I do not know what an Internationalist is;" but they tell me it is a system by which the working-men from London to Gibraltar, from Moscow to Paris, can clasp hands. Then I say God speed, God speed, to that or any similar movement.

Now, let me tell you where the great weakness of an association of working-men is. It is that it cannot wait. It does not know where it is to get its food for next week. If it is kept idle for ten days, the funds of the society are exhausted. Capital can fold its arms, and wait six months; it can wait a year. It will be poorer, but it does not get to the bottom of the purse. It can afford to wait; it can tire you out, and starve you out.

* Wendell Phillips, *Speeches, Lectures, and Letters* (Boston, 1892), pp. 169–70, 172–76.

Except to Walk Free

And what is there against that immense preponderance of power on the part of capital? Simply organization. *That makes the wealth of all, the wealth of every one.* So I welcome organization. I do not care whether it calls itself Trades-union, Crispin, International, or Commune; anything that masses up the units in order that they may put in a united force to face the organization of capital, anything that does that, I say *amen* to it. One hundred thousand men! It is an immense army. I do not care whether it considers chiefly the industrial or the political questions; it can control the nation if it is in earnest. The reason why the Abolitionists brought the nation down to fighting their battle is that they were really in earnest, knew what they wanted, and were determined to have it. Therefore they got it. The leading statesmen and orators of the day said they would never urge abolition; but a determined man in a printing-office said that they should, and they did it. . . .

Let me tell you why I am interested in the Labor Question. Not simply because of the long hours of labor; not simply because of a specific oppression of a class. I sympathize with the sufferers there; I am ready to fight on their side. But I look out upon Christendom, with its three hundred millions of people, and I see, that, out of this number of people, one hundred millions never had enough to eat. Physiologists tell us that this body of ours, unless it is properly fed, properly developed, fed with rich blood and carefully nourished, does no justice to the brain. You cannot make a bright or a good man in a starved body; and so this one third of the inhabitants of Christendom, who have never had food enough, can never be what they should be.

Now, I say that the social civilization which condemns every third man in it to be below the average in the

Transition

nourishment God prepared for him, did not come from above; it came from below; and the sooner it goes down, the better. Come on this side of the ocean. You will find forty millions of people, and I suppose they are in the highest state of civilization; and yet it is not too much to say, that out of that forty millions, ten millions, at least, who get up in the morning and go to bed at night, spend all the day in the mere effort to get bread enough to live. They have not elasticity enough, mind or body, left to do anything in the way of intellectual or moral progress. . . .

I hail the Labor movement for two reasons; and one is, that it is my only hope for democracy. At the time of the Antislavery agitation, I was not sure whether we should come out of the struggle with one republic or two; but republics I knew we should still be. I am not so confident, indeed, that we shall come out of this storm as a republic, unless the labor movement succeeds. Take a power like the Pennsylvania Central Railroad and the New York Central Railroad, and there is no legislative independence that can exist in its sight. As well expect a green vine to flourish in a dark cellar as to expect honesty to exist under the shadow of those upas-trees. Unless there is a power in your movement, industrially and politically, the last knell of democratic liberty in this union is struck; for as I said, there is no power in one State to resist such a giant as the Pennsylvania road. We have thirty-eight one-horse legislatures in this country; and we have got a man like Tom Scott, with three hundred and fifty million dollars in his hands; and, if he walks through the States, they have no power. Why, he need not move at all. If he smokes, as Grant does, a puff of the waste smoke out of his mouth upsets the legislature.

Except to Walk Free

Now, there is nothing but the rallying of men against money that can contest with that power. Rally industrially if you will; rally for eight hours, for a little division of profits, for co-operation; rally for such a banking-power in the government as would give us money at three per cent.

Only organize, and stand together. Claim something together, and at once; let the nation hear a united demand from the laboring voice, and then, when you have got that, go on after another; but get something. . . .

7. THE GREAT UPRISING*

1877

Probably the best contemporary account of the 1877 strike was written by Joseph A. Dacus, an editor of the St. Louis *Republican*. Though obsessed by the hobgoblin of socialist revolution, Dacus tried to be fair, and he blamed the railroad companies for having provoked the workers to rebel.

Startling as was the collision on Friday night, in the streets of Baltimore, that event had become but an episode—an incident no longer to be remembered before the close of another day. The smaller and less important was lost in the greater and more momentous events transpiring all over the country. What mattered a few volleys, what importance could longer attach to the death of ten or twelve obscure individuals in Baltimore, when the whole country was in an uproar, when no human foresight could determine that a reign of devastation and death, such as had never before afflicted the world, might not commence at any time? The appearance of the Commune, bold, audacious, apparently organized, was a matter for more serious concern than the death of a few roughs, and some innocent citizens by the fatal discharge of musketry in the streets of Baltimore. Strikes were occurring almost every hour. The great State of Pennsylvania was in an uproar; New Jersey was afflicted

* Joseph A. Dacus, *Annals of the Great Strikes of the United States*, pp. 88–90, 205–9, 214–16.

Except to Walk Free

by a paralyzing dread; New York was mustering an army of militia; Ohio was shaken from Lake Erie to the Ohio river; Indiana rested in a dreadful suspense. Illinois, and especially its great metropolis, Chicago, apparently hung on the verge of a vortex of confusion and tumult. St. Louis had already felt the effect of the premonitory shocks of the uprising wave of popular passion.

And yet in the public mind, there was no well defined fear of dreadful deeds to be committed by railroad strikers. The public mind was settled in the conviction that the strikers would interrupt traffic on the highways of commerce by quitting their posts, and even by threats and violence preventing others from taking their places, but such acts, if lawless, were regarded at most as but venial faults. There was an abiding confidence in the good character and honorable disposition of the working men as a class. The public refused to believe that a class of persons who had contributed so much toward building up the country by their toil, and devotion to duty, could in the short space of a few days become untamed savages —merciless plunderers and murderers.

It was not, therefore the fusilades, and the bloody results of the collision at Baltimore that engaged public attention. It was that which appeared "beneath the surface." The event itself was nothing, but that which was revealed by it, was everything. Behind the strikers men beheld a more dreadful force. It was the awful presence of that socialism, which has more than once made Europe tremble on account of its energy, its despotism, its fearful atrocities. The smoke had scarcely cleared away from the streets, when the character of the Baltimore mob was revealed in all its hideousness. The Commune had found a place in America. Taking advantage of the disorders caused by the strike, these socialistic disorganizers appeared on the scene, and displayed a boldness and energy really awe-inspiring. Who could say that the *Red Lady* might not soon appear to garner a ghastly harvest of bodiless heads? . . .

Baltimore and Pittsburgh had not been forgotten. The great strikes continued. There was still in the minds of men disquieting thoughts. When would the troubles end? How would the difficulty conclude? What was to be the result of all the turmoil, the bitterness, the hate aroused? These were questions present in the minds of men, and for them there were no answers. Nearly a hundred lives had already been extinguished, five times a hundred human beings had been maimed and mangled since the strikes began. Property worth millions of dollars had vanished amid smoke and flames. The country was in a feverish state of excitement from Boston to San Francisco; from the Lakes to the Gulf. Men lived, thought, and acted more in a day, than they ordinarily do in a week. Since the first European landed on the shores of America, no such scenes as those transpiring had ever before arrested the attention of the whole people of the country. It was a time of fear and anxiety. Who would be the next victim, what city next be given over to devouring flames, and the rapacity of a lawless mob? Who could tell?

It was on the 23d day of July, 1877—just seven days after the commencement of the first strike on the Baltimore and Ohio Railroad, at South Baltimore and Martinsburg. Already momentous events had happened. Baltimore, Pittsburgh, and Cumberland had successively attracted the attention of those who cared to observe the course of the remarkable movement among the working classes. Hornellsville, Harrisburgh, Phillipsburg, and Buffalo had been the scene of actions, startling in their nature. Where would the next center of interest be located? It was not

Except to Walk Free

necessary to wait long for an answer to this question. For some days there had been trouble on the Philadelphia and Reading Railroad, and among the miners in that vicinity. Reading was favorably situated to become the central point of the movement in that region.

At this time Pennsylvania was in arms, from the Delaware to the Monongahela. There were many militia officers who were anxious to immortalize themselves by the performance of some heroic action. The Knight of La Mancha has imitators in this age, and in this land. Up to the 22nd, no trouble had occurred at Reading. There were some men on a strike, and trains had been stopped, but the crowds that gathered about the stations, were citizens drawn to those places to satisfy an idle curiosity.

But the scene was destined to change. There was in that division of Pennsylvania a notable military commander, Major-General William J. Bolton, who commanded the Second Division of the National Guards of Pennsylvania. To this puissant warrior the railroad authorities appealed, and he sent one of his trusted Lieutenants, Brigadier-General Frank Reeder, to Reading, with the Fourth and Sixteenth Regiments. These warriors, even, according to the sworn statement of their commander, succeeded in making for themselves an odious record ere they left Reading—at least, may this be said of the Fourth Regiment, and particularly of the "Easton Greys." Reading mourns the folly of the militia yet.

On account of the unmilitary conduct of some companies of General Reeder's regiment, we are compelled to add another story of slaughter to the bloody records of Baltimore and Pittsburgh. Without one word of warning, these militia fired upon an assembled crowd of citizens, in the very heart of the city of Reading, and killed thir-

Transition

teen people, shot five policemen, and altogether severely wounded twenty-seven persons.

Night had just settled upon the city, and North Seventh street, for two squares, was lined with people, sitting in the enjoyment of the cool air of evening, in front of their homes. The main line of the Philadelphia and Reading Railroad Company's road passes through the city on Seventh street. Penn street is the main thoroughfare, running in an opposite direction from the course of the railroad, and crosses Seventh street at right angles. From Penn street northward for two squares, two lines of track are laid, leading to the new depot. These are laid through a deep cut, with a heavy stone wall, twenty feet high on either side. On this section of track the bloody work was done. At ten minutes after eight o'clock the military marched in toward Penn street, through the cut, from the depot. They were about three hundred and fifty strong, and they marched, to the tap of a few drums that could not be heard a square away. Few people were aware of their arrival in the city, and fewer still knew they were advancing upon the crowd.

Steadily they approached, when suddenly three hundred rifles were discharged in volleys, and five men dropped to the pavements. The report that the troops had shot blank cartridges, of course, was incorrect. When the troops fired their first volleys, they were given broadsides of rocks and stones from the tops of the walls. Quite a number of revolver shots were returned by parties in the crowd. The troops continued their firing, and men, women and children fled in fear. They had assembled on Seventh street to look at the train that had been stopped, and they were recklessly and indiscriminately shot by the militia. The citizens were almost universal in their condemnation of these proceedings. In five minutes the streets were cleared,

Except to Walk Free

stores were closed, and hotels and restaurants were locked up. Business had been proceeding as usual, and just before the firing, not a single merchant, or business man was aware of the coming of the military. The streets resembled a small battle field, and the pavements were stained with many pools of blood. It was absolutely dangerous for men to come from the alleyways and from behind the brick walls, to go to the assistance of the dying. The heroic militia stood to their guns, and were valiantly disposed to shoot down any citizen who might cross the line of their vision. Finally the sufferers, groaning and shrieking for water, were carried to the drug stores to have their wounds dressed. . . .

The presence of the military did not curb the spirit of the rioters. On the contrary they grew bolder and more threatening. For some days after the fight open attacks on the trains were made.

The strikers mounted a passing loaded coal train, put on the brakes, stopped the train and pushed back the caboose and several loaded cars, thus virtually blockading the down track. One of the eight-ton cars was dumped on the rails. At ten minutes after four o'clock, July 25th, the down express train came along slowly on the other track. The strikers were led by a large man wearing a dark shirt and dark pants. His hair looked as if it had been recently shaved from his head.

Fully two hundred strikers would rush right up squarely to the front of the approaching locomotive, wave their hands, shake their clenched fists, and by many devices intimidate and threaten the engine driver and train employes. An up freight train was compelled to go back, and the crew made to desert the cars. At one time it was feared they would run the engine into the river below the city. The up passenger and express train came through the city

Transition

at a fearful speed, with the engine whistling lustily. As she sped through the crowd, Engineer Saracool bent low in his cab and gave the engine full stroke, in order to successfully pass the enraged men.

The freight up from Philadelphia and the market train were compelled to halt and go no further. At this point the passenger train down, was stopped in the cut, where the fighting took place. The crew was compelled to desert and the passengers were obliged to leave. These high handed proceedings continued until about seven o'clock, when nearly all the strikers left the ground for parts unknown. Not one of the rioters was either killed or wounded.

The majority, in fact all the unfortunates, were law-abiding, peaceable citizens, who had assembled at Seventh and Penn streets simply to gratify their curiosity.

A large body of Coal and Iron Police, from the coal regions, were quartered at the Company's mammoth car shops, which works the strikers threatened to burn. A large crowd of the friends of the railroad men procured about fifty muskets for the strikers, and there was imminent danger of a desperate conflict.

The military companies engaged in the fight were the Hamburg Rifles, Slatington Rifles, Allentown Continentals, Company I, infantry, of Catasqua, Easton Greys, and a company from Portland, Northampton county. They arrived at eight o'clock in the evening. A number of the military, after their bloody work was done, threw down their arms, and asked for citizens' clothes.

At a quarter after eleven o'clock, the night of the 25th, the strikers had torn down the watch boxes at the street corners, and proceeded down the road to tear up the tracks. They signalized their departure by a perfect hurricane of yells and cheering, as they proceeded in their on-

Except to Walk Free

ward march of ruin and destruction. The city had become turbulent again, and the outlook indicated desperate work. The cry among the men was, "Wages and revenge."

The Sheriff issued his proclamation, and Mayor Evans returned home from Ocean Grove, on a special train, in answer to an urgent telegram. Town meetings were held to take steps to prevent any repetition of the dark deeds which had cast a gloom over the whole community at Reading.

Before the militia were withdrawn from Reading, there was a narrow escape from a bloody scene. It was the night after the horrible fusilades. Large crowds had gathered at the scene of that conflict, and about the same time several companies of the Fourth Regiment marched down Seventh to Penn street. Here they met a company of the Sixteenth Regiment, and a fight between the military seemed imminent. The crowd treated the Easton Greys to a shower of stones. This company immediately levelled their pieces, when they were notified by Colonel Scholl of the Sixteenth Regiment that no indiscriminate slaughter would be permitted. All the troops then passed down Penn and out Fifth street, followed by the mob, who fairly threw insults in the teeth of the soldiery.

The Morristown company of the Sixteenth Regiment subsequently stacked their arms, and refused absolutely to operate against the rioters. Some of them threw their guns away, and distributed the cartridges among the crowd. The company left for home shortly afterwards, as did all the militia engaged in the firing on the citizens. Mayor Evans issued a proclamation, calling for one thousand volunteers to do patrol duty in the city, until quiet and order was restored. A special force of policemen were sworn in, and other measures taken to preserve order in the city.

8. THE KNIGHTS OF LABOR: 2*

1878

This is the Preamble to the Knights of Labor Constitution, adopted in 1878.

The recent alarming development and aggression of aggregated wealth, which, unless checked, will invariably lead to the pauperization and hopeless degradation of the toiling masses, render it imperative, if we desire to enjoy the blessings of life, that a check should be placed upon its power and upon unjust accumulation, and a system adopted which will secure to the laborer the fruits of his toil; and as this much desired object can only be accomplished by the thorough unification of labor, and the united effort of those who obey the divine injunction that "In the sweat of thy brow shalt thou eat bread," we have formed the * * * * * with a view of securing the organization and direction, by co-operative effort, of the power of the industrial classes; and we submit to the world the object sought to be accomplished by our organization, calling upon all who believe in securing "the greatest good to the greatest number" to aid and assist us:—

I. To bring within the folds of organization every department of productive industry, making knowledge a standpoint for action, and industrial and moral worth, not wealth, the true standard of individual and national greatness.

II. To secure to the toilers a proper share of the wealth

---

* Terence V. Powderly, *Thirty Years of Labor* (Columbus, Ohio, 1889), pp. 243-44.

that they create; more of the leisure that rightfully belongs to them; more societary advantages; more of the benefits, privileges, and emoluments of the world, all those rights and privileges necessary to make them capable of enjoying, appreciating, defending, and perpetuating the blessings of good government.

III. To arrive at the true condition of the producing masses in their educational, moral, and financial condition, by demanding from the various governments the establishment of bureaus of Labor Statistics.

IV. The establishment of co-operative institutions, productive and distributive.

V. The reserving of the public lands—the heritage of the people—for the actual settler;—not another acre for railroads or settlers.

VI. The abrogation of all laws that do not bear equally upon capital and labor, the removal of unjust technicalities, delays, and discriminations in the administration of justice, and the adopting of measures providing for the health and safety of those engaged in mining, manufacturing, or building pursuits.

VII. The enactment of laws to compel chartered corporations to pay their employes weekly, in full, for labor performed during the preceding week, in the lawful money of the country.

VIII. The enactment of laws giving mechanics and laborers a first lien on their work for their full wages.

IX. The abolishment of the contract system on national, state, and municipal work.

X. The substitution of arbitration for strikes, whenever and wherever employers and employes are willing to meet on equitable grounds.

XI. The prohibition of the employment of children in

Transition

workshops, mines, and factories before attaining their fourteenth year.

XII. To abolish the system of letting out by contract the labor of convicts in our prisons and reformatory institutions.

XIII. To secure for both sexes equal pay for equal work.

XIV. The reduction of the hours of labor to eight per day, so that the laborers may have more time for social enjoyment and intellectual improvement, and be enabled to reap the advantages conferred by the labor-saving machinery which their brains have created.

XV. To prevail upon governments to establish a purely national circulating medium, based upon the faith and resources of the nation, and issued directly to the people, without the intervention of any system of banking corporations, which money shall be a legal tender in payment of all debts, public or private.

9. THE ANARCHOCOMMUNISTS*

1883

> The anarchocommunist movement reached its high-water mark in 1883. That was the year hundreds of anarchocommunists—German-Americans from east of the Mississippi, native Americans from west of it—convened in Pittsburgh and put out a manifesto of their beliefs. They did so in the name of the Anarchist, or Black, International (as distinguished from the defunct Marxist, or Red, International).

Agitation for the purpose of organization; organization for the purpose of rebellion. In these few words the ways are marked, which the workers must take if they want to be rid of their chains, as the economic condition is the same in all countries of so-called "civilization," as the governments of all Monarchies and Republics work hand in hand for the purpose of opposing all movements of the thinking part of the workers, as finally the victory in the decisive combat of the proletarians against their oppressors can only be gained by the simultaneous struggle along the whole line of the bourgeois (capitalistic) society, so therefore the international fraternity of peoples, as expressed in the International Working People's Association, presents itself a self-evident necessity.

True order should take its place. This can only be achieved when all implements of labor—the soil and other premises of production, in short, capital produced

* Richard T. Ely, *The Labor Movement in America* (New York, 1886), pp. 360–63.

Transition

by labor—is changed into societary property. Only by this presupposition is destroyed every possibility of the future spoliation of man by man. Only by common, undivided capital can all be enabled to enjoy in their fulness the fruits of the common toil. Only by the impossibility of accumulating individual (private) capital can every one be compelled to work who makes a demand to live.

This order of things allows production to regulate itself according to the demand of the whole people, so that nobody need work more than a few hours a day, and that all nevertheless can satisfy their needs. Hereby time and opportunity are given for opening to the people the way to the highest possible civilization; the privileges of higher intelligence fall with the privileges of wealth and birth. To the achievement of such a system the political organizations of the capitalistic classes—be they monarchies or republics—form the barriers. These political structures (States), which are completely in the hands of the propertied, have no other purpose than the upholding of the present order of expoliation.

All laws are directed against the working people. In so far as the opposite appears to be the case, they serve on one hand to blind the worker, while on the other hand they are simply evaded. Even the school serves only the purpose of furnishing the offspring of the wealthy with those qualities necessary to uphold their class domination. The children of the poor get scarcely a formal elementary training, and this, too, is mainly directed to such branches as tend to producing prejudices, arrogance, and servility; in short, want of sense. The Church finally seeks to make complete idiots out of the mass and to make them forego the paradise on earth by promising a fictitious heaven. The capitalistic press, on the other hand, takes care of the confusion of spirits in public life. All these institutions, far from aiding in the education of the masses, have for their object the keeping in ignorance of the people. They are all in the pay and under the direction of the capitalistic classes. The workers can therefore expect no help from any capitalistic party in their struggle against the existing system. They must achieve their liberation by their own efforts. As in former times a privileged class never surrendered its tyranny, neither can it be expected that the capitalists of this age will give up their rulership without being forced to do it.

If there ever could have been any question on this point, it should long ago have been dispelled by the brutalities which the bourgeoisie of all countries—in America as well as in Europe—constantly commits, as often as the proletariat anywhere energetically move to better their condition. It becomes, therefore, self-evident that the struggle of the proletariat with the bourgeoisie must have a violent revolutionary character.

We could show by scores of illustrations that all attempts in the past to reform this monstrous system by peaceable means, such as the ballot, have been futile, and all such efforts in the future must necessarily be so, for the following reasons:—

The political institutions of our time are the agencies of the propertied class; their mission is the upholding of the privileges of their masters; any reform in your own behalf would curtail these privileges. To this they will not and cannot consent, for it would be suicidal to themselves.

That they will not resign their privileges voluntarily we know; that they will not make any concessions to us we likewise know. Since we must then rely upon the kindness of our masters for whatever redress we have, and knowing that from them no good may be expected, there

Transition

remains but one recourse—FORCE! Our forefathers have not only told us that against despots force is justifiable, because it is the only means, but they themselves have set the immemorial example.

By force our ancestors liberated themselves from political oppression, by force their children will have to liberate themselves from economic bondage. "It is, therefore, your right; it is your duty," says Jefferson; "to arms!"

What we would achieve is, therefore, plainly and simply,—

First, Destruction of the existing class rule, by all means, *i.e.*, by energetic, relentless, revolutionary, and international action.

Second, Establishment of a free society based upon co-operative organization of production.

Third, Free exchange of equivalent products by and between the productive organizations without commerce and profitmongery.

Fourth, Organization of education on a secular, scientific, and equal basis for both sexes.

Fifth, Equal rights for all without distinction to sex or race.

Sixth, Regulation of all public affairs by free contracts between the autonomous (independent) communes and associations, resting on a federalistic basis.

Whoever agrees with this ideal let him grasp our outstretched brother hands!

Proletarians of all countries, unite!

Fellow-Workmen, all we need for the achievement of this great end is ORGANIZATION and UNITY.

There exists now no great obstacle to that unity. The work of peaceful education and revolutionary conspiracy well can and ought to run in parallel lines.

The day has come for solidarity. Join our ranks! Let

the drum beat defiantly the roll of battle, "Workmen of all lands, unite! You have nothing to lose but your chains; you have a world to win!"

Tremble, oppressors of the world! Not far beyond your purblind sight there dawns the scarlet and sable lights of the JUDGMENT DAY.

10. HENRY GEORGE*

1885

> Every speech Henry George gave echoed the radically agrarian theme he set forth in his great opus *Progress and Poverty*. Here he presents it to an audience of Knights of Labor at the Burlington Opera House on April 1, 1885. Thousands of copies of the speech (entitled "The Crime of Poverty") were distributed throughout the country.

Now why is it that men have to work for such low wages? Because if they were to demand higher wages there are plenty of unemployed men ready to step into their places. It is this mass of unemployed men who compel that fierce competition that drives wages down to the point of bare subsistence. Why is it that there are men who cannot get employment? Did you ever think what a strange thing it is that men cannot find employment? Adam had no difficulty in finding employment; neither had Robinson Crusoe; the finding of employment was the last thing that troubled them.

If men cannot find an employer, why cannot they employ themselves? Simply because they are shut out from the element on which human labour can alone be exerted. Men are compelled to compete with each other for the wages of an employer, because they have been robbed of the natural opportunities of employing themselves; be-

---

* Henry George, *Our Land and Land Policy* (New York, 1901), pp. 204–5, 215–16, 218.

Except to Walk Free

cause they cannot find a piece of God's world on which to work without paying some other human creature for the privilege.

I do not mean to say that even after you had set right this fundamental injustice, there would not be many things to do; but this I do mean to say, that our treatment of land lies at the bottom of all social questions. This I do mean to say, that, do what you please, reform as you may, you never can get rid of wide-spread poverty so long as the element on which and from which all men must live is made the private property of some men. It is utterly impossible. Reform government—get taxes down to the minimum—build railroads; institute co-operative stores; divide profits, if you choose, between employers and employed—and what will be the result? The result will be that the land will increase in value—that will be the result—that and nothing else. Experience shows this. Do not all improvements simply increase the value of land—the price that some must pay others for the privilege of living? . . .

It is so all over the United States—the men who improve, the men who turn the prairie into farms and the desert into gardens, the men who beautify your cities, are taxed and fined for having done these things. Now, nothing is clearer than that the people of New York want more houses; and I think that even here in Burlington you could get along with more houses. Why, then, should you fine a man who builds one? Look all over this country—the bulk of the taxation rests upon the improver; the man who puts up a building, or establishes a factory, or cultivates a farm, he is taxed for it; and not merely taxed for it, but I think in nine cases out of ten the land which he uses, the bare land, is taxed more than the adjoining lot or the adjoining 160 acres that

Transition

some speculator is holding as a mere dog in the manger, not using it himself and not allowing anybody else to use it.

I am talking too long; but let me in a few words point out the way of getting rid of land monopoly, securing the right of all to the elements which are necessary for life. We could not divide the land. In a rude state of society, as among the ancient Hebrews, giving each family its lot and making it inalienable we might secure something like equality. But in a complex civilisation that will not suffice. It is not, however, necessary to divide up the land. All that is necessary is to divide up the income that comes from the land. In that way we can secure absolute equality; nor could the adoption of this principle involve any rude shock or violent change. It can be brought about gradually and easily by abolishing taxes that now rest upon capital, labour and improvements, and raising all our public revenues by the taxation of land values; and the longer you think of it the clearer you will see that in every possible way will it be a benefit.

Now, supposing we should abolish all other taxes direct and indirect, substituting for them a tax upon land values, what would be the effect? In the first place it would be to kill speculative values. It would be to remove from the newer parts of the country the bulk of the taxation and put it on the richer parts. It would be to exempt the pioneer from taxation and make the larger cities pay more of it. It would be to relieve energy and enterprise, capital and labour, from all those burdens that now bear upon them. What a start that would give to production! In the second place we could, from the value of the land, not merely pay all the present expenses of the government, but we could do infinitely more. In the city of San Francisco James Lick left a few

Except to Walk Free

blocks of ground to be used for public purposes there, and the rent amounts to so much, that out of it will be built the largest telescope in the world, large public baths and other public buildings, and various costly works. If, instead of these few blocks, the whole value of the land upon which the city is built had accrued to San Francisco what could she not do? . . .

But all such benefits as these, while great, would be incidental. The great thing would be that the reform I propose would tend to open opportunities to labour and enable men to provide employment for themselves. That is the great advantage. We should gain the enormous productive power that is going to waste all over the country, the power of idle hands that would gladly be at work. And that removed, then you would see wages begin to mount. It is not that everyone would turn farmer, or everyone would build himself a house if he had an opportunity for doing so, but so many could and would, as to relieve the pressure on the labour market and provide employment for all others. And as wages mounted to the higher levels, then you would see the productive power increased. The country where wages are high is the country of greatest productive powers. Where wages are highest, there will invention be most active; there will labour be most intelligent; there will be the greatest yield for the expenditure of exertion. The more you think of it the more clearly you will see that what I say is true. I cannot hope to convince you in an hour or two, but I shall be content if I shall put you upon inquiry. Think for yourselves; ask yourselves whether this wide-spread fact of poverty is not a crime, and a crime for which every one of us, man and woman, who does not do what he or she can do to call attention to it and do away with it, is responsible.

11. THE KNIGHTS OF LABOR: 3*

1886

Hoping to avert a showdown with the Knights, several trade-union leaders got together in May 1886 and drew up a "Treaty" which they offered to the Knights' executive board, due to meet in Cleveland later in the month. It should more appropriately have been called an ultimatum, for it left no room for compromise.

In our capacity as a committee of six selected by the conference of the chief officers of the National and International trade unions held in Philadelphia, Pa., May 18, 1886, beg leave to submit for your consideration and with hope of approval the following terms with a view to secure complete harmony of action and fraternity of purpose among all the various branches of organized labor:

Treaty

1st. That in any branch of labor having a National or International Trade Union, the Knights of Labor shall not initiate any person or form any assembly of persons following a trade or calling organized under such National or International Union without the consent of the nearest Local Union of the National or International Union affected.

2d. No person shall be admitted to membership in the Knights of Labor who works for less than the regular

* *Proceedings of the General Assembly of the Knights of Labor* (Cleveland, 1886), p. 12.

Except to Walk Free

scale of wages fixed by the trade union of his craft or calling, and none shall be admitted into the Knights of Labor who have ever been convicted of "scabbing," "ratting," embezzlement or any other offense against the union of his trade or calling until exonerated by said union.

3d. The charter of any Knights of Labor Assembly of any trade having a National or International Union shall be revoked, and the members of the same be requested to join a mixed Assembly or form a local union under the jurisdiction of their National or International Trade Union.

4th. That any organizer of the Knights of Labor who endeavors to induce trade unions to disband or tampers with their growth or privileges, shall have his commission forthwith revoked.

5th. That wherever a strike of any trade union is in progress, no Assembly or District Assembly of the Knights of Labor shall interfere until settled to the satisfaction of the trade union affected.

6th. That the Knights of Labor shall not establish nor issue any trade mark or label in competition with any trade mark or label now issued, or that may be hereafter issued by any National or International Trade Union.

12. THE KNIGHTS OF LABOR: 4*

1886

> The Knights' executive board gave what might appear to be a reasonable reply to the unions. It agreed to confer with them, to find a way of working out differences. But the unions had demanded immediate action. The reply was equivalent to a rejection, and the war was on.

To the Officers and Members of all National and International Trades' Unions of the United States and Canada, Greeting:

Brothers in the Cause of Labor:—We, the Knights of Labor, in General Assembly convened, extend our heartiest greeting to all branches of honorable toil, welcoming them to the most friendly union in a common work.

This organization embraces within its folds all branches of honorable toil and all conditions of men, without respect to trades, occupations, sex, creed, color or nationality. We seek to raise the level of wages and reduce the hours of labor; to protect men and women in their occupations, in their lives and limbs, and in their rights as citizens. We seek also to secure such legislation as shall tend to prevent the unjust accumulation of wealth, to restrict the power of monopolies and corporations, and to enact such wise and beneficent legislation as shall promote equity and justice, looking forward to the day when coöperation shall supersede the wage system, and the

* *Proceedings of the General Assembly of the Knights of Labor* (Cleveland, 1886), p. 13.

Except to Walk Free

castes and classes that now divide men shall be forever abolished.

We recognize the service rendered to humanity and the cause of labor by trades-union organizations, but believe that the time has come, or is fast approaching, when all who earn their bread *by the sweat of their brow* shall be enrolled under one general head, as we are controlled by one common law—the law of our necessities; and we will gladly welcome to our ranks or to protection under our banner any organization requesting admission. And to such organizations as believe that their craftsmen are better protected under their present form of government, we pledge ourselves, as members of the great army of labor, to cooperate with them in every honorable effort to achieve the success which we are unitedly organized to obtain; and to this end we have appointed a Special Committee to confer with a like committee of any National or International Trades' Union which shall desire to confer with us on the settlement of any difficulties that may occur between the members of the several organizations.

We have received a communication from a committee of the national officers of some of the National and International Trades' Unions, requesting certain specific legislation at our hands; but as we believe that the object sought and stated in the preamble to the communication above referred to can best be accomplished by a conference between a committee of this Association and a committee of any other organization, and as the propositions contained therein are inconsistent with our duty to our members, we therefore defer action upon said propositions until a conference of committees can be held.

The basis upon which we believe an agreement can be reached would necessarily include the adoption of some plan by which all labor organizations could be protected

Transition

from unfair men, men expelled, suspended, under fine, or guilty of taking places of union men or Knights of Labor while on strike or while locked out from work; and that as far as possible a uniform standard of hours of labor and wages should be adopted, so that men of any trade, enrolled in our Order, and members of trades' unions, may not come in conflict because of a difference in wages or hours of labor. We also believe that a system of exchanging working cards should be adopted, so that members of any craft belonging to different organizations could work in harmony together—the card of any member of this Order admitting men to work in any union shop, and the card of any union man admitting him to work in any Knights of Labor shop.

We further believe that, upon a demand of increase of wages or shorter hours of labor made by either organization, a conference should be held with the organized labor men employed in the establishment where the demand for increase of wages or reduction of hours is contemplated—action upon a proposed reduction of wages or other difficulty to be agreed upon in like manner; and that, in the settlement of any difficulties between employers and employees, the organizations represented in the establishment shall be parties to the terms of settlement.

Trusting that the method proposed herein will meet with your approval, and that organized labor will move forward and onward in harmony of effort and of interest, we are

    Yours fraternally,

                Committee.

III
The A.F. of L. 1883-1929

On November 15, 1881, representatives of local and national trade unions (i.e., typographers, iron molders, carpenters, cigar makers, and glassworkers) met in Pittsburgh for the purpose of establishing a new labor organization. Though most of them belonged to the Knights of Labor and had no quarrel with its egalitarian philosophy, its celebration of the working man, they had come to the conclusion that the specific needs of trade unions, especially those demanding legislative remedy—factory reform, child and convict labor, etc.—could best be served by their own organization.

Their model was the British Trades Union Congress, which in its brief history had demonstrated how much labor could accomplish, even from a hostile Parliament, once it mobilized its resources and acted as a cohesive special-interest group. It was in hopes of emulating the British success that the American trade unionists gathered in Pittsburgh for the first convention of the Federation of Organized Trades and Labor Unions of the United States and Canada, as they called themselves.

The Federation (or F.O.T.L.U.) started out as the Knights' partner in a common endeavor, each with its own constituency. But this amiable arrangement soon broke down. The phenomenal expansion of the Knights, particularly in 1885-86, placed an intolerable strain on the unions. For the Knights' district assemblies tended, as they grew in size, to swamp the unions. Skilled workers found themselves at the mercy of the unskilled, of people from other trades, even of rival unions. Attempts to reconcile differences failed. The trade unionists concluded that their organization, F.O.T.L.U., had to be strengthened, their solidarity reaffirmed, in preparation for the struggle to come. In December 1886, in Columbus, Ohio, they brought forth the American Federation of Labor.

The A.F. of L. refined and extended the principle that its progenitor had enunciated, namely that the supreme value of a labor organization was its survival, its durability, as an independent, self-governing entity. Accordingly, under the provisions of its constitution, the A.F. of L. could make no demands on its member unions, could not even require that they aid one another, such aid (e.g., strike funds) to be voluntary. In fact, nothing was required of them beyond the payment of dues (the merest trifle at that) to support a modest administration indeed (the president was to receive a salary of 1,000 dollars a year plus a tiny office). The national trade unions, then, gave the A.F. of L. only minimal powers: the power to prevent encroachment on their autonomy; the power to speak for them in the councils of government and to the world at large. It might more aptly have been called the American *Confederation* of Labor.

Yet, in its quiet, unprepossessing way, the A.F. of L. represented something new in the history of American labor. It proclaimed that a trade union was not a transitory means to a larger end, one possibility among many. It was an end in itself, and whatever other goals individual workers might value—political, social, religious, ethnic,

The A.F. of L.

etc.—the trade union representing them was sovereign in its sphere.

In proclaiming this, the A.F. of L. was also serving notice that workers could not expect to become something other than what they were. They could not expect to be self-reliant artisans or entrepreneurs or homesteaders or communitarians or the like, these hopes being so many departures from reality—reality defined as the recognition of the industrial system, of a universe divided irreversibly between capital and labor, between those who owned the means of production and those who owned their bodies and their skills. Only by acknowledging economic reality, only by perceiving themselves as they were and would always be, could workers win their freedom. Only then would they act in such a way as to resist the power of industrial capitalism. The A.F. of L., in short, was the first labor organization to embody a consciousness appropriate to industrial society.

In effect, the A.F. of L. was attempting to do what the socialists or Marxists had been urging all along, what the North American Branch of the First International had sought but failed to do. Nor was it an accident that the architects of the A.F. of L., chief among them Samuel Gompers, its first president (and only president, except for one year, until his death, in 1924), were schooled in the Marxist tradition. Being socialists, Gompers and the other founding fathers assumed as a matter of course that workers were inescapably circumscribed by their class. But they had also learned from their experience as workers and organizers that class consciousness, to be effective, must be transmuted into trade-union consciousness, that before *all* workers can be organized, one must begin with the organizable—those who labored in the same trade, who shared similar concerns and backgrounds and were

139

Except to Walk Free

united by the solidarity of the workbench and the craft they practiced.

The leaders of the A.F. of L. were not abandoning their class orientation or their wish to bring about radical reform. They were only separating the immediate, day to day, pragmatic needs of their members—improved working conditions, control of machinery and the labor supply, more leisure and dignity—from their ultimate ends: a classless society, the co-operative commonwealth. Inevitably, tensions arose between the immediate and the ultimate ends, between trade-union interests and class interests. They were the tensions, however, that accompanied the workers' capacity to act, to organize, to administer their affairs and thus exercise some limited measure of autonomy over their lives. Marx himself, after all, favored the trade unions, conservative as they were, and supported their efforts to secure factory reforms, higher wages, the elimination of child labor, etc. Marx, too, separated the *hic et nunc* from the distant future, palliatives from revolution.

In any case, the A.F. of L. had evidently discovered the right formula; it endured. In the prosperous years of the late 1880s and early '90s its membership rose perceptibly, thanks in part to the collapse of the Knights of Labor. Its unions were winning the right to bargain collectively and were securing contracts for an eight-hour day; Gompers was as wise as Solomon in settling jurisdictional problems between national unions, thereby laying the foundation for further growth. Most impressive of all was the A.F. of L.'s ability to weather the 1893 depression in fairly good shape. In previous depressions the trade unions suffered catastrophic losses or dissolved altogether. The A.F. of L. more than held its own.

Its character, however, was changing in response to the

The A.F. of L.

great labor and social troubles of the 1890s. Constantly tested on the anvil of conflict, the A.F. of L. emerged a vastly different organization from the one that had been formed a decade earlier.

There was its response to the massive strikes of the period, notably the 1892 Homestead, Pennsylvania, strike of steelworkers against the Carnegie Steel Company and, two years later, the American Railway Union strike (led by Eugene V. Debs) against the Pullman Palace Car Company. The workers were routed in both these strikes, their unions demolished. The A.F. of L., of course, sympathized with the strikers, but it refused to join them; indeed it conspicuously kept its distance from them. The message of its inaction could hardly be misconstrued: The A.F. of L. was not going to jeopardize the welfare of its unions merely out of kinship for other workers, however great their trials, however grievous their conflicts.

Second was its response to the challenge posed by the socialists. In the early 1890s the Socialist Labor Party, now directed by the redoubtable Daniel De Leon, attempted to gain a foothold in the A.F. of L. ("boring-from-within") with a view to eventually taking it over. De Leon argued that trade unions must consolidate into industrial unions, must transcend all craft distinctions and embrace all workers within a particular industry, this process to be carried out under Socialist Labor Party leadership. Should the A.F. of L. fail to do so, the trade unions would be overwhelmed by the industrial trusts and the power of the state serving as their agent. Gompers was able to beat back this assault (though it cost him the presidency of the A.F. of L. in 1894), maintaining that unions must never compromise their independence and integrity, never commit themselves to a political line or ideology no matter how attractive.

Except to Walk Free

De Leon developed a fierce hatred for Gompers and the A.F. of L. A master of invective, a relentless polemicist, De Leon continually referred to Gompers and the A.F. of L. ("A.F. of Hell") as "labor fakirs," "labor lieutenants of capitalism," "mis-leaders of labor," and the like. Despite the epithets, De Leon was articulating a view held by radicals in general, even those who otherwise disagreed with him or were offended by his language. The function of the A.F. of L., according to this view, was to keep the working class divided and so help prevent class consciousness and class struggle from crystallizing. It was no exaggeration, therefore, to hold up the A.F. of L. leaders as traitors to the cause of working-class emancipation.

The ferocity of the conflict between himself and the radicals drove Gompers farther and farther to the right, as though he were determined to justify De Leon's caricature of him. Gompers became an active opponent of socialism. As long as the capitalist class and the government did not interfere with trade-union autonomy, Gompers had no quarrel with the status quo. In fact, he saw much to commend in it. Gone, at any rate, was any notion of ultimate ends, of support for far-reaching social change. The everyday struggle for better working conditions and for a more sympathetic public opinion—an ethic of immediate ends—was all that remained of the original spirit of the A.F. of L.

Under the circumstances, the A.F. of L. withdrew, as it were, from the working class at large. Gompers now affirmed the distinctiveness and exclusivity of the A.F. of L. Its members were proud of being a privileged stratum, the "aristocracy of labor," occupying as they did an intermediate zone between capitalists and proletariat. And so, threatened from below by those who presumed to represent the proletariat, the A.F. of L. identified more and more with the capitalists above—or at least those among them who were sufficiently enlightened to recognize the value of "responsible" trade unionism and were willing to come to terms with it.

His critics were not surprised, therefore, when Gompers joined the Civic Federation, an organization of just such enlightened capitalists and statesmen (e.g., Mark Hanna, August Belmont, Grover Cleveland, William H. Taft, George Perkins), men dedicated to maintaining industrial peace and order. The Civic Federation's definition of peace and order was also Gompers': recognition of, and collective bargaining with, conservative craft unions (the A.F. of L.); opposition to socialism, class conflict, and the unionization of mass-production industries.

On some social issues, the A.F. of L. adopted positions as reactionary as any in the country. Hostility to non-Western immigrants was its fixed policy. Prejudice ran deep against eastern and southern Europeans, who comprised the bulk of the immigrants and the non-skilled work force after 1890. The A.F. of L.'s hatred of Asians, that is, Chinese and Japanese, was pathological. Gompers, who carried the prevailing racism of the times to obsessive lengths, regarded "Asiatics" as humanoids, a subrace deserving to be treated as such.

His attitude toward blacks was somewhat more open and generous. He had fought for the admission of blacks into trade unions, and on occasion he even refused to charter unions that had written lily-white clauses into their constitutions. But by 1900 the A.F. of L. was itself practically lily-white (it contained a few all-black locals), a condition that Gompers accepted, with a shrug of the shoulders, as inevitable.

Its critics might cavil and issue dire prophecies, but the

Except to Walk Free

A.F. of L. was obviously doing something right. Between 1897 and 1904 its membership increased over 500 per cent —from 265,000 to 1,676,000—especially in construction, the needle trades, and coal mining (the United Mine Workers being the largest single union in the A.F. of L.), and though it ceased to grow for the next several years (indeed it lost some members) no one could any longer doubt that it had become a permanent feature of American life, a force to contend with, one capable of rewarding its friends and punishing its enemies. Trade unionism had arrived. And so had Samuel Gompers—a Jew, an immigrant, a onetime socialist cigar maker of the Lower East Side, who now moved in the highest circles of the land, where his counsel was sought and his opinions respected.

The astonishing fact was that a significant number of A.F. of L. unions, almost a third of the total, were led by socialists. These socialists naturally favored the industrial-union principle and despised Gompers and all that Gompers stood for, yet they were not going to break away and establish their own rival organization. De Leon had tried that in the 1890s, with disastrous results. No, the socialist unions would continue to work within the A.F. of L., would capture its machinery and eventually join hands with the emergent Socialist Party to bring the co-operative commonwealth into being.

But unskilled workers remained unorganized, and as far as revolutionists such as De Leon were concerned, the Socialist Party was no less guilty of betraying the proletariat than Gompers; more guilty, perhaps, since Gompers did not pretend to be a socialist. For such revolutionists, and for all others who were fed up with the A.F. of L.—chiefly trade unions (e.g., the Western Federation of Miners, the Brewery Workers) that had failed to receive its support in recent strikes—the time had come to create a rival labor

The A.F. of L.

organization, one that would embrace all workers as brethren and consecrate itself, here and now, to the realization of a classless society.

And so, at a convention held in Chicago in June 1905 attended by De Leon and Debs, among other assorted revolutionists, along with leaders of a number of militant unions, was born the Industrial Workers of the World. And the constitution they framed was consistent with the ideology they professed. Under its provisions, all the crafts and trades were to take their place in their appropriate industry-wide departments or syndicates (manufacturing, mining, transportation, agriculture, etc.). These would be sovereign in their realms, but subordinate to the I.W.W. as a whole—the I.W.W. being co-terminous with the nation as a whole. Thus united, the working class would abolish the capitalist state and institute government by industrial departments.

This hope was soon dashed. The I.W.W. underwent a startling metamorphosis, becoming, within three years of its founding, an out-and-out anarchosyndicalist body, declaring itself at war with politics and the legal system and in favor of direct action, including sabotage of industry. By now it was scarcely an organization at all. Debs and De Leon and the unions were out, and it consisted for the most part of West Coast farm laborers, lumber workers, and longshoremen, a few thousand at most.

Its extravagant revolutionary rhetoric, its dauntless, free-spirited approach to life (celebrated in countless songs and poems), its willingness to go among the poorest, most neglected victims of industry, whom it tried to organize and whom it led in hopeless strikes (a few of which, though, miraculously it won), its tendency to call forth the most hostile response from authority—these gave the I.W.W. a magnificent notoriety and invested it with a

Except to Walk Free

legendary aura. But the I.W.W. was never more than a noble ideal. Its worldly accomplishments were few, and it died of inanition long before its martyrdom at the hands of the government during World War I.

The A.F. of L., meanwhile, stood poised for even greater triumphs. In 1910 the slight decline that had taken place over the past five years was arrested and the unions began to grow again. When the First World War broke out, in Europe, and the country entered a new era of prosperity, the pace of growth quickened, and when the United States itself became involved, the A.F. of L. reached the summit of its possibilities. By 1920 its membership had swelled to over four million—80 per cent of all trade unionists and 12 per cent of all non-agricultural workers.

Throughout these years of expansion, the A.F. of L. had a warm friend in President Woodrow Wilson. His administration sponsored much pro-labor legislation, especially the Clayton Act, which excluded unions from the reach of the anti-trust laws. And during the war Wilson gave the A.F. of L. considerable responsibility for the handling of government labor policies and war industries, in effect placing the government's seal of approval upon the union as labor's legitimate representative.

The war also enabled Gompers and the A.F. of L. to settle accounts with their socialist enemies. Nearly all socialists, moderate and revolutionary alike, opposed American entry into the war, and for this the government punished them without mercy. Their publications were not allowed to go through the mails. Many Socialist Party leaders, notably Debs, went to jail for violating the Espionage Act of 1917. Others went underground for the duration. The I.W.W.—what was left of it—was extirpated, its best known spokesman, "Big Bill" Haywood, escaping

The A.F. of L.

to Russia soon after the Bolshevik Revolution. The A.F. of L. seized the chance to expel or suppress the socialists in its ranks. It was aided in this by the government as well as a sizable contingent of conservative Catholics for whom trade unions meant defense of family, property, religion, and country. They shaped the A.F. of L. in *their* image.

At war's end the A.F. of L. was everything Gompers had hoped it would be. It was strong and respectable. It stood for both progress and the status quo, and it could never be accused of harboring foreign or anti-American ideologies. And it could expect to prosper as America prospered.

By rights, then, the 1920s should have been red-letter years for the A.F. of L. They were, after all, among the most prosperous years in American history. A host of new industries came into their own: automobile (and all the others connected with it), telephone, electric-utility, electronics, chemical, appliance, entertainment (movies, radio, etc.), to name a few. Wages and real income rose significantly. Yet, instead of expanding, as one would have anticipated, the A.F. of L. contracted sharply, its membership dropping to just under three million in 1929, its proportion of non-agricultural labor falling to about 7 per cent. The biggest declines were registered by the more industrial unions: coal mining (which was decimated), transportation, clothing, and steel (which was completely wiped out after the 1919 strike). The newer, mass-consumption industries successfully resisted unionism. Only in the building trades—the A.F. of L.'s traditional bailiwick—did the unions do well. More than ever, they dominated the organization.

The sudden change in the political climate was one reason, certainly, why the A.F. of L. as a whole fared so

Except to Walk Free

poorly. The Republican administrations of Harding, Coolidge, and Hoover were, to say the least, inhospitable to unions. So were the courts, which—reinvoking the doctrine of *laissez faire* in employer-employee relations—voided federal laws that regulated child labor and minimum wages for women, and gave companies the freedom to do as they wished, however inequitable, to prevent workers from joining unions (widespread use of "yellow dog" contracts, lockouts, spies, etc.).

Companies, for their part, applied the carrot as well as the stick. Many of them set up their own "unions." (By 1929 a million and a half workers belonged to such "unions.") Some companies also set up pension and profit-sharing plans for their employees. Whatever their cost, these plans were far cheaper than resisting strong, independent workers' organizations.

The cause of trade unionism suffered, too, from the absence of a viable radical movement. The Socialist Party, once so large and so confident of the future, was reduced to a sect. The Communists (or Workers' Party) were hardly more numerous. The left was moribund in the 1920s, and such energies as it did muster, it expended in factional struggles revolving around Soviet policies.

But mostly the A.F. of L. had itself to blame for the malaise of the 1920s. It had hardened into an impermeable special-interest group, a privileged enclave for its diminishing rank and file. It was simply unequipped, temperamentally, ideologically, jurisdictionally, to go out and organize workers—even essay the attempt—in the new, mass-production industries. Craft unionism had just about run its course, gone as far as it could. It was entirely appropriate, therefore, that Gompers (who died in 1924) should be succeeded by William Green, lately of the United Mine Workers. Chosen by the most stalwart

The A.F. of L.

of the old-line leaders, Green was the business unionist par excellence. With him at the helm—or, rather, in front of it as a figurehead—the crafts rested secure. As for workers at large—they would have to fend for themselves.

1. THE A.F. OF L.: 1*

1883

Samuel Gompers gave a pithy explanation of the principles that governed the A.F. of L. (three years before its formal establishment) when, in 1883, he testified before a Senate committee looking into the burgeoning conflict between capital and labor.

... When we strike as organized working men, we generally win, and that is the reason of the trouble that our employers go to when they try to show that strikes are failures, but you will notice that they generally or always point to unorganized workers. That is one reason also why when the employers know that the working men are organized and have got a good treasury strikes are very frequently avoided. There are fewer strikes among organized working men, but when they do strike they are able to hold out much longer than the others, and they generally win. The trades unions are not what too many men have been led to believe they are, importations from Europe: if they are imported, then, as has been said, they were landed at Plymouth Rock from the *Mayflower*. Modern industry evolves these organizations out of the existing conditions where there are two classes in society, one incessantly striving to obtain the labour of the other class for as little as possible, and to obtain the largest

* U. S. Senate Committee on Education and Labor, *Relations Between Labor and Capital*, 48th Congress, 1885, vol. I, pp. 374–75.

amount or number of hours of labour; and the members of the other class being, as individuals, utterly helpless in a contest with their employers, naturally resort to combinations to improve their condition, and, in fact, they are forced by the conditions which surround them to organize for self-protection. Hence trades unions. Trades unions are not barbarous, nor are they the outgrowth of barbarism. On the contrary they are only possible where civilization exists. Trades unions cannot exist in China; they cannot exist in Russia; and in all those semi-barbarous countries they can hardly exist, if indeed they can exist at all. But they have been formed successfully in this country, in Germany, in England, and they are gradually gaining strength in France. In Great Britain they are very strong; they have been forming there for fifty years, and they are still forming, and I think there is a great future for them yet in America. Wherever trades unions have organized and are most firmly organized, there are the right[s] of the people most respected. A people may be educated, but to me it appears that the greatest amount of intelligence exists in that country or that State where the people are best able to defend their rights, and their liberties as against those who are desirous of undermining them. Trades unions are organizations that instill into men a higher motive-power and give them a higher goal to look to. The hope that is too frequently deadened in their breasts when unorganized is awakened by the trades unions as it can be by nothing else. . . .

Q. The outside public, I think, very largely confound the conditions out of which the trades union grows or is formed, with the, to the general public mind, somewhat revolutionary ideas that are embraced under the names of socialism and communism. Before you get through, won't you let us understand to what extent the trades union is

Except to Walk Free

an outgrowth or an evolution of those ideas, and to what extent it stands apart from them and is based on different principles?

A. The trades unions are by no means an outgrowth of socialistic or communistic ideas or principles, but the socialistic and communistic notions are evolved from some of the trades unions' movements. As to the question of the principles of communism or socialism prevailing in trades unions, there are a number of men who connect themselves as working men with the trades unions who may have socialistic convictions, yet who never gave them currency; who say, 'Whatever ideas we may have as to the future state of society, regardless of what the end of the labour movement as a movement between classes may be, they must remain in the background, and we must subordinate our convictions, and our views and our acts to the general good that the trades-union movement brings to the labourer.' A large number of them think and act in that way. . . .

2. THE A.F. OF L.: 2*

1886

The preamble to the A.F. of L. constitution will give some idea of the radical roots from which it sprung. The rest of the constitution remained virtually unchanged for the next sixty-nine years —until the establishment of the A.F.L.-C.I.O.

Preamble

WHEREAS, a struggle is going on in all the nations of the civilized world, between the oppressors and the oppressed of all countries, a struggle between the capitalist and the laborer, which grows in intensity from year to year, and will work disastrous results to the toiling millions, if they are not combined for mutual protection and benefit,

It therefore behooves the representatives of the Trades and Labor Unions of America, in Convention assembled, to adopt such measures and disseminate such principles among the mechanics and laborers of our country as will permanently unite them, to secure the recognition of the rights to which they are justly entitled.

We therefore declare ourselves in favor of the formation of a thorough Federation, embracing every Trade and Labor Organization in America.

Constitution

ARTICLE I—NAME

Section 1. This association shall be known as "The American Federation of Labor," and shall consist of such

* *Report of Proceedings of the First Annual Convention of the American Federation of Labor* (Columbus, Ohio, 1886), pp. 3-4.

Trade and Labor Unions as shall conform to its rules and regulations.

Article II—Objects

Section 1. The objects of this Federation shall be the encouragement and formation of local Trades Labor Unions, and the closer Federation of such societies through the organization of Central Trades and Labor Unions in every city, and the further combination of such bodies into state, territorial, or provincial organizations, to secure legislation in the interests of the working masses.

Sec. 2. The establishment of National and International Trades Unions, based upon a strict recognition of the autonomy of each trade, and the promotion and advancement of such bodies.

Sec. 3. An American Federation of all National and International Trades Unions, to aid and assist each other; and, furthermore, to secure National Legislation in the interests of the working people, and influence public opinion, by peaceful and legal methods, in favor of Organized Labor.

Sec. 4. To aid and encourage the labor press of America. . . .

Article IV—Representation

Section 1. The basis of representation in the Convention shall be: From National or International Unions, for less than four thousand members, one delegate; four thousand or more, two delegates; eight thousand or more, three delegates; sixteen thousand or more, four delegates; thirty-two thousand or more, five delegates, and so on; and from each Local or District Trades Union, not connected with, or having a National or International head, affiliated with this Federation, one delegate.

Sec. 2. No organization which has seceded from any Local, National, or International organization, shall be allowed a representation or recognition in this Federation.

Article V—Officers

Section 1. The Officers of the Federation shall consist of a President, two Vice-Presidents, a Secretary, and a Treasurer, to be elected by the Convention. . . .

Article VI—Executive Council

Section 1. The Officers shall be an Executive Council with power to watch legislative measures directly affecting the interests of working people, and to initiate, whenever necessary, such legislative action as the Convention may direct.

Sec. 2. The Executive Council shall use every possible means to organize new National or International Trades Unions, and to organize local Trades Unions and connect them with the Federation, until such time as there are a sufficient number to form a National or International Union, when it shall be the duty of the President of the Federation to see that such organization is formed.

Sec. 3. While we recognize the right of each trade to manage its own affairs, it shall be the duty of the Executive Council to secure the unification of all labor organizations, so far as to assist each other in any justifiable boycott, and with voluntary financial help in the event of a strike or lock-out, when duly approved by the Executive Council.

Sec. 4. When a strike has been approved by the Executive Council, the particulars of the difficulty, even if it be a lock-out, shall be explained in a circular issued by the President of the Federation to the unions affiliated

Except to Walk Free

therewith. It shall then be the duty of all affiliated societies to urge their Local Unions and members to make liberal financial donations in aid of the working people involved. . . .

Article VIII—Miscellaneous

Section 1. In all questions not covered by this Constitution, the Executive Council shall have power to make rules to govern the same, and shall report accordingly to the Federation.

Sec. 2. Charters for the Federation shall be granted by the President of the Federation, by and with the consent of the Executive Council, to all National and International and Local bodies affiliated with this Federation.

Sec. 3. Any seven wage workers of good character, and favorable to Trades Unions, and not members of any body affiliated with this Federation, who will subscribe to this Constitution, shall have the power to form a local body, to be known as a "Federal Labor Union," and they shall hold regular meetings for the purpose of strengthening and advancing the Trades Union movement, and shall have the power to make their own rules in conformity with this Constitution, and shall be granted a local charter. . . .

Sec. 5. Where there are one or more Local Unions in any city, belonging to a National or International Union, affiliated with this Federation, it shall be their duty to organize a Trades Assembly, or Central Labor Union, or join such body if already in existence. . . .

3. THE PULLMAN STRIKE: 1*

1894

> Here is the moving statement made by the Pullman Palace Car workers on June 15, 1894, to the American Railway Union, imploring support for their strike. Eugene V. Debs, head of the union, urged caution, but the union voted to go along with the strike by refusing to handle Pullman cars. The railroad companies refused to allow this. Thus began the struggle that ended the following month with the defeat of the strike and the destruction of the union.

Mr. President and Brothers of the American Railway Union: We struck at Pullman because we were without hope. We joined the American Railway Union because it gave us a glimmer of hope. Twenty thousand souls, men, women, and little ones, have their eyes turned toward this convention today, straining eagerly through dark despondency for a glimmer of the heaven-sent message you alone can give us on this earth.

In stating to this body our grievances it is hard to tell where to begin. You all must know that the proximate cause of our strike was the discharge of two members of our grievance committee the day after George M. Pullman, himself, and Thomas H. Wickes, his second vice-president, had guaranteed them absolute immunity. The more remote causes are still imminent. Five reductions in wages, in work, and in conditions of employment swept

* United States Strike Commission, *Report on the Chicago Strike of June–July, 1894* (Washington, 1895), pp. 87–88.

Except to Walk Free

through the shops at Pullman between May and December, 1893. The last was the most severe, amounting to nearly thirty per cent, and our rents had not fallen. We owed Pullman $70,000 when we struck May 11. We owe him twice as much today. He does not evict us for two reasons: One, the force of popular sentiment and public opinion; the other because he hopes to starve us out, to break through in the back of the American Railway Union, and to deduct from our miserable wages when we are forced to return to him the last dollar we owe him for the occupancy of his houses.

Rents all over the city in every quarter of its vast extent have fallen, in some cases to one-half. Residences, compared with which ours are hovels, can be had a few miles away at the price we have been contributing to make a millionaire a billionaire. What we pay $15 for in Pullman is leased for $8 in Roseland; and remember that just as no man or woman of our 4,000 toilers has ever felt the friendly pressure of George M. Pullman's hand, so no man or woman of us all has ever owned or can ever hope to own one inch of George M. Pullman's land. Why, even the very streets are his. His ground has never been platted of record, and today he may debar any man who has acquiring rights as his tenant from walking in his highways. And those streets; do you know what he has named them? He says after the four great inventors in methods of transportation. And do you know what their names are? Why, Fulton, Stephenson, Watt, and Pullman.

Water which Pullman buys from the city at 8 cents a thousand gallons he retails to us at 500 per cent advance and claims he is losing $400 a month on it. Gas which sells at 75 cents per thousand feet in Hyde Park, just north of us, he sells for $2.25. When we went to tell him our grievances he said we were all his "children."

The A.F. of L.

Pullman, both the man and the town, is an ulcer on the body politic. He owns the houses, the schoolhouses, and churches of God in the town he gave his once humble name. The revenue he derives from these, the wages he pays out with one hand—the Pullman Palace Car Company, he takes back with the other—the Pullman Land Association. He is able by this to bid under any contract car shop in this country. His competitors in business, to meet this, must reduce the wages of their men. This gives him the excuse to reduce ours to conform to the market. His business rivals must in turn scale down; so must he. And thus the merry war—the dance of skeletons bathed in human tears—goes on, and it will go on, brothers, forever, unless you, the American Railway Union, stop it; end it; crush it out.

4. THE PULLMAN STRIKE: 2*

1894

Debs's testimony before a House committee tells how the court injunction, which the railroad companies and federal government had jointly brought against the union, broke the back of the strike. Refusing to comply with the order, Debs was found guilty of contempt of court and went to jail for six months. The whole experience hastened Debs' evolution to socialism. In 1897 (at a convention of the American Railway Union—or what remained of it) he launched the Social Democratic Party, under whose auspices, three years later, he ran for President of the United States.

... On the second day of July, I was served with a very sweeping injunction that restrained me, as president of the union, from sending out any telegram or any letter or issuing any order that would have the effect of inducing or persuading men to withdraw from the service of the company, or that would in any manner whatsoever, according to the language of the injuction, interfere with the operation.... That injunction was served simultaneously, or practically so, by all of the courts embracing or having jurisdiction in the territory in which the trouble existed. From Michigan to California there seemed to be concerted action on the part of the courts in restraining us from exercising any of the functions of our offices. That

* United States Strike Commission, *Report on the Chicago Strike of June–July, 1894* (Washington, 1895), pp. 142–44.

The A.F. of L.

resulted practically in the demoralization of our ranks. Not only this, but we were organized in a way that this was the center, of course, of operations. It is understood that a strike is war; not necessarily a war of blood and bullets, but a war in the sense that it is a conflict between two contending interests or classes of interests. There is more or less strategy resorted to in war, and this was the center in our operations. Orders were issued from here, questions were answered, and our men were kept in line from here. . . .

As soon as the employees found that we were arrested and taken from the scene of action, they became demoralized, and that ended the strike. It was not the soldiers that ended the strike; it was not the old brotherhoods that ended the strike; it was simply the United States courts that ended the strike. Our men were in a position that never would have been shaken under any circumstances if we had been permitted to remain upon the field, remain among them; but once that we were taken from the scene of action and restrained from sending telegrams or issuing the orders necessary, or answering questions; when the minions of the corporations would be put to work at such a place, for instance, as Nickerson, Kansas, where they would go and say to the men that the men at Newton had gone back to work, and Nickerson would wire me to ask if that were true; no answer would come to the message, because I was under arrest, and we were all under arrest. The headquarters were demoralized and abandoned, and we could not answer any telegrams or questions that would come in. Our headquarters were temporarily demoralized and abandoned, and we could not answer any messages. The men went back to work, and the ranks were broken, and the strike was broken up by the Federal courts of the United States, and not by the

Except to Walk Free

Army, and not by any other power, but simply and solely by the action of the United States courts in restraining us from discharging our duties as officers and representatives of the employees. . . .

5. DANIEL DE LEON*

1896

> Thrown out of the A.F. of L. and the Knights of Labor, the Socialist Labor Party under De Leon's leadership established its own union, the Socialist Trade and Labor Alliance. Here, in Boston, before an S.L.P. audience, De Leon castigates the assorted traitors and "ignoramuses" and defends the S.L.P.'s revolutionary approach to trade unionism.

The Socialist, in the brilliant simile of Karl Marx, sees that a lone fiddler in his room needs no director; he can rap himself to order, with his fiddle to his shoulder, and start his dancing tune, and stop whenever he likes. But just as soon as you have an orchestra, you must also have an orchestra director—a central directing authority. If you don't, you may have a Salvation Army powwow, you may have a Louisiana negro breakdown; you may have an orthodox Jewish synagogue, where every man sings in whatever key he likes, but you won't have harmony—impossible. (Applause.)

It needs this central directing authority of the orchestra master to rap all the players to order at a given moment; to point out when they shall begin; when to have these play louder, when to have those play softer; when to put in this instrument, when to silence that; to regulate the time of all and preserve the accord. The orchestra director is not an oppressor, or his baton an insignia of tyr-

* Daniel De Leon, *Reform or Revolution* (New York, 1896).

anny; he is not there to bully anybody; he is as necessary or important as any or all of the members of the orchestra.

Our system of production is in the nature of an orchestra. No one man, no one town, no one State, can be said any longer to be independent of the other; the whole people of the United States, every individual therein, is dependent and interdependent upon all the others. The nature of the machinery of production; the subdivision of labor, which aids co-operation, and which co-operation fosters, and which is necessary to the plentifulness of production that civilization requires, compel a harmonious working together of all departments of labor, and thence compel the establishment of a Central Directing Authority, of an Orchestral Director, so to speak, of the orchestra of the Co-operative Commonwealth. (Loud applause.)

Such is the State or Government that the Socialist revolution carries in its womb. Today, production is left to Anarchy, and only Tyranny, the twin sister of Anarchy, is organized.

Socialism, accordingly, implies organization; organization implies directing authority; and the one and the other are strict reflections of the revolutions undergone by the tool of production. Reform, on the other hand, skims the surface, and with "Referendums" and similar devices limits itself to external tinkerings. . . .

Fake Movements.

Then, again, with this evil of miseducation, the working class of this country suffers from another. The charlatans, one after the other, set up movements that proceeded upon lines of ignorance; movements that were denials of scientific facts; movements that bred hopes in the hearts of the people; yet movements that had to collapse. A movement must be perfectly sound, and scientifi-

The A.F. of L.

cally based or it cannot stand. A falsely based movement is like a lie, and a lie cannot survive. All these false movements came to grief, and what was the result?—disappointment, stagnation, diffidence, hopelessness in the masses.

K. of L.

The Knights of Labor, meant by Uriah Stephens, as he himself admitted, to be reared upon the scientific principles of Socialism—principles found today in no central or national organization of labor outside of the Socialist Trade & Labor Alliance (loud applause)—sank into the mire. Uriah Stephens was swept aside; ignoramuses took hold of the organization; a million and a half men went into it, hoping for salvation; but, instead of salvation, there came from the veils of the K. of L. Local, District and General Assemblies the developed ignoramuses, that is to say, the Labor Fakirs, riding the working man and selling him out to the exploiter. (Applause.) Disappointed, the masses fell off.

A.F. of L.

Thereupon bubbled up another wondrous concern, another idiosyncrasy—the American Federation of Labor, appropriately called by its numerous English organizers the American Federation of Hell. (Laughter.) Ignoramuses again took hold and the lead. They failed to seek below the surface for the cause of the failure of the K. of L.; like genuine ignoramuses, they fluttered over the surface. They saw on the surface excessive concentration of power in the K. of L., and they swung to the other extreme—they built a tapeworm. (Laughter.) I call it a tapeworm, because a tapeworm is no organism; it is an aggregation of links with no cohesive powers worth men-

Except to Walk Free

tioning. The fate of the K. of L. overtook the A.F. of L. Like causes brought on like results: false foundations brought on ruin and failure. Strike upon strike proved disastrous in all concentrated industries; wages and the standard of living of the working class at large went down; the unemployed multiplied; and again the ignorant leaders naturally and inevitably developed into approved Labor Fakirs: the workers found themselves shot, clubbed, indicted, imprisoned by the identical Presidents, Governors, Mayors, Judges, etc.—Republican and Democratic—whom their misleaders had corruptly induced them to support. Today there is no A.F. of L.—not even the tapeworm—any more. If you reckon it up, you will find that, if the 250,000 members which it claims paid dues regularly every quarter, it must have four times as large a fund as it reports. The fact is the dues are paid for the last quarter only; the fakirs see to this to the end that they may attend the annual rowdidow called the "A.F. of L. Convention"—and advertise themselves to the politicians. That's all there is left of it. It is a ship, never seaworthy, but now stranded and captured by a handful of pirates; a tapeworm pulled to pieces, contemned by the rank and file of the American proletariat. (Applause.) Its career only filled still fuller the workers' measure of disappointment, diffidence, helplessness.

Single Tax.

The Henry George movement was another of these charlatan booms, that only helped still more to dispirit people in the end. The "Single Tax," with its half-antiquated, half-idiotic reasoning, took the field. Again great expectations were raised all over the country—for a while. Again a social-economic lie proved a broken reed to lean on. Down came Humpty Dumpty, and all the

The A.F. of L.

king's horses and all the king's men could not now put Humpty Dumpty together again. (Applause.) Thus the volume of popular disappointment and diffidence received a further contribution. . . .

[*The S.L.P. The Head of The Column*]

. . . At such a season, it is the duty of us, revolutionists, to conduct ourselves in such manner as to cause our organization to be better and better known, its principles more and more clearly understood, its integrity and firmness more and more respected and trusted—then, when we shall have stood that ground well and grown steadily, the masses will in due time flock over to us. In the crash that is sure to come and is now just ahead of us, our steadfast Socialist organization will alone stand out intact above the ruins; there will then be a stampede to our party—but only upon revolutionary lines can it achieve this; upon lines of reform it can never be victorious. (Applause.)

6. THE A.F. OF L. AND THE BLACKS*

1898

The February 1898 number of the *American Federationist*, official publication of the A.F. of L., carried a lead article by a union representative (Will H. Winn by name) on "The Negro: His Relation to Southern Industry" which pretty well sums up the A.F. of L.'s position on black workers.

. . . While there are many exceptions, of course, to the general rule, it is a fact patent to every observing man who has studied the negro from contact that as a race, he does not give evidence of a possession of those peculiarities of temperament such as patriotism, sympathy, sacrifice, etc., which are peculiar to most of the Caucasian race, and which alone make an organization of the character and complicity of the modern trade union possible —sufficiently to warrant a hope that his condition might be improved by organization corresponding with the good results obtained through white organization.

Those well-meaning but misguided philanthropists (and others) who would attempt a solution of the negro problem in the South on the supposition that his character, his needs and adaptabilities are similar to those of the white race, do not appear to take into consideration certain well-known traits of negro character, prominent among which is his distrust of his fellows in black and his deep-seated prejudice against the white working man, the ignorance of the adults, and his abandoned and reckless

* *American Federationist*, vol. IV, pp. 269–71.

disposition. I said that there were many exceptions to this, but, as applicable to the race, the truthfulness of the above is universally recognized in the South, and may be easily verified.

It would be well for all union men, irrespective of section or opinion, to understand correctly the negro's position in the Southern labor movement, as, I believe, he is yet to bring about a complete readjustment of the Southern industrial problem. We must deal honestly and fearlessly with conditions as they are, and not as we would have them be. . . .

But even admitting as possible a thorough organization of the negroes, it is hardly probable that the white workers generally could be induced to recognize them as union men—that is, brothers in a common cause—and without such recognition or federation or understanding between the two organized races whereby concerted action might be engendered, I submit that organization would be worse than worthless.

From a Southern view, colonization would be a practical and mutually agreeable solution of the negro-labor problem. Bishop Turner, of this State, and many others of the prominent negro divines and educators, all over the South, favor the emigration or colonization scheme, and are now working to that end in favor of the negro republic of Liberia. The only opposition these men encounter is from the capitalistic class (of course), and its chief tool—a hireling press. The negroes themselves are friendly to the proposition, as witnessed by the fact that some 19,000 of them have emigrated to the black republic, although the prosperity of Liberia has been very obvious, it is a poor country; its climate is bad, and its native surroundings unfavorable to the purpose.

The country most suitable in every respect, and at pres-

Except to Walk Free

ent the most available for negro colonization, is Cuba, "Queen of the Antilles," and the garden spot of the continent. There the negro would thrive and prosper as he would nowhere else on earth. And with this end in view the United States might well afford to put an end to the horrible conditions now prevalent on that unhappy isle. I believe 90 per cent of the Southern negroes would hail with delight this opportunity.

And the white toilers of the South, once freed from this disorganizing competition and a consequent wage and hour system the most demoralizing of any section of America, would easily demand and receive a just compensation for a reasonable amount of labor.

Reader, this article is not intended to influence your opinion against the negro. No fair-minded man would blame him for that which he cannot help, considering that he, like all humanity, derives his natural character from a source which we dare not assail. I would place him on a higher level, open his way for greater possibilities and rejoice with him in his happiness, but I would also help those whom his competition unwittingly injures.

I have thus laid before you an unprejudiced statement of the negro's position in the Southern industrial problem.

7. GOMPERS AND THE SOCIALISTS: 1

1924

At most A.F. of L. conventions Gompers would tangle with his socialist critics. What he thought of them may be gathered from these remarks, a synthesis of his statements on the subject over the years, excerpted from the article on socialism in the American Federation of Labor History, Encyclopedia, Reference Book, *published in 1919–24.*

... [T]he trade union form of organization is the historic and natural form of associated effort of the working people. The nearer and closer we hew to the line of trade unionism, exercising the functions of trade unions, the more direct and successful will be the progress of our movement. I heard a delegate on the floor of the convention say, that if you elected six Socialist Congressmen in the U.S., you will have very many changes. I respectfully call the delegate's attention to the fact that in the German Parliament there are nearly 100 Socialists, and there we find the most backward of all European countries in the interest of labor. The man who is held up to typify Socialism is [K]arl Marx. There is not a socialist that can find in all his utterances one word for a co-operative commonwealth. During his life, he wrote not only his work, "Das Kapital," but he wrote a number of other works, and in one of them, replying to Proudhon, he denounced the socialists as the worst enemies of the laboring classes. I know that the socialists have taken that

Except to Walk Free

pamphlet and made a foot-note on it, and said that [K]arl Marx, in writing that, did not have the socialist of today in mind, but I call the attention of the gentlemen who made that foot-note that it was made when [K]arl Marx was dead, not when he was alive, when he would have had an opportunity of repudiating those who wanted to expurgate the statement that he made.

Attention has been called to the conduct of the men who clothed themselves in the mantle of Socialism, and assumed a position of superiority, mentally, in honesty, in work, and in ennobling purposes. It is because their professions are in entire discord with their actions in this Convention that it is necessary to call their position in question. I shall not refer at this time to their very many detailed acts of treachery to the trade union movement; but I shall refer to some of the declarations made upon the floor of the Convention by delegates participating in this discussion, and show you that though they may believe themselves to be trade unionists, they are at heart, and logically, the antagonists of our movement. Our friends, the Socialists, always when with us have an excellent conception of the trouble in our industrial life. They say, as we say, and as every intelligent man or woman says, that there are miseries which surround us. We recognize the poverty, we know the sweatshops, we can play on every string of the harp, and touch the tenderest chord of human sympathy; but while we recognize the evil and would apply the remedy, our Socialist friends would look forward to the promised land, and wait for "the sweet by-and-by." . . .

. . . I want to tell you, Socialists, that I have studied your philosophy; read your works upon economics, and not the meanest of them; studied your standard works, both in English and German—have not only read, but

The A.F. of L.

studied them. I have heard your orators and watched the work of your movement the world over. I have kept close watch upon your doctrines for thirty years; have been closely associated with many of you, and know how you think and what you propose. I know, too, what you have up your sleeve. And I want to say that I am entirely at variance with your philosophy. I declare to you, I am not only at variance with your doctrines, but with your philosophy. Economically, you are unsound; socially, you are wrong; industrially, you are an impossibility.

8. EUGENE V. DEBS

1910

Since becoming a socialist in 1897, Debs's views on the relation between socialist politics and trade unionism never varied. Following—an excerpt from his article "Working Class Politics," in the November 1910 number of the International Socialist Review—*is a typical expression of them.*

... We live in the capitalist system, so-called because it is dominated by the capitalist class. In this system the capitalists are the rulers and the workers the subjects. The capitalists are in a decided minority and yet they rule because of the ignorance of the working class.

So long as the workers are divided, economically and politically, they will remain in subjection, exploited of what they produce and treated with contempt by the parasites who live out of their labor.

The economic unity of the workers must first be effected before there can be any progress toward emancipation. The interests of the millions of wage workers are identical, regardless of nationality, creed or sex, and if they will only open their eyes to this simple, self-evident fact, the greatest obstacle will have been overcome and the day of victory will draw near.

The primary need of the workers is industrial unity and by this I mean their organization in the industries in which they are employed as a whole instead of being separated into more or less impotent unions according to

The A.F. of L.

their crafts. Industrial unionism is the only effective means of economic organization and the quicker the workers realize this and unite within one compact body for the good of all, the sooner will they cease to be the victims of ward-heeling labor politicians and accomplish something of actual benefit to themselves and those dependent upon them. In Chicago where the labor grafters, posing as union leaders, have so long been permitted to thrive in their iniquity, there is especially urgent need of industrial unionism, and when this is fairly under way it will express itself politically in a class-conscious vote of and for the working class.

So long as the workers are content with conditions as they are, so long as they are satisfied to belong to a craft union under the leadership of those who are far more interested in drawing their own salaries and feathering their own nests with graft than in the welfare of their followers, so long, in a word, as the workers are meek and submissive followers, mere sheep, they will be fleeced, and no one will hold them in greater contempt than the very grafters and parasites who fatten out of their misery.

It is not Gompers, who banquets with Belmont and Carnegie, and Mitchell, who is paid and pampered by the plutocrats, who are going to unite the workers in their struggle for emancipation. The Civic Federation, which was organized by the master class and consists of plutocrats, politicians and priests, in connivance with so-called labor leaders, who are used as decoys to give that body the outward appearance of representing both capital and labor, is the staunch supporter of trade unions and the implacable foe of industrial unionism and socialism, and this in itself should be sufficient to convince every intelligent worker that the trade union under its present leadership and, as now used, is more beneficial to the capitalist

Except to Walk Free

class than it is to the workers, seeing that it is the means of keeping them disunited and pitted against each other, and as an inevitable result, in wage slavery.

The workers themselves must take the initiative in uniting their forces for effective economic and political action; the leaders will never do it for them. They must no longer suffer themselves to be deceived by the specious arguments of their betrayers, who blatantly boast of their unionism that they may traffic in it and sell out the dupes who blindly follow them. I have very little use for labor leaders in general and none at all for the kind who feel their self-importance and are so impressed by their own wisdom that where they lead, their dupes are expected to blindly follow without a question. Such "leaders" lead their victims to the shambles and deliver them over for a consideration and this is possible only among craft-divided wage slaves who are kept apart for the very purpose that they may feel their economic helplessness and rely upon some "leader" to do something for them.

Economic unity will be speedily followed by political unity. The workers once united in one great industrial union will vote a united working-class ticket. Not only this, but only when they are so united can they fit themselves to take control of industry when the change comes from wage slavery to economic freedom. It is precisely because it is the mission of industrial unionism to unite the workers in harmonious cooperation in the industries in which they are employed, and by their enlightened interdependence and self-imposed discipline prepare them for industrial mastery and self-control when the hour strikes, thereby backing up with their economic power the verdict they render at the ballot box, it is precisely because of this fact that every Socialist, every class-conscious worker should be an industrial unionist and strive

The A.F. of L.

by all the means at his command to unify the workers in the all-embracing bonds of industrial unionism.

The Socialist Party is the party of the workers, organized to express in political terms their determination to break their fetters and rise to the dignity of free men. In this party the workers must unite and develop their political power to conquer and abolish the capitalist political state and clear the way for industrial and social democracy.

But the new order can never be established by mere votes alone. This must be the result of industrial development and intelligent economic and political organization, necessitating both the industrial union and the political party of the workers to achieve their emancipation.

In this work, to be successfully accomplished, woman must have an equal part with man. If the revolutionary movement of the workers stands for anything it stands for the absolute equality of the sexes and when this fact is fully realized and the working woman takes her place side by side with the working man all along the battlefront the great struggle will soon be crowned with victory.

9. GOMPERS AND THE SOCIALISTS: 2*

1914

An extraordinary encounter took place in Washington, D.C., on May 22, 23, and 24, 1914. Samuel Gompers, president of the A.F. of L., and Morris Hillquit, a very prominent spokesman for the Socialist Party of America, questioned each other at length before the Industrial Relations Commission. The entire colloquy was published under the title *The Double Edge of Labor's Sword*. It is a remarkable summary of the differences between the official Socialist Party position and the A.F. of L. leadership on the meaning of trade unionism.

Mr. GOMPERS: When Mr. Debs says: "The American Federation of Labor has numbers, but the capitalist class do not fear the American Federation of Labor. Quite the contrary." Do you regard that utterance as a friendly expression for the American Federation of Labor?

Mr. HILLQUIT: I do not, nor do I regard it as an authorized utterance of the Socialist Party.

Mr. GOMPERS: Speaking of the American Federation of Labor and of some Socialists, he says: "There are these who believe that this form of unionism can be changed from within. They are very greatly mistaken." Do you agree with Mr. Debs on that utterance?

Mr. HILLQUIT: I do not agree. I think, on the contrary, the American Federation of Labor is being forced,

* *The Double Edge of Labor's Sword* (New York, 1914), pp. 45–46, 50, 130–32.

The A.F. of L.

and will be forced more and more to gradually change its form of organization, to adjust itself to the forms of modern industrial conditions.

Mr. Gompers: I read this, and ask you for your opinion. Mr. Debs says in that speech: "There is but one way to effect this change, and that is for the working man to sever his relation with the American Federation."

Mr. Hillquit: I do not agree with that, nor does the Socialist Party agree with that. And, to make our position clear once for all, Mr. Gompers, I will say that it will be quite useless to quote Mr. Debs on his attitude to the American Federation of Labor. Mr. Debs took part in the organization of the Industrial Workers of the World. I think he has now lived to regret it, but whether he does or not, the fact is that he acted entirely on his own accord and on his own responsibility; that the Socialist Party at no time approved, directly or indirectly, of that stand, and at no time have endorsed the Industrial Workers of the World as against the American Federation of Labor. And I will say further that the Socialist Party at no time made fundamental criticisms against the American Federation of Labor, although I am just as frank to add that the Socialist Party, or at least the majority of its members, do believe that the present leadership of the American Federation of Labor is somewhat archaic, somewhat antiquated, too conservative and not efficient enough for the objects and purposes of the American Federation of Labor. That is the general Socialist position.

Mr. Gompers: Of course as to the leadership, that must be determined. The leadership of the American Federation of Labor, I assume, must be determined by the membership of the organization, as it can best give expression to its preference.

Mr. Hillquit: Entirely so.

Except to Walk Free

Mr. Gompers: Are you aware that the leadership to which you refer, has been elected and re-elected by practically unanimous vote for several years past?

Mr. Hillquit: We do not contest the election nor the legitimacy of office of the officials of the A.F. of L. We only wish they were a little more abreast of the time, and that they would keep pace with industrial developments. . . .

Mr. Gompers: All right, Mr. Chairman. Now, of course, Mr. Hillquit, you understand that the articles or editorials which I have written and published in the American Federationist, all of them have been caused by the defensive attitude which the American Federation has been forced to take against the aggressiveness and hostility of the Socialist Labor Party and the Socialist Party?

Mr. Hillquit: I don't think so at all, Mr. Gompers. If you ask me about my understanding of it, my understanding is that those articles have been caused by your fear of the increasing growth of Socialism in the ranks of the Federation. That is my understanding of it.

Mr. Gompers: Well, of course, you would not attribute to me very great fear of anything, would you?

Mr. Hillquit: Of anything?

Mr. Gompers: Of anything.

Mr. Hillquit: If you want my opinion, Mr. Gompers, I should say you are a very brave man, but you do hate to see the American Federation of Labor turning Socialistic. . . .

Mr. Hillquit: Mr. Gompers, you are familiar with industrial conditions as few men in this country. You know perfectly well that the most important industries in the United States are managed and operated by corporations, and you know that the income from such industries is

The A.F. of L.

distributed very largely in the form of dividends on stocks and interest on bonds, don't you?

Mr. Gompers: Yes, sir.

Mr. Hillquit: Now, I am asking you this question: As the President of the American Federation of Labor do you consider that the vast sum of money paid annually by industry in the shape of such dividends on stock and interest on bonds in the various industries are a legitimate and proper charge upon the product of labor, or do you not?

Mr. Gompers: I do not.

Mr. Hillquit: That is an answer. Then the stockholders or bondholders of modern corporations receive a workless income from the product of the workers who have produced it. Is that your opinion?

Mr. Gompers: Unquestionably.

Mr. Hillquit: And the efforts of the American labor movement to secure a larger share are directed against that class who gets such improper income?

Mr. Gompers: Against all who——

Mr. Hillquit: Against all who obtain a workless income which comes from the product of labor. Is that correct?

Mr. Gompers: Well, all who illegitimately stand between the workers and the attainment of a better life.

Mr. Hillquit: Which means, or does it not mean, those who derive an income without work by virtue of their control of the industry?

Mr. Gompers: No.

Mr. Hillquit: Whom do you except?

Mr. Gompers: I except, as I have before called attention to, honest investment, honest enterprise.

Mr. Hillquit: Have the efforts of the workers in the American Federation of Labor and in other labor or-

Except to Walk Free

ganizations to obtain a larger share of the product, met a favorable reception from those who obtain what we may call the unearned part of the product?

MR. GOMPERS: If you mean the employers——

MR. HILLQUIT: Employers, stockholders, bondholders, the capitalist class generally.

MR. GOMPERS: As a matter of fact, there has been very much opposition to the efforts of the working people to secure improved conditions.

MR. HILLQUIT: And that opposition is based upon the desire of the beneficiaries of the present system of distribution to retain as much as possible of their present share or to increase it, is it not?

MR. GOMPERS: I suppose it is not difficult to determine that that is one of the reasons. But one additional reason is that there are employers who live in the 20th century and have the mentality of the 16th century in regard to their attitude toward working people. They still imagine that they are the masters of all that serve, and that any attempt on the part of the working people to secure improvement in their condition is a species of rebellion—a rebellious spirit which must be bounded down. But we find this, Mr. Hillquit, that after we have had some contests with employers of such a character, whether we have won the battle or lost it, if we but maintain our organization, there is less difficulty thereafter in reaching a joint agreement or a collective bargain involving improved conditions for the working people.

MR. HILLQUIT: That is, if you retain your organization?

MR. GOMPERS: Yes, sir.

MR. HILLQUIT: And the stronger the organization, the more likelihood of securing such concessions, is that correct?

The A.F. of L.

Mr. Gompers: Unquestionably.

Mr. Hillquit: Then it is not on account of the changed sentiment of the employer, that he is ready to yield, but on account of greater strength shown by the employees, is that correct?

Mr. Gompers: Not entirely.

Mr. Hillquit: No, why not?

Mr. Gompers: Not entirely, for, as a matter of fact, the employer changes his sentiment when he is convinced that the working men have demonstrated that they have the right to have a voice in determining the questions affecting the relations between themselves and their employers, as evidenced, if you please, by the late Mr. Baer, who, you may recall, once declared that he would not confer with the representative of the miners or anyone who stood for them; that he and his associates were the trustees of God in the administration of their property, and appointed to take care of the rights and interests of the working people. Well, he lived to revise his judgment, as many other employers live to revise their judgments, and have come to agreements with their workmen.

Mr. Hillquit: Now, Mr. Gompers, the employers as a class, being interested in retaining their share of the general product or increasing it, and the workers as you say, being determined to demand an ever greater and greater share of it, would you say that the economic interests between the two classes are harmonious or not?

Mr. Gompers: I say they are not, and as I am under affirmation before this Commission, I take this opportunity of saying that no man within the range of my acquaintance has ever been so thoroughly misrepresented on that question as I have. . . .

10. THE I.W.W.*

1915

William D. (Big Bill) Haywood, secretary-treasurer of the I.W.W., was another labor leader who testified (on May 12, 1915) before the Industrial Relations Commission. He was very candid and open in his explanation of the anarcho-communist philosophy behind the I.W.W., its ideal of One Big Union.

Mr. Haywood. . . . We say to you frankly that there can be no identity of interests between labor, who produces all by their own labor power and their brains, and such men as John D. Rockefeller, Morgan, and their stockholders, who neither by brain or muscle or by any other effort contribute to the productivity of the industries that they own. We say that this struggle will go on in spite of anything that this commission can do or anything that you may recommend to Congress; that the struggle between the working class and the capitalistic class is an inevitable battle; that it is a fight for what the capitalistic class has control of—the means of life, the tools and machinery of production. These, we contend, should be in the hands of and controlled by the working class alone, independent of anything that capitalists and their shareholders and stockholders may say to the contrary.

Personally I don't think that this can be done by political action. . . .

* *Commission on Industrial Relations*, 64th Congress, 1st Session, Senate Document 415 (Washington, 1916), vol. XI, pp. 10575, 10582–83.

The A.F. of L.

Commissioner O'CONNELL. Have you in mind some other method by which it can?

MR. HAYWOOD. Yes, sir; I think it can be done by direct action. I mean by organization of the forces of labor. Take, for instance, the organization that you know, the United Mine Workers of America. They have about one-half of the miners of this country organized. At least a sufficient number to control them all. I think the United Mine Workers can say to the mine owners, "You must put these mines in order, in proper shape, or we won't work in them." They can compel the introduction of safety appliances, of ventilation systems, and save in that way thousands of lives every year. I don't think anybody will deny that they have that power to bring about that improvement. If they have the power to do that by direct action, they have the power to reduce their hours; they have the power to increase or at least to better the laboring conditions around the mines and have better houses. It seems to me there is no reason in the world why the miner should not enjoy, even in a mining camp, some of the advantages that the worker has in the city. And I think that free organization of miners, organized in one big union, having no contract with the boss, have no right to enter into a contract with the employer or any other combination of labor, to my mind. There can be each division of industry, each subdivision, be brought into a whole, and that will bring about the condition that I have described to you. . . .

Commissioner WEINSTOCK. Now, will you tell this commission, Mr. Haywood, as an authority on the subject, wherein, assuming that you and the Socialists and the American Federationists have the same objective in mind; that is, the betterment of the worker—will you point out to this commission as clearly and concisely as you can

Except to Walk Free

wherein your methods differ and are better than the method of the Socialists, and of the American Federationists? . . .

Mr. Haywood. Without saying—without criticizing trade-unions, which I regard as having accomplished great good in their time, there are many things in the workings of trade-unions where they recognize the right of the bosses. The Industrial Workers of the World do not recognize that the bosses have any rights at all. We have founded the organization on the basis of the class struggle, and on that basis it must work out its ultimate.

The trade-union says, "Well, the boss has some right here, and we are going to enter into a contract with him." How long is it going to take to solve this problem if you have continuity of contracts? That is the thing we say.

The trade-union is organized on the basis of the tools they work with. Now, the tools are changing, and it is driving trade-unions out of business. For instance, the glass blowers—glass was made by workmen who blew through a tube. A glass maker, a glass blower himself contrived a machine whereby this blowing is done automatically, and the glass blower, he is wheeling sand to that machine now.

We believe that everybody that works around that machine ought to be organized just as before; we believe that everybody that works around the glass factory ought to be organized, organized with regard to the welfare of each other. . . .

Can you conceive of anything that labor can not do if they were organized in one big union? If labor was organized and self-disciplined it could stop every wheel in the United States tonight—every one—and sweep off

The A.F. of L.

your capitalists and State legislatures and politicians into the sea. Labor is what runs this country, and if they were organized, scientifically organized—if they were class-conscious, if they recognized that the worker's interest was every worker's interest, there is nothing but what they can do.

Commissioner WEINSTOCK. Granting an organization so colossal in its character would have great power for good, would it not have great power for ill?

MR. HAYWOOD. Yes, it would have great power for ill—that is, it would be ill for the capitalists. Every one of them would have to go to work.

Commissioner WEINSTOCK. Would it not also have great power in doing this—in establishing a new slavery? If the wage earner claims that under [the] present system of things he is in slavery, would not the colossal power of your plan simply be slavery with new masters?

MR. HAYWOOD. Such a labor organization would be a fine sort of slavery. I would like to work for my union in a shop that I owned best.

Commissioner WEINSTOCK. If you were the "big Injun" chief?

MR. HAYWOOD. No; to go right back in the mine that I came from. That is the place that I would like to go, right tomorrow, and receive for my labor, without any stockholder, without any Rockefeller taking off any part of it, the social value of what my labor contributed to society.

Commissioner WEINSTOCK. To that degree, then, I take it, the I.W.W.'s are Socialistic?

MR. HAYWOOD. All right.

Commissioner WEINSTOCK. Let me see if I understand the distinction correctly between socialism and I.W.W.'-ism.

Except to Walk Free

As I understand it, I.W.W.'ism is socialism with this difference—

Mr. Haywood (interrupting). With its working clothes on.

11. THE LUDLOW MASSACRE*

1915

The Ludlow Massacre was one of the most atrocious in the unhappy history of American labor. There had been a succession of strikes against the Colorado Fuel and Iron Company dating back to the 1880s. In September 1913 the workers (many of whom had been brought in as scabs for the previous strike) went out again, trekking their families from their company-owned homes to a series of tent communities set up by the United Mine Workers. The largest of these was in a place called Ludlow. Sporadic fighting broke out as company police and local militia sought to protect scabs from attack by the striking miners. On April 20, 1914, the militiamen burned down the tent city at Ludlow. Three workers were killed. Two women and eleven children died in the fire. President Wilson dispatched troops and ended the violence. Then he established a commission to investigate the massacre and recommend a solution. It did so, but the company refused to accept the recommendations. Colorado Fuel was one of John D. Rockefeller's absentee properties. He claimed never to have had any interest in how the company ran its affairs and so disavowed any responsibility for what transpired at Ludlow. Below is the testimony of John R. Lawson, a leader of the United Mine Workers, before the Industrial Relations Commission.

* *Commission on Industrial Relations*, 64th Congress, 1st Session, Senate Document 415 (Washington, 1916), vol. VIII, pp. 8004–6.

Except to Walk Free

... In those first days, when he might have been expected to possess a certain enthusiasm in his vast responsibilities, Colorado was shaken by the coal strike of 1903-4. It is a matter of undisputed record that a mercenary militia, paid openly by the mine operators, crushed this strike by the bold violation of every known constitutional right that the citizen was thought to possess. Men were herded in bull pens like cattle, homes were shattered, the writ of habeas corpus suspended, hundreds were loaded on cars and dumped into the desert without food or water, others were driven over the snow of the mountain ranges, a governor elected by 15,000 majority was unseated, a man never voted on for that office was made governor, and when there came a thing called peace, the blacklist gave 6,000 miners the choice between starvation or exile. The Colorado Fuel & Iron Co. organized and led that attack on the liberties of freemen, and yet you heard from Mr. Rockefeller's own lips that he never inquired into the causes of the strike, the conduct of his executives or the fate of those who lost. So little interest did he take in the affair, so faint was the impression it made upon him, that he could not even answer your questions as to its larger facts.

To take the place of the banished workers, thousands were imported, and the extent of the company's dragnet for new material may be judged from the fact that over thirty languages and dialects have been spoken in the mines since 1904.

Ten years pass, and in 1913 Colorado is once more pushed to the verge of bankruptcy by another strike. Many strikebreakers of 1903, reaching the limit of human endurance, followed the example of those whose places they had taken, choosing hunger and cold in tents on the mountain side and plains in preference to a continuance

The A.F. of L.

of unbearable conditions in the mines. By actual count, the union was supporting 21,508 men, women, and children in the various colonies in January, 1914.

What course did Mr. Rockefeller pursue in connection with this upheaval of employees? His duty was clear, for he is on record with this admission, "I think it is the duty of every director to ascertain the conditions as far as he can, and if there are abuses, to right them." Putting their justice to one side, the fact remains that we claimed many abuses and cited them specifically.

The statute law of Colorado ordered a semimonthly pay day, checkweightmen so that we might not be cheated, the right to form unions, the eight-hour day, and payment in cash—not scrip. We charged that the Colorado Fuel & Iron Co. had violated these and other laws, and in addition we told of evil housing conditions, high rents, company-store extortions, saloon environment, armed guards, and the denial of freedom in speech, education, religion, and politics. When 12,000 men back up such claims by taking their wives and children into windswept tents, surely they would seem to be deserving of consideration.

Yet upon the stand, throughout three whole days this week, John D. Rockefeller, Jr., insisted that he was absolutely ignorant of every detail of the strike. He stated that he had not received reports on labor conditions, he could not tell within several thousands how many men worked for him in Colorado, he did not know what wages they received or what rent they paid, he had never considered what the proper length of a working day should be, he did not know what constituted a living wage, and, most amazing of all, he had never even read the list of grievances that the strikers filed with the governor of Colorado and gave to the world through the press. He

Except to Walk Free

did not know whether or not fifty per cent of his employees worked twelve hours a day, and when asked whether or not he considered twelve hours a day in front of a blast furnace to be a hardship he answered that he was not familiar enough with the work to judge. He did not know how many of his employees worked seven days a week the year around, but judged that it would be a hardship, yet when asked what part of a year could be worked under such conditions without hardship, he refused to approximate an opinion.

He knew that there was a system by which injured men or their families were compensated, yet he did not know what the system was, and when a list was read showing the beggarly amounts paid to crippled, mangled miners, he would say nothing but that they were not matters that a board of directors would pass on. He did not know that his company's control of the courts had resulted in a condition where not one damage suit has been filed against it in years, and he did not know that men were treated like criminals for daring to mention unionism. . . .

These, Messrs. Commissioners—this record of indifference respecting human life and human happiness—are vital causes of industrial discontent. An employer who is never seen, and whose power over us is handed down from man to man until there is a chain that no individual can climb; our lives and our liberties passed over as a birthday gift or by will; our energies and futures capitalized by financiers in distant cities; our conditions of labor held of less account than dividends; our masters too often men who have never seen us, who care nothing for us, and will not, or can not, hear the cry of our despair.

There is another cause of industrial discontent, and

The A.F. of L.

this, too, flows from a Rockefeller source. This is the skillful attempt that is being made to substitute philanthropy for justice. There is not one of these foundations now spreading their millions over the world in showy generosity that does not draw those millions from some form of industrial injustice. It is not their money that these lords of commercialized virtue are spending, but the withheld wages of the American working class.

I sat in this room and heard Mr. Rockefeller read the list of activities that his foundation felt calculated "to promote the well-being of mankind." . . . A wave of horror swept over me during that reading, and I say to you that that same wave is now rushing over the entire working class in the United States. Health for China, a refuge for birds, food for the Belgians, pensions for New York widows, university training for the elect, and never a thought or a dollar for the many thousands of men, women, and children who starved in Colorado, for the widows robbed of husbands, children of their fathers, by law-violating conditions in the mines, or for the glaring illiteracy of the coal camps. There are thousands of Mr. Rockefeller's ex-employees in Colorado today who wish to God that they were in Belgium to be fed or birds to be cared for tenderly.

12. THE YELLOW-DOG CONTRACT*

1916

> Under yellow-dog agreements, workers, as the condition of their employment, had to agree never to join a union except with the express approval of the company. The legality of such agreements came before the Supreme Court in 1916, in the case of *Hitchman Coal and Coke Co.* v. *Mitchell* (Mitchell had been president of the United Mine Workers). Thanks to the Court's decision, the yellow-dog contract became common in the 1920s.

About the 1st of June a self-appointed committee of employees called upon plaintiff's president, stated in substance that they could not remain longer on strike because they were not receiving benefits from the Union, and asked upon what terms they could return to work. They were told that they could come back, but not as members of the United Mine Workers of America; that thenceforward the mine would be run non-union, and the company would deal with each man individually. They assented to this, and returned to work on a nonunion basis. Mr. Pickett, the mine superintendent, had charge of employing the men, then and afterwards, and to each one who applied for employment he explained the conditions, which were that while the company paid the wages demanded by the Union and as much as anybody else, the mine was run nonunion and would continue so to run; that the company would not recognize the

* *Hitchman Coal and Coke Co.* v. *Mitchell,* 245 U.S. 240, 250.

The A.F. of L.

United Mine Workers of America; that if any man wanted to become a member of that union he was at liberty to do so; but he could not be a member of it and remain in the employ of the Hitchman Company; that if he worked for the company he would have to work as a nonunion man. To this each man employed gave his assent, understanding that while he worked for the company he must keep out of the Union. . . .

That the plaintiff was acting within its lawful rights in employing its men only upon terms of continuing nonmembership in the United Mine Workers of America is not open to question. Plaintiff's repeated costly experiences of strikes and other interferences while attempting to "run union" were a sufficient explanation of its resolve to run "nonunion," if any were needed. But neither explanation nor justification is needed. Whatever may be the advantages of "collective bargaining," it is not bargaining at all, in any just sense, unless it is voluntary on both sides. The same liberty which enables men to form unions, and through the union to enter into agreements with employers willing to agree, entitles other men to remain independent of the union and other employers to agree with them to employ no man who owes any allegiance or obligation to the union. In the latter case, as in the former, the parties are entitled to be protected by the law in the enjoyment of the benefits of any lawful agreement they may make. This court repeatedly has held that the employer is as free to make nonmembership in a union a condition of employment, as the working man is free to join the union, and that this is a part of the constitutional rights of personal liberty and private property, not to be taken away even by legislation, unless through some proper exercise of the paramount police power. . . .

13. W. E. B. DUBOIS ON THE A.F. OF L.*

1918

W. E. B. DuBois, the great black sociologist and historian, had taken a liberal or progressive position on most issues in his early life (i.e., before the 1930s), believing it to be the most realistic, if not necessarily the best, hope for the advancement of black people. And so he had given a seal of qualified approval to the A.F. of L., despite its racism. It was the East St. Louis race riot of July 1917 (one hundred blacks killed in one day) that prompted DuBois to openly attack the A.F. of L. in the pages of his magazine, *The Crisis*. White trade unionists had participated prominently in the riot, but Gompers conspicuously refrained from condemning them at the 1918 A.F. of L. convention.

I AM among the few colored men who have tried conscientiously to bring about understanding and cooperation between American Negroes and the labor unions. I have sought to look upon the Sons of Freedom as simply a part of the great mass of the earth's Disinherited, and to realize that world movements which have lifted the lowly in the past and are opening the gates of opportunity to them today are of equal value for all men, white and black, then and now.

I carry on the title page, for instance, of this magazine the union label, and yet I know, and every one of my Negro readers knows, that the very fact that this label is

* *The Crisis*, March 1918.

The A.F. of L.

there is an advertisement that no Negro's hand is engaged in the printing of this magazine, since the International Typographical Union systematically and deliberately excludes every Negro that it dares from membership, no matter what his qualifications.

Even here, however, and beyond the hurt of mine own, I have always striven to recognize the real cogency of the union argument. Collective bargaining has, undoubtedly, raised modern labor from something like chattel slavery to the threshold of industrial freedom, and in this advance of labor white and black have shared.

I have tried, therefore, to see a vision of vast union between the laboring forces, particularly in the South, and hoped for no distant day when the black laborer and the white laborer, instead of being used against each other as helpless pawns, should unite to bring real democracy in the South.

On the other hand, the whole scheme of settling the Negro problem, inaugurated by philanthropists and carried out during the last twenty years, has been based upon the idea of playing off black workers against white. That it is essentially a mischievous and dangerous program no sane thinker can deny, but it is peculiarly disheartening to realize that it is the labor unions themselves that have given this movement its greatest impulses and that today, at last, in East St. Louis have brought the most unwilling of us to acknowledge that in the present union movement, as represented by the American Federation of Labor, there is absolutely no hope of justice for an American of Negro descent.

Personally, I have come to this decision reluctantly and in the past have written and spoken little of the closed door of opportunity, shut impudently in the faces of black men by organized white working men. I realize

Except to Walk Free

that by heredity and century-long lack of opportunity one cannot expect in the laborer that larger sense of justice and duty which we ought to demand of the privileged classes. I have, therefore, inveighed against color discrimination by employers and by the rich and well-to-do, knowing at the same time in silence that it is practically impossible for any colored man or woman to become a boilermaker or bookbinder, an electrical worker or glassmaker, a worker in jewelry or leather, a machinist or metal polisher, a papermaker or piano builder, a plumber or a potter, a printer or a pressman, a telegrapher or a railway trackman, an electrotyper or stove mounter, a textile worker or tile layer, a trunkmaker, upholsterer, carpenter, locomotive engineer, switchman, stonecutter, baker, blacksmith, boot- and shoemaker, tailor, or any of a dozen other important well-paid employments, without encountering the open determination and unscrupulous opposition of the whole united labor movement of America. That, further than this, if he should want to become a painter, mason, carpenter, plasterer, brickmaker or fireman he would be subject to humiliating discriminations by his fellow union workers and be deprived of work at every possible opportunity, even in defiance of their own union laws. If, braving this outrageous attitude of the unions, he succeeds in some small establishment or at some exceptional time at gaining employment, he must be labeled as a "scab" throughout the length and breadth of the land and written down as one who, for his selfish advantage, seeks to overthrow the labor uplift of a century.

The recent convention of the American Federation of Labor, at Buffalo, is no proof of change of heart. Grudgingly, unwillingly, almost insultingly, this Federation yields to us inch by inch the status of half a man, denying and withholding every privilege it dares at all times.

14. THE STEEL STRIKE*

1919

Mary Heaton Vorse was a well-known foreign correspondent when she gravitated toward radical politics and the labor movement after World War I. Her accounts of the industrial wars of the '20s and '30s are among the best extant. She would always emphasize the human and personal side of the event—as she did in *Men and Steel,* her fine book on the great 1919 steel strike (from which the following passage is taken).

The National Committee for Organizing Iron and Steel Workers

In 1918 the American Federation of Labor voted to organize the workers. The agreement between the workers and employers of the War Labor Board still existed. On one hand the workers had agreed not to strike; on the other the employers had agreed not to interfere with the organization of labor.

A sparse band of organizers began work in South Chicago in 1918. They organized South Chicago; they organized Joliet and the Calumet basin; they organized Gary where no organization had ever been. They worked in the East. At last all the workers in the steel mills moved and stirred together. In ten states and fifty towns thousands and thousands of men thought together; thousands and thousands of workers who would never know each

* Mary Heaton Vorse, *Men and Steel* (London, 1922), pp. 48–51, 60–61, 99–100, 152–53.

Except to Walk Free

other, who would never see one another, thought the same thoughts. The disturbance throughout all the steel towns was like a slow, heavy ground swell. There were very few organizers and a great number of steel workers. There was very little money for so great a campaign. And yet, steel was organized.

The mass of workers heaved and swayed—a long, slow upheaval. It was as though they advanced on a deep unhurried wave. It was like the heaving of mid-ocean.

How did they come to do this? The book that tells of the properties of the United States Steel Company is a very large book. It tells of holdings so great that the ordinary mind cannot grasp its implied power. The men who own the steel mills and the mines and the railways that brought the steel ore down to the water-front and the boats that carried it across the lake, own other things in Alleghany County. They control the law courts. The mounted state police are at their call. The political power—with all burgesses and sheriffs—they own also. In the steel country government is possessed nakedly by those iron and steel masters and their friends.

The steel workers' revolt was a dumb revolt, a revolt as deep as has been the workers' patience. This mute rebellion of the steel workers had for its background the sullen, coiling smoke, the perpetual soot, the ugly streets; all these things, the long day, the long oppression, were the foundation of the steel strike and they were its background.

The men struck even against the paternalism of the steel masters who knew so little of what was in the workers' minds as to imagine that men who wanted freedom would be content with welfare work.

The memory of Homestead, the upheaval in Youngstown, the killing in Braddock, all were part of the strike.

The A.F. of L.

The flag of hope, the white curtains of the steel makers' wives were part of its fabric. The steel strike was not made of a simple pattern. The strike was about all these things, but it had a deeper portent.

The concern of these towns is not Life; it is Industry. The making of steel has become a monstrous preoccupation. Production a game where men's lives are used.

Life is about human beings. Human beings revolt when their existence is used for the pleasure of kings or for making imperialistic wars or for the profits of industry.

That is why the organization was successful in spite of the power of the steel masters. Organizing went on underground, it went on through a fleet whispered word. Everywhere were spies; everywhere was repression. In spite of this 300,000 steel workers struck. There was something almost mystical in their unanimous action. Stickers appeared which said: "Strike September 22."

The Strike Demands

1. Right of collective bargaining.
2. Reinstatement of all men discharged for union activities with pay for time lost.
3. Eight hour day.
4. One day's rest in seven.
5. Abolition of 24-hour shift.
6. Increases in wages sufficient to guarantee American standard of living.
7. Standard scales of wages in all trades and classification of workers.
8. Double rates of pay for all overtime after 8 hours, holiday and Sunday work.
9. Check-off system of collecting union dues.
10. Principles of seniority to apply in the maintenance, reduction and increase of working forces.

Except to Walk Free

11. Abolition of company unions.
12. Abolition of physical examination of applicants for employment. . . .

John Fitzpatrick and William Z. Foster

Samuel Gompers was first chairman of the National Committee. He resigned in favor of John Fitzpatrick, President of the Chicago Federation of Labor and most beloved by the rank and file of all labor leaders. He conducted the Chicago end of the stike but the responsibility of the Steel Strike rested on William Z. Foster. He presented the resolution for organizing the iron and steel workers to the Chicago Federation of Labor in 1918. He was then engaged in organizing the packing industry. Largely through Foster's ability this industry whose organization had been totally destroyed in 1907, was reorganized. They won their demands without striking.

Foster imagined organizing steel under wartime conditions, without striking steel. Through lack of money and loss of time his first plan was not realized. He worked with what materials he had. It had been said steel could never be organized. Foster and the men working with him organized steel.

Foster is a long New Englander from Taunton, Mass. He has a thin face, a kind mouth and eyes, and he can work from morning to night, interrupt his work to receive a hundred people, and never turn a hair. He is composed, confident, unemphatic and imperishably unruffled. The waves of the strike break around him, there come to him the incessant news of arrests, there come to him daily multitudinous problems for decisions. All the minutiæ of this strike flung over the surface of the whole country, involving the destinies of the men of a whole great indus-

The A.F. of L.

try come to him. Never for a moment does Foster hasten his tempo.

One of the reasons of this is that he seems completely without ego. Foster never thinks of Foster. He lives completely outside the circle of self. Absorbed ceaselessly in the ceaseless stream of detail which confronts him. A ceaseless stream whose sum spells the fate of 500,000 men, and all those dependent upon them.

I have never heard him express himself in any abstraction. But the sum of my impression of him is this. It is as though he said:

"All I can do is my best. This is not a fight of to-day nor of to-morrow, it is part of the fight that was going on at the time of the Cæsars. This great steel strike is only an incident."

Once in a while he gets angry over the stupidity of man; then you see his quiet is the quiet of a high tension machine moving so swiftly it barely hums.

He is swallowed up in the strike's immensity. What happens to Foster does not concern him. I do not believe that he spends five minutes in the whole year thinking of Foster or Foster's affairs. . . .

Mother Jones

Mother Jones wove in and out of the steel strike. She was never long away. During her absence from Pittsburgh one could hear of her being in Joliet or in the Calumet Basin. She had greater intimacy with the workers than any one else in America.

She is their "Mother."

The foreign workers rarely meet Americans. The only Americans that some meet are bosses, landlords or tradesmen.

Except to Walk Free

Mother Jones is the only American woman that thousands of them have ever spoken to. She goes about surrounded with the protecting love of young men whose names she does not know. She goes up and down the country, and with her walks the memory of the long fight of the working people of America. It is a matter of record that her home is wherever there is a fight for justice. No minor prophet ever foretold the downfall of an arrogant city in bitterer words than she foretells the downfall of what she calls "the ruling powers."

When the convention ended I went with Mother Jones to Ohio. She sat beside me in the train talking; she talked almost as to herself. You might fancy that you heard the heart of the workers muttering.

"There was never a convention like this before. They never met before to talk only about liberty. Oh, it's coming; it's coming! . . . There's a terrible bitter tide rolling up and welling up in this country. There's gall mixed with the mud that's churned under the workers' feet in the city alleys. . . .

"Look at these towns; look out of the window. Nothing to rest the eyes. I say to you there has never been a crueler despotism than there is in this country to-day. Look out there! Look at the stacks of the mills like trees in a black forest! Look at the blast furnaces and smoke as far as your eye can reach, and the wealth that comes out of it made by the blood of slaves."

She cannot endure the suffering of the workers' children. She cannot endure the indifference of rich women. The two in her mind are sharply related. The indifferent women are blood-stained creatures to her. Brutal, cruel, abandoned, she makes you feel this. Exaggerations in her mouth become real. She talks about "Brutal women hung about with the decorations they have bought with the blood of children." This is to her a literal fact.

"Oh, God, the little children—to face it all! And our women are so brutal. They don't dream that in the great upheaval that's coming, their own children will meet with the same conditions. Then people go to church! They're mad as they were in the days of Babylon!" . . .

Johnstown Mob

After the strike had lasted some weeks, people said openly in the towns that the strike could not be broken peacefully. Members of the Chamber of Commerce said it, leading citizens. They formed vigilance committees. The Steel Company officials helped them.

James Maurer, President of the Pennsylvania State Federation of Labor was threatened by a mob of dubious origin. It was said that money was spent by Chambers of Commerce in their effort to terrorize him. Boys formed the mob and hoodlums. Maurer was dangerous. Maurer had said if he had the power he would stop every wheel in the state if the steel workers' rights and liberties were not returned to them, so terror whined at his heels.

In many towns these terroristic groups, under the name of citizens' committees, were organizing to stampede the strikers, to drive out organizers. This was done in towns where the strike had been peaceful, where there had been no conflicts with the police.

Johnstown was such a town. The first week in November Foster went there to speak. At that station they warned him it would be dangerous. He went on. Conboy and Foster were walking up the street; they were going up to the hall. A mob of men bore down on them; they were surrounded and separated. They took Foster to the train, a gun in his ribs. There was no police protection for

Except to Walk Free

Foster. The state constabulary were quiet. When mobs are made up of leading citizens, mobs are unmolested. They put Foster on the train.

That night the mob surrounded the strikers' hall. They drove the organizers out of town. They pried open the mills. The scene was set for the mills to open. It was more spectacular than the Youngstown opening. It was advertised through the papers. Of the 18,000 men on strike only 800 went back. But the opening had been made. Smoke rolled up to the sky. In these mills where no smoke had been, the fire of the blast took their heart from the men. The sense of disaster deepened in all the towns. The small striking communities were steeped in doubt; the bosses went around to the women undermining their courage, threatening that if their men did not go back there would never be any work for them. In isolated places every power the company knew was brought to bear on the strikers to make them believe that they alone were hanging on, to make them believe the strike was over everywhere else, and that people were only striking in this town. . . .

They Will Wait

Weeks after the strike was over I walked again down Braddock's alleys. The outward flow had set in. Many of my acquaintances had gone back to their own countries. The derelict old man, whose son had died of rage, had gone. The family was scattered.

There were no outward changes. The women's curtains were still drying on frames. The children played in the litter. Smoke rolled down the valley. Gusts of white steam arose behind the mill walls.

A woman was sitting beside her door with a child in her arms, another playing at her feet. Her mild eyes gazed on vacancy, as though not seeing the monotony of the squalid street that ended with the red cylinders of the mills, vast structures rearing their monstrous tank-like bulk far into the air and above which rolled the somber magnificence of the smoke.

The woman had the patience of eternity in her broad quiet face.

"I have waited," she seemed to say. "I am eternal. This strife is about me and mine. If my brothers do not change this, my sons will. I can wait."

IV
The C.I.O. 1935–41

Passivity, acquiescence, was the initial American response to the Great Depression. It was as though people had been struck by a natural catastrophe: All they could do was wait until it passed. The Hoover administration encouraged this view with its claim that "prosperity is just around the corner." And as the catastrophe deepened, as unemployment rose to a third of the labor force by 1932, as poverty entered the desperate stage, so, it seemed, did the passivity deepen too. Americans were brought up on the ethic of self-reliance, they were taught to believe that each of them was the author of his own destiny, and they tended to blame themselves for their wretched condition. The economic system they accepted as given, as unquestionable.

On the margins of American life, however, the left was stirring. Their long sleep was over. Their prophecies had been borne out, and to an extent that surprised them too. They had been saying all along that capitalism was bound to fail, that only the working class could replace it by taking matters into its own hands—by organizing into industrial unions, seizing political power, and socializing the means of production. On this general formula

Except to Walk Free

all socialists could agree, however they differed in doctrine and strategy.

And increasingly they were finding an audience. They were staging demonstrations and marches and signing up recruits, and not alone among students and intellectuals. The Communists formed the Trade Union Unity League and the Workers' Ex-Servicemen's League; the Socialist Party established the Workers' Alliance; the Reverend A. J. Muste (a remarkable revolutionary pacifist, an authentic worker-priest) and his followers set up the National Unemployment League. The left was no longer a minuscule cloud on the distant horizon.

As for the trade-union structure—the A.F. of L. and the railroad brotherhoods—it was as decrepit and inert as ever. The free-enterprise system found its most loyal defender in the A.F. of L. If anything, its attitude toward social reform was to the right of the Hoover administration's. Circumstances compelled President Hoover to initiate some modest (and grudging) government programs to help the poor and the unemployed. But the A.F. of L. opposed government intervention, on the grounds that any benefits to workers should come "voluntarily" from contracts between unions and employers, or from gratuitous acts of philanthropy. Meanwhile, A.F. of L. membership had dwindled to 2,127,000; relatively, it was back to where it had been at the turn of the century.

The advent of the New Deal—the administration of Franklin D. Roosevelt—marked a decisive turn in the fortunes of American labor. In its early years, when recovery was the order of the day, the New Deal sought to organize the major economic sectors, business and labor and agriculture, into mammoth cartels or syndicates. They could then, under government direction,

The C.I.O.

plan all aspects of prodution and distribution: prices, wages, profits, hours of work, and so forth. Planning through cartelization was the basis of the sweeping National Industrial Recovery Act of 1933, which specified (Section 7a) that workers had the right to "organize and bargain collectively through representatives of their own choosing." Roosevelt appointed a special Labor Board to make certain that Section 7a was observed. The federal government was thus declaring that only through unions could industrial workers be adequately represented and industrial peace obtained. This was what the union movement had been saying all along.

Thanks largely to Roosevelt and the New Deal, Americans—workers in particular—were not as intimidated as they had been by the forces pressing down on them. They discovered new reserves of energy in themselves. Workers defied the laws of political economy (which decreed that unions do not arise in periods of high unemployment—when there is a buyers' market for labor) and joined unions en masse. The A.F. of L. suddenly experienced an epiphany. It was vivified, pumped up with a new spirit. By the end of 1934, hundreds of thousands of members had enrolled, and many, many more were clamoring to get in. William Green spoke of 15 million members.

A growing body of workers felt sufficiently strong to rebel by more direct means. Strikes rose very sharply in 1934—it was, in fact, the greatest strike year in American history—as the NIRA machinery for handling disputes functioned poorly (the Labor Board being impotent), as workers began to perceive that the companies were not observing the law, or worse, were conspiring with government officials to undermine it (hence the expression "National Runaround" for the way the NIRA was being administered).

Except to Walk Free

The most eventful of the 1934 strikes were led by socialists of one persuasion or another. Their strategy was to exploit the general discontent in behalf of the union—to enlist, that is, the support of the community as a whole and, if possible, bring off a general strike. In most instances where such a strategy was tried, the employers did capitulate after a long and often violent struggle, and recognized the union as the workers' bargaining agent. This was what happened in Toledo, where A. J. Muste and the National Unemployment League participated in the Auto-Lite strike; in San Francisco where Harry Bridges (who had close ties to the Communist Party) led the longshoremen's strike; and in Minneapolis, where a group of talented Trotskyists (notably James Cannon, Farrell Dobbs, and the Dunne brothers) directed the truck drivers' strike. Not since the 1877 uprisings had the country seen anything like it. But with this difference: now the insurgents were successful.

The largest corporations were, of course, thoroughly alarmed, and they determined to do something. Nor did they scruple about the means. They expanded the size and scope of their own "unions" (the membership of which reached two and a half million by the end of 1935). Companies also planted numerous spies among the workers to find out who the activists were, circulated blacklists throughout industry, hired agents to provoke violence and repression, and employed their own private police to break up meetings and strikes. Business enterprise served notice that Toledo, San Francisco, and Minneapolis were not going to set the pattern for the future; that it had only begun to fight.

In the meantime, business had discovered an ally worth more than all the goons, spies, provocateurs, and private police combined—namely, the American Federation of

The C.I.O.

Labor. Between big business and the A.F. of L. the new unionism was halted dead in its tracks.

In theory, the A.F. of L. welcomed all workers to its fold, regardless of occupation and background and even race. But (as we have noted at tedious length) its practice was quite another thing, especially when hordes of workers from the mass-production industries were streaming in under "federal" charters—those granted temporarily by the A.F. of L president. At once, grave jurisdictional problems arose. How were the various craft unions going to assimilate the recruits? Given the fact that each industry contained a number of specialized trades (in autos, to take one example, it was tool-and-die, carpentry, machine-repair, electric, etc.), how would the new members who engaged in them be parceled out among the corresponding craft unions? And, assuming that difficulty was overcome, how would these craft unions unite to negotiate with a giant employer such as General Motors or Ford? And even if that difficulty were overcome too, the recruits still had no guarantee that the union representing their trades would admit them. Those left out would simply float about in limbo, or be dropped from the rolls altogether.

Mass-production workers, in other words, fell victim to the A.F. of L's hopelessly archaic structure and modus operandi. There was no way—in practice—that it could accommodate large numbers of industrial workers. Its watchword, now as ever, was: Better not to organize at all than jeopardize vested privileges and ancient fiefdoms. Small wonder so many workers tore up their union cards in disgust. Small wonder why, in one industry after another—steel, auto, rubber, electric, etc.—union membership declined about as vertiginously in 1935 as it had risen the year before.

Except to Walk Free

But it was also true that the A.F. of L. was no monolith. It had a handful of industrial unions—mainly the United Mine Workers, the Amalgamated Clothing Workers, and the International Ladies Garment Workers Union—which had grown considerably of late and were among the largest within the Federation, the U.M.W. alone numbering over half a million members. By 1935 these industrial unions had joined forces to become an insurgent bloc. They were seeking to change the A.F. of L.'s policies and ultimately its structure of power. They were challenging its craft-union hegemony, its domination by the most retrograde elements of the labor movement: the building trades, the teamsters, the machinists, and the carpenters.

That the two garment unions took such a position was hardly surprising. They embodied what remained of the prewar socialist tradition in the A.F. of L. Their rank and file, mostly Jewish immigrants from eastern Europe, and their presidents, Sidney Hillman of the Amalgamated and David Dubinsky of the I.L.G.W.U., were committed to class solidarity and the ideal (remote to be sure) of a socialist commonwealth.

That the United Mine Workers chief, John L. Lewis, should also take such a position, that he should assume leadership of the insurgent camp—this was surprising indeed. Throughout his life Lewis had been a conservative, a Republican of the McKinley-Coolidge stamp, an apostle of untrammeled free enterprise. He ruled his own domain with a mailed fist, as his opponents—those who lived to tell about it—could testify. But he was, by common acknowledgment, the most talented labor leader in the country, a brilliant organizer and negotiator and a magisterial public figure (he had few peers as a speaker). His A.F. of L. colleagues feared and distrusted him (which

The C.I.O.

was why they denied him the presidency on Gompers' death). To the left he summed up all that was grotesque and loathsome in the American labor movement.

No one, therefore, was quite prepared for the astonishing metamorphosis that took place in 1935—for the man who suddenly emerged, at the age of fifty-five, from the chrysalis of the past. As much as any revolutionary, Lewis was now a crusader for the unorganized workers of America, all of them, even the humblest and most despised. He smote both the craft unions and the capitalists hip and thigh, bringing to mind the likes of Eugene Debs and Bill Haywood and the other martyrs to industrial unionism. Not that Lewis had adopted their radical principles, their views of society at large. Farthest from it. His call for the organization of the entire working class implied strictly limited ends. He never went beyond the advocacy of trade unionism pure and simple. And on most social issues he was as hidebound as he had always been. But this was exactly why he was such a fortress of strength: *He* could not be accused of being a revolutionist; *he* represented no alien presence in the land; *his* credentials were impeccable.

Lewis placed his union's treasure where his sentiments lay. He readily supplied the money needed to launch the organizing campaign. (So, to the limits of their capacity, did the other unions in the insurgent bloc.) A cadre of organizers had to be hired. And here again Lewis gave striking evidence of his changed character. Laying aside previous antipathies, he willingly worked with any radical, any personal opponent—no questions asked—for the sake of the industrial-union cause. Lewis was like a general whose only concern was to win the battle and who could not care less where his troops came from or who they were as long as they fought well and obeyed his commands.

And just when they needed it, Lewis and the A.F. of L. insurgents received valuable encouragement from the Roosevelt administration—the President throwing his support, in effect, behind any future mass organizing campaign. In May 1935 the Supreme Court had invalidated the N.I.R.A., thereby depriving labor of its legal protection under Section 7a. Congress, however, promptly passed the National Labor Relations (or Wagner) Act, which not only incorporated the main features of Section 7a (the right to form unions, the right to bargain collectively); it backed them up with strict enforcement provisions while explicitly prohibiting company unions.

Now there should be no illusions about the Administration's motives. It was not love of labor and the oppressed that prompted passage of the law; it was the desire to ensure long-term social peace. For according to fixed New Deal doctrine, industrial order required the coexistence of strong unions and large corporations. This doctrine played directly into the hands of the industrial-union movement.

The conflict between the A.F. of L. insurgents and hard-liners came to a boil in the famous November 1935 convention in Atlantic City. There Lewis and his cohorts officially put forward a resolution asking the A.F. of L. to approve the chartering of autonomous industrial unions. After long and acrimonious argument (punctuated by the fistfight between Lewis and Big Bill Hutcheson, head of the carpenters' union), the convention, as expected, turned the insurgents down by nearly two to one. The insurgents went ahead anyway, establishing their own Committee for Industrial Organization within the A.F. of L. William Green denounced the C.I.O. as a

The C.I.O.

species of dual unionism, the least forgivable sin a trade unionist could commit. It was tantamount to a declaration of war.

Fortunate in its enemies, the C.I.O. was successful beyond its wildest calculations. Within a year and a half of its founding it had organized unions and secured recognition as bargaining agent in every major industry. And it had captured the greatest prizes of all: General Motors and United States Steel.

But these triumphs were achieved only after protracted, sometimes violent struggles. Workers relied increasingly on such tactics as sit-down strikes—in effect, taking over the factory (private property!) and challenging the owners to do their worst: dismiss them, lock them out, bring in scabs or police. Workers were thus raising the ante higher and higher, threatening to wreak terrible destruction on companies that refused to bargain with them, threatening—it was but one step further—outright class war. That is why General Motors' capitulation in February 1937 to the United Auto Workers, who had been occupying the Fisher and Chevrolet plants in Flint, Michigan, was an event of transcendant importance. It meant that the most powerful segment of big business took the workers' threats seriously and, when the chips were down, preferred peace on the union's terms to war.

Now the C.I.O.'s task would have been more difficult had fortune not sided with it once again. For one thing, the economy experienced a demonstrable improvement in 1936–37, and business, hoping to resume full-scale production, wanted to avoid labor troubles. And for another, the Supreme Court, in April 1937, upheld the Wagner Act, thereby giving the government the authority it needed to protect the rights of organized labor. The handwriting, then, was on the wall, and even the most intractable holdouts—i.e., Ford and the smaller steel companies—could not help noticing it.

By 1938 the C.I.O. (now the *Congress* of Industrial Organizations) was solidly established, its four million members constituting a mighty power, the equal, certainly, of the A.F. of L. Its president, John L. Lewis, was honored (or reviled) as the Samson of the industrial-union movement. By his active support of, and participation in, the great strikes he, more than any other person, had brought that movement to fruition. And the fact that he was soon to undergo a sort of reverse metamorphosis and return to his pre-1935 persona—conservative, parochial, mean-spirited—does not diminish in the least the magnitude of his accomplishment, his place in history.

Under Lewis' aegis a remarkable new breed of labor leader emerged: young, defiant, committed to one or another radical ideology, whether socialism or Trotskyism or communism or militant New Dealism. And though their differences, or hatreds, cut deep, they all agreed that the destiny of labor lay beyond narrow and transient gain, that their own specific mission was to serve as its "vanguard"—to educate the working class, raise its consciousness, guide it to more distant goals of social reconstruction. The contrast between them—the Reuther brothers, Bridges, Carey, et al.—and the gerontocracy that ran the A.F. of L. provided the aptest commentary on the types of unionism that now existed side by side in America.

Yet, no less than the A.F. of L. hierarchs, could these new men of the C.I.O. afford to neglect their everyday responsibilities to the rank and file. They had to be effective trade unionists in the pragmatic, bread-and-butter sense of the term. Their survival depended on their abil-

The C.I.O.

ity to strike a nice balance between immediate and ultimate ends. And they, too, would discover in the course of time—as the A.F. of L. had back in the 1880s and '90s—that the balance could not be maintained indefinitely, that success might end up another kind of failure.

1. THE WAGNER ACT: 1*

1935

> Business enterprise did not take the Wagner Act seriously at the time of its passage. It was widely assumed that the Supreme Court would invalidate this law as it had the previous ones, thereby depriving organized labor of its great charter.

Sec. 1. . . . The inequality of bargaining power between employees who do not possess full freedom of association or actual liberty of contract, and employers who are organized in the corporate or other forms of ownership association substantially burdens and affects the flow of commerce, and tends to aggravate recurrent business depressions, by depressing wage rates and the purchasing power of wage earners in industry and by preventing the stabilization of competitive wage rates and working conditions within and between industries.

Experience has proved that protection by law of the right of employees to organize and bargain collectively safeguards commerce from injury, impairment, or interruption, and promotes the flow of commerce by removing certain recognized sources of industrial strife and unrest, by encouraging practices fundamental to the friendly adjustment of industrial disputes arising out of differences as to wages, hours, or other working conditions, and by restoring equality of bargaining power between employers and employees.

It is hereby declared to be the policy of the United

* The National Labor Relations Act, 1935, 49 Stat. 449–50.

The C.I.O.

States to eliminate the causes of certain substantial obstructions to the free flow of commerce and to mitigate and eliminate these obstructions when they have occurred by encouraging the practice and procedure of collective bargaining and by protecting the exercise by workers of full freedom of association, self-organization, and designation of representatives of their own choosing, for the purpose of negotiating the terms and conditions of their employment or other mutual aid or protection. . . .

Sec. 3. (a) There is hereby created a Board, to be known as the "National Labor Relations Board," which shall be composed of three members, who shall be appointed by the President, by and with the advice and consent of the Senate. . . .

Sec. 6. (a) The Board shall have authority from time to time to make, amend, and rescind such rules and regulations as may be necessary to carry out the provisions of this Act. . . .

Sec. 7. Employees shall have the right of self-organization, to form, join, or assist labor organizations, to bargain collectively through representatives of their own choosing, and to engage in concerted activities, for the purpose of collective bargaining or other mutual aid and protection.

Sec. 8. It shall be an unfair labor practice for an employer—

(1) To interfere with, restrain, or coerce employees in the exercise of the rights guaranteed in section 7.

(2) To dominate or interfere with the formation or administration of any labor organization or contribute financial or other support to it. . . .

(3) By discrimination in regard to hire or pay, tenure of employment or any term or condition of employment to encourage or discourage membership in any labor organization. . . .

2. THE C.I.O. INSURGENTS*

1935

> Following is the "Minority Report of the Resolutions Committee on Organization Policies," submitted by the industrial-union insurgents to the A.F. of L. convention on October 18, 1935. The report was turned down by a vote of 18,024 to 10,933—a foregone conclusion. The next day its authors, headed by John L. Lewis, met to form an organizing committee of their own. This was the germ of the C.I.O.

During the fifty-five years the American Federation of Labor has existed its declared purpose has been to organize the unorganized industrial workers of the nation. The contributions from its numerous affiliates have been made in the belief that organization would be advanced for the purpose of adding economic strength to the various units and that the organization policies would at all times be molded to accomplish the main purpose of organizing the unorganized workers in the industrial field.

During the existence of the American Federation of Labor and since the date many of the charters were granted to National and International Unions upon craft lines, the changes in industrial methods have been such that the duties of millions of industrial workers are of a nature that did not exist at the time many National and International charters were issued. This makes it apparent

* *Report of Proceedings of the Fifty-fifth Annual Convention of the American Federation of Labor* (Washington, 1935), pp. 523–24.

The C.I.O.

that jurisdiction over these new classes of work could not have been anticipated and included in the jurisdictional outlines of charters issued to National and International Unions at a time when the work that is now performed by these millions of industrial workers did not exist.

We refuse to accept existing conditions as evidence that the organization policies of the American Federation of Labor have been successful. The fact that after fifty-five years of activity and effort we have enrolled under the banner of the American Federation of Labor approximately three and one-half millions of members of the thirty-nine millions of organizable workers is a condition that speaks for itself.

We declare the time has arrived when common sense demands the organization policies of the American Federation of Labor must be molded to meet present day needs. In the great mass production industries and those in which the workers are composite mechanics, specialized and engaged upon classes of work which do not fully qualify them for craft union membership, industrial organization is the only solution. Continuous employment, economic security and the ability to protect the individual workers depends upon organization upon industrial lines.

In those industries where the work performed by a majority of the workers is of such nature that it might fall within the jurisdictional claim of more than one craft union, or no established craft union, it is declared that industrial organization is the only form that will be acceptable to the workers or adequately meet their needs. Jurisdictional claims over small groups of workers in these industries prevent organization by breeding a fear that when once organized the workers in these plants will be separated, unity of action and their economic power destroyed by requiring various groups to transfer to National and International Unions organized upon craft lines.

To successfully organize the workers in industrial establishments where conditions outlined herein obtain there must be a clear declaration by the American Federation of Labor. It must recognize the right of these workers to organize into industrial unions and be granted unrestricted charters which guarantee the right to accept into membership all workers employed in the industry or establishment without fear of being compelled to destroy unity of action through recognition of jurisdictional claims made by National or International Unions.

It is not the intention of this declaration of policy to permit the taking away from National or International craft unions any part of their present membership, or potential membership in establishments where the dominant factor is skilled craftsmen coming under a proper definition of the jurisdiction of such National or International Unions. However, it is the declared purpose to provide for the organization of workers in mass production and other industries upon industrial and plant lines, regardless of claims based upon the question of jurisdiction.

The Executive Council of the American Federation of Labor is expressly directed and instructed to issue unrestricted charters to organizations formed in accordance with the policy herein enunciated. The Executive Council is also instructed to enter upon an aggressive organization campaign in those industries in which the great mass of the workers are not now organized, issue unrestricted charters to workers organized into independent unions, company-dominated unions, and those organizations now affiliated with associations not recognized by the American Federation of Labor as bonafide labor organizations.

3. THE CRAFT-UNION PRINCIPLE*

1935

At its 1935 convention the main defense of the A.F. of L.'s policies on industrial unions fell to John P. Frey, chief of the Metal Trades Department and long an articulate and intelligent spokesman for the craft unions. Here he rebuts the argument of the industrial-union insurgents.

There are in this country a few unions which are thoroughly industrial, or thoroughly vertical, if you want that term. There are some unions in Europe that are thoroughly industrial, that is, all the members employed in the industry are members of one union. The only thoroughly industrial unions I know of in this country are company unions, organized by the employers, who compel the office workers and the manual workers to belong to the organization they form. In Russia there were free trade unions. I knew their officers and corresponded with them. When the Bolsheviks gained control and formed the Soviet they destroyed these trade unions, they assassinated most of the officers, and in their place the government created twelve industrial unions—only twelve for everyone employed in Russia. Those who joined these unions had no choice but to be in an organization composed of laborers, skilled mechanics and technical experts.

When Mussolini gained control in Italy he destroyed

* *Report of Proceedings of the Fifty-fifth Annual Convention of the American Federation of Labor* (Washington, 1935), pp. 553-56.

Except to Walk Free

all the free trade unions, and in their place organized three industrial unions to which everyone must belong who worked for wages. And I submit to you that while this has no direct bearing upon the question we are considering that the only thoroughly industrial unions in the world are the company unions or the type of organization forced upon the work men in Russia, in Italy, and recently in Germany, by dictators brought into existence only after free institutions and free expression had been suppressed.

We have been organized as we are up to the present time for fifty-five years. During all of these years so-called industrial unions and so-called craft unions have cooperated as best they could. We have made some progress. I have heard our trade union movement condemned for ineffectiveness. Employers have done that, the press has done that, and I am not altogether disheartened after listening to some of the remarks that have been made here. I believe that the American Federation of Labor is going to carry on just as it has in the past.

Now, when men propose that an organization such as ours shall change its entire construction, shall alter all that it has been acquainted with and use a new method, so far as I am concerned, they must bring to me something much more effective and convincing than either eloquence or sarcasm. And, as a number of international unions support the change in our form of organization, it seems to me that we have a right to put some searching questions to them.

There are a number of delegates in this hall with whom I have had the privilege of associating for many years. The newer ones can easily learn the record. We have had for fifty-five years so-called industrial unions which never, by the wildest stretch of imagination, cov-

The C.I.O.

ered the entire industry; and we have had the so-called craft unions, many of which are more industrial than those so called. We have worked with them side by side, and I want to ask those who have had more of an industrial form of organization than others whether their form of organization has enabled them, during the years, to show a better record of accomplishments than the so-called craft unions which now are accused of standing in the way of progress. Those who come in and accuse one type of union of standing in the way of progress must be prepared to answer those questions, and those of us who reply must be willing to ask certain questions that cut to the bone.

I want to ask some organizations which favor this complete change, and which for years have been affiliated with the American Federation of Labor, whether they can show a better record of accomplishments than the craft unions? I want to ask them whether it is the craft unions that have come into these conventions year after year for all of the assistance which we were generously willing to give? Or which have been coming into these conventions with such a problem on their hands that they dumped it into our laps and we were called upon, not only to finance them, but to turn over our organizers to help them to organize.

Is it the craft unions that have done that? Is it some of the so-called industrial unions which now ask us to throw overboard the type of organization we have built up, without which they would have passed out of existence many years ago? If an organization wants to convince me that the form they have adopted is more effective than my own International Molders' Union they will have to show me that they made more progress. . . .

In the steel industry there is an employer who owns

Except to Walk Free

and operates his own coal mines. He does that because he wants to have control of his own industry, and so we have a program to organize the automobile industry along industrial lines, which, up to the present time, doesn't include the coal miners. The same thing is true of steel. In the steel mills, or among some of them, they, too, operate and own their own coal mines. And so if we are to have an industrial union in the steel industry the question arises, is it or is it not to be an industrial union? Is everybody employed by these great steel corporations to be made members of an industrial union, or are we to draw the line at certain organizations and say, "We believe in industrial unionism, but you cannot have these men?"

Now I submit to you that I might look upon the question a little differently if, in the interest of thoroughgoing industrial unionism, the eloquent gentleman who preceded will say: "To prove my sincerity and my deep conviction in this matter, and my conviction is that the only way to organize industry is to organize along industrial lines, I am going to assert that the coal miners working for the automobile industry shall belong to the automobile industrial union and that the coal miners working for the steel industry, in order that they may have an industrial union, shall also belong to the steel workers' industrial union."

There is nothing new about this question we are discussing, but it seems to me that every generation has to learn its own lesson over, and that the experience of the past is either meaningless or is forgotten. We have heard this form of organization advocated in the past, and not only that, but the very organizations which applied it, and there is only a tombstone now to mark the fact that they existed. . . .

4. AKRON: THE FIRST SIT-DOWN*

1936

The first of the sit-down strikes, and in many ways the model for those that followed, broke out at the Firestone plant in Akron (precipitated by the laying off of a rubber worker named Dicks) in late January 1936. It is beautifully described in Ruth McKenney's *Industrial Valley*. McKenney, a native of Akron, later established a name for herself as a best-selling novelist.

John L. Lewis, January 19, 1936

The swirling snow of a winter blizzard swept Akron. The wind screamed on the armory front lawn as thousands of rubberworkers, their scanty coats pulled tight around their lean tall frames, filed into the big drafty hall to hear John L. Lewis, President of the United Mine Workers of America, make a speech.

Lewis, the chunky, powerful, heavy-faced miners' leader, came to Akron at the precise moment when rubberworkers were ready and eager, once again, to hear union talk. The Goodyear eight-hour-day policy threatened every fourth man with starvation. Everybody knew, for the company had taken pains to demonstrate it, that the Industrial Assembly wasn't worth a pinch of salt. In desperation, the men in the Akron valleys cocked a receptive ear once more to the idea of a union.

They turned up this Sunday, dubious, doubtful, ready

* Ruth McKenney, *Industrial Valley* (New York, 1939), pp. 248–51, 257–58, 262–63, 267–68. Reprinted by permission of Harcourt, Brace, Jovanovich.

Except to Walk Free

to be shown. Some of them knew Lewis from the days when they worked in West Virginia mines. Others remembered his fight in the A.F. of L. convention. More came because the U.R.W.A. workers in the shops had talked day and night for a week of this meeting, this great man.

Lewis faced the mountaineer workers of Akron calmly. He had taken the trouble to prepare himself with exact information about the rubber industry and The Goodyear Tire and Rubber Company. He made no vague, general speech, the kind the rubberworkers were used to hearing from Green. Lewis named names and quoted figures. His audience was startled and pleased when he called Cliff Slusser by name, described him, and finally denounced him. The A.F. of L. leaders who used to come into Akron in the old days were generally doing well if they remembered who Paul Litchfield was.

The Lewis speech was a battle cry, a challenge. He started off by recalling the vast profits the rubber companies had always made, even during the deepest days of the Depression. He mentioned the Goodyear labor policy, and quoted Mr. Litchfield's pious opinions about the partnership of labor and capital.

"What," he said in his deep, passionate voice, "have Goodyear workers gotten out of the growth of the company?" His audience squirmed in its seats, listening with almost painful fervor.

"Partnership!" he sneered. "Well, labor and capital may be partners in theory, but they are enemies in fact."

He paused, looking out at his audience, and caught the tenseness, the eagerness, the unfolding hope. He raised his voice, "That is what is basically wrong with American economic life and American industry. Here is the record of one great corporation in the rubber industry that has

The C.I.O.

made untold millions throughout the years and yet it has been a constant struggle for its workers to live at all."

"The only way out," he said with slow emphasis, "is to organize the workers into unions that can raise articulate voices."

The rubberworkers listened to this with surprise and great excitement. William Green used to tell them about the partnership of labor and capital nearly as eloquently as Paul Litchfield. Here was a man who put into words—what eloquent and educated and even elegant words—facts they knew to be true from their own experience. Here was a man who said things that made real sense to a guy who worked on a tire machine at Goodyear.

"Organize!" Lewis shouted, and his voice echoed from the beams of the armory. "Organize!" he said, pounding the speaking pulpit until it jumped. "Organize! Go to Goodyear and tell them you want some of those stock dividends. Say, So we're supposed to be partners, are we? Well, we're not. We're enemies."

He said these words to an increasingly excited audience. He evoked a dream in the minds of men, a dream of security, and a dream of freedom.

Suddenly he stopped speaking. There was a long pause. Then he said quietly, and very earnestly, "I hope you will do something for yourselves."

The crowd cheered Lewis for minutes. The men walked out into the blizzard so excited that they hardly noticed the bitter winds. They walked home through swirling snow talking fast and hard. Boy, here was a guy who knew something! Jesus, this guy could certainly put a finger on the truth! And, boy, did he give it to old Green? What a talker!

The Akron rubberworkers admired, and found deeply moving, Lewis's rather florid style of speech. Simple men

Except to Walk Free

of simple speech themselves, they liked hearing their dreams, their problems, their suffering, cloaked in Biblical phrases. They felt proud that a workers' leader could use so many educated words with such obvious fluency, and they were pleased and a little flattered by hearing their own fate discussed in such rolling periods and such dramatic phrases.

The Lewis speech made a profound impression in Akron. His audience went out of that chilly hall to make John L. the most talked of man in town. A hero to his listeners, he was next morning a hero to every second man in the rubber shops. . . .

[*The First Sit-down, January 29–31, 1936*]

The men were talking quietly but with fierce excitement. They had just decided to give Murphy one more chance: Reinstate Dicks and give him back pay for his time lost, or else.

"He'll say 'or else what' and that would be bad," one of the men objected. He was, like his friends, tall above the average, with tremendous shoulders, but very thin and gaunt, with deep hollows in his young weatherbeaten face and at his big neck bones.

"Yeah, that's right," someone answered from the outer circle around the stove. "We don't want to give him no hint. This has got to come off quick and easy. It's got to be a big surprise. That's what was the matter last year. We was all the time talkin' and didn't do nothin'."

"Yeah," a tirebuilder whose heavy boots were sizzling against the very belly of the stove replied, "yeah, and we let a lot of guys do the talkin' for us. This time we run it ourselves, and we don't tell nobody, and we don't ask nobody if it suits them either."

"Yep," the men in the circle murmured. They sat

The C.I.O.

quietly in their wooden chairs, close to the smelly stove, thinking. They seemed tired. Mostly blond men, freckled on the high cheekbones, with blue eyes, big red ears covered with soft blond fuzz, big heavy noses and wide mouths, they had still, after years away from their mountains, the look of outdoor men. Awkward in repose, their big feet reached out in a dozen queer angles. But even as they lounged silently, their lanky bodies revealed swiftness of action, power in motion.

And indeed these men who sat now, brooding, were said by expert industrial engineers to be the most highly skilled workmen in American mass industry. They built truck tires, partly by machine, partly by hand. They worked at a speed unequaled even in the auto shops. Their tires shoed the busses and heavy motor vans of the world.

In the quiet, the faces of these men were profoundly unhappy. They had been pushed into making plans for desperate action, a final resistance against the way of their lives. Most of them were married, and had three or four young children. During the past years many of them had been off and on relief as they were taken on and laid off again at the factory. Since they were the aristocrats of the rubber shops, they made about $25 a week when they worked—if they worked. They could not feed their growing families on this average annual wage of a thousand dollars or less. With the eight-hour day in the offing, every fourth man would lose his job forever.

Just before midnight the men in the union hall buttoned their jackets and crossed the street to ring in. Murphy had said "No" again to a hasty telephone call. Their minds were made up. The signals were arranged. Everything was ready. Some of the men had trouble slipping their timecards into the punch. They were nervous and

Except to Walk Free

their throats felt dry. This was really a hell of a thing they were going to do. Nobody had ever done such a thing before—at least not in this country. It made a man sort of upset. . . .

It was 1:57 A.M. January 29, 1936.

The tirebuilders worked in smooth frenzy, sweat around their necks, under their arms. The belt clattered, the insufferable racket and din and monotonous clash and uproar went on in steady rhythm. The clock on the south wall, a big plain clock, hesitated, its minute hand jumped to two. A tirebuilder at the end of the line looked up, saw the hand jump. The foreman was sitting quietly staring at the lines of men working under the vast pools of light. Outside, in the winter night, the streets were empty, and the whir of the factory sounded faintly on the snow-swept yard.

The tirebuilder at the end of the line gulped. His hands stopped their quick weaving motions. Every man on the line stiffened. All over the vast room, hands hesitated. The foreman saw the falter, felt it instantly. He jumped up, but he stood beside his desk, his eyes darting quickly from one line to another.

This was it, then. But what was happening? Where was it starting? He stood perfectly still, his heart beating furiously, his throat feeling dry, watching the hesitating hands, watching the broken rhythm.

Then the tirebuilder at the end of the line walked three steps to the master safety switch and, drawing a deep breath, he pulled up the heavy wooden handle. With this signal, in perfect synchronization, with the rhythm they had learned in a great mass-production industry, the tirebuilders stepped back from their machines.

Instantly, the noise stopped. The whole room lay in perfect silence. The tirebuilders stood in long lines, touch-

The C.I.O.

ing each other, perfectly motionless, deafened by the silence. A moment ago there had been the weaving hands, the revolving wheels, the clanking belt, the moving hooks, the flashing tire tools. Now there was absolute stillness, no motion anywhere, no sound.

Out of the terrifying quiet came the wondering voice of a big tirebuilder near the windows: "Jesus Christ, it's like the end of the world."

He broke the spell, the magic moment of stillness. For now his awed words said the same thing to every man, "We done it! We stopped the belt! By God, we done it!" And men began to cheer hysterically, to shout and howl in the fresh silence. Men wrapped long sinewy arms around their neighbors' shoulders, screaming, "We done it! We done it!"

For the first time in history, American mass-production workers had stopped a conveyor belt and halted the inexorable movement of factory machinery.

"John Brown's body," somebody chanted above the cries. The others took it up. "But his soul," they sang, and some of them were nearly weeping, racked with sudden and deep emotion, "but his soul goes marchin' on."

Downstairs, the echo of the song burst on the first quiet. Men heard the faint music and picked up the familiar words. They leaned out the windows into the cold winter's night air. "He is trampling out the vintage where the grapes of wrath are stored," they sang.

Across the street, in the union hall, men ran to the door and heard the faint faraway song, and said, full of wonder and a deep pride, "Jesus Christ! They done it! Listen to 'em! They're singing! They're singing!"

Over the snow-swept yard, in the winds of January, the song floated out to the whole valley, a song that promised never to die away, a song that promised to live

Except to Walk Free

on, fresh and unafraid, in the hearts of working men, a song that promised to spread from Akron to Detroit, to New York, and across the whole land of America.

"Glory, Glory, Hallelujah!" the tirebuilders sang. "And his soul goes marchin' on."

The foremen heard the song and retreated. They locked the fire doors and, five minutes later, opened them on demand. They were amazed by the organization of these revolting workmen. After the first hysteria had died down, the confusion disappeared at once. The ringleader, the man who switched the current off, climbed on the foreman's desk and shouted, "O.K., fellows. Now any of you guys here who ain't with us can get the hell out right now. Go home and stay home and don't let's see your yellow-livered face around here again. Anybody want to leave?"

Nobody did. "O.K.," the speaker went on. "Now we got a lot of things to do. First, we got to have a committee to visit other departments, and let's have some volunteers who ain't chicken-livered." The whole truck-tire department wanted to go. The leader picked half a dozen. "You go downstairs and combine with the auto boys' committee and, listen, it's up to you guys to shut this whole goddamned plant down, see?"

"O.K.," the speaker continued quickly. "Now we got to have a committee to police the floor. We don't want no machinery broken we can get blamed for, and we got to keep the place clean. No gamblin' for money either, and absolutely no drinking. We frisk everybody who comes in, for bottles. We don't take nobody's word for it. A couple of drunks would make this sitdown strike look punk."

"Sitdown strike," the crowd repeated. It was a good

The C.I.O.

phrase. The tirebuilders had never heard it before. They liked it.

"That's what I call it," the speaker said, "because we're sittin' down, ain't we, instead of working?"

"Yeah," the men answered and grinned.

"Now," the leader went on. "We're going to elect a committee to talk to Murphy. We figure we got to stay shut down until Murphy takes back Dicks and fixes the base rate. . . ."

The management of the rubber shops were stunned by the news. Here was something they had never heard of before, something frightening and queer. How did you deal with it? How did you break it up? One thing they were sure of: Firestone must be very firm. Not by any chance should the sitdowners be allowed to think they had won their peculiar strike. That would be fatal. That would give the new idea just the proper halo of success to make it spread, and then heaven only knew what would happen next.

The Firestone management agreed at first. For twenty-four hours Murphy refused even to discuss settlement with the negotiation committee. He said the plant would have to be cleared before he would talk about the Dicks case or the base rate either. The second twenty-four hours Murphy began to change his mind. It was all very well for Goodrich and Goodyear to beef about being firm and holding out and standing together. They were making tires, and he wasn't. Their factories were running smoothly and his was a bedlam.

Still Murphy hesitated. But at the beginning of the third full day of the sitdown, after fifty-three hours, his foremen brought terrible news. All of Plant Two was ready to sitdown in sympathy unless there was an immediate settlement. The Plant Two pitworkers had already

Except to Walk Free

voted to stand by their curing boxes and cut off the steam. Murphy shuddered, and in his mind's eye, he could see the beginning of a real strike, a strike for union recognition or something of the kind. His spies told him there was plenty of talk about spreading the strike and increasing the demands. Now this terrible news about the men in Plant Two!

Murphy sent for the negotiating committee and consigned to hell the opinions of his fellow factory superintendents at Goodrich and Goodyear. It was all very well to talk about a solid employer front, but in the face of something like this, a man had to act quickly or the whole situation would simply blow up in his face.

The settlement allowed Dicks' immediate reinstatement and three hours' pay for every day lost. It promised immediate negotiation on the base rate. It offered three hours' pay per day to all workers who had lost time during the sitdown.

When the committee, breathless and excited, brought the news to the men up in the truck-tire department for a vote, they could hardly talk, they were so jubilant. And the strikers were quite beside themselves. They were getting paid, paid, mind you, for sittingdown! And Dicks was back, with pay. And the rate would be negotiated. Glory Hallelujah!

The sitdowners marched out singing, and the sound of their voices went everywhere in the valley. The Firestone sitdowners had won! They won! They won! This sitdown business worked.

5. THE GENERAL MOTORS SIT-DOWN: 1[*]

1937

> The sit-down strikes at the Fisher and Chevrolet plants in Flint were successfully under way—that is, were jeopardizing the entire General Motors operation—when the company president, Alfred P. Sloan himself, sent a letter to all his employees vowing not to surrender the sacred principle of the open shop. But larger forces were closing in on Sloan. Both the governor of Michigan and President Roosevelt, rather than send troops into the factories to defend property rights, were urging the company to negotiate with the United Auto Workers. Following is Sloan's letter.

In view of the fact that several of our manufacturing plants have been forced to close down, possibly necessitating similar closing on the part of others in the not distant future, and realizing that this means a great deal to you and your families, as well as to the business, it seems only fair that I should tell you the circumstances that have brought this about in order that you may better understand and therefore judge more intelligently.

First, let me say that General Motors products were never in greater demand than today. This good business insures plenty of jobs, with generous hours of employment for some time to come. Wages are higher today, by far, than the corporation ever paid before. And, not only

[*] "Statement by General Motors Corporation," *N.A.M. Labor Relations Bulletin* (January 22, 1937), p. 8.

Except to Walk Free

that, but the amount that each dollar buys is importantly greater than it was during the last period of good business, say in 1929.

Again, important progress has been made in providing steadier work through the year; thus on these and every other count General Motors workers are earning more than they ever have in the entire history of General Motors, and as much, if not more, than the workers of any other business. No one can honestly say otherwise.

Yet under these conditions you are being forced out of your jobs by sit-down strikes, by widespread intimidation, and by shortage of materials produced by similar tactics in many allied industries.

Your employments and wages and the welfare of your families are being endangered by actions beyond your control and that of your company. The same ruthless tactics are threatening the general recovery of business, in which the automobile industry had the leading part.

You are being told you had better join a union. You are being told that to bargain collectively you must be a member of a labor organization. You are being told that the automotive industry is to be run as a closed shop. You are being told that if you do not join now it will be impossible for you to work in any automobile plant when the union wins, unless you pay. In other words, you will be without a job, therefore you must sign up, pay dues; or else.

I want to say to you most frankly, that this is positively not so. Do not be misled. Have no fear that any union or any labor dictator will dominate the plants of General Motors Corporation. No General Motors worker need join any organization to get a job or keep a job. . . .

6. THE GENERAL MOTORS SIT-DOWN: 2*

1937

> Mary Heaton Vorse, at the scene of action as always, writes on the victorious conclusion of the Flint strike, General Motors having just capitulated to the U.A.W.

A man in a red mackinaw walks down the steep steps leading from Chevrolet 4 toward the gate. He takes a key from his pocket. Bob Travis appears at the top of the steps, a crowd of strikers behind him. Accompanying him is a detachment of soldiers. Opposite, the plant militia, newspaper and camera men stand around a roaring fire. The street is empty and very quiet as if awaiting some momentous event. At the top of the street a crowd stands behind the barrier of the guard.

The man in the red mackinaw unlocks the high gate of Chevrolet 4. None had passed through it since the momentous sit down of February 1, which had affirmed the workers' power and brought about the conference for settlement.

Now the man in the red mackinaw unlocked that closely guarded gate. Bob Travis walks down Chevrolet avenue to Fisher 2 with the guard beside him. He goes into Fisher 2.

There is a roar of an approaching crowd. This one street still guarded by troops is the only quiet street left on the line of march. The peace terms have already

---

* Mary Heaton Vorse, "New Life Begins for Auto Workers," *United Automobile Worker*, February 13, 1937.

Except to Walk Free

been accepted down in Fisher 1 and these men have marched out accompanied by the cheers of several thousand people. In front of Fisher 2 now, the loud speaker is addressing the crowd which is increasing every moment.

Inside Fisher 2 Bob Travis stood on a chair and told the terms of peace to the Fisher 2 boys. Here were the boys who had been on the front of the battle line. They were young but they had the tempered and matured faces which a long fight gives. Here they had sat for 44 days and nights. Suspense had been heavy and long drawn out in Fisher No. 2. Here they had created a disciplined world of their own. Here they had risked their lives as the bullet holes through the windows on the second floor still tell. They had won their first battle, for everyone of these shock troops of unionism knew that the battle for the union was only the beginning.

The plant had been left in perfect order. We walked through its empty spaces peopled by half made cars and parts of cars. The great rooms were dim and ghostly. There was a curious almost breathless quiet here as if the cars and the silent machinery were waiting for life to begin its flow again. Outside, the roar of the rejoicing crowd came nearer. The barrier of soldiers had drawn aside while they swept past. The crowd with flags had marched cheering into the guarded zone.

The strikers were coming out of Chevrolet 4, flags preceding them. There were flags on the steps and flags on the street. Great flares lighted up the scene. Cheers for Governor Murphy filled the air with a tremendous rejoicing sound. Strikers' wives are waving to husbands they have not seen for days. A woman holds up a baby. The procession marches down the street. Another tremendous roar fills all space.

The Fisher 2 boys have marched out. They march out

The C.I.O.

in military formation from the quiet of the empty, waiting plant carrying neat bundles of their possessions. They make part of the huge joyful crowd, by now bright with confetti. People are carrying toy balloons. The whole scene is lit by the burst of glory of the photographers' flares. The big flags punctuate the crowd with color.

They are shouting to the rhythm of "Freedom, Freedom, Freedom!"

Chevrolet avenue is packed from bridge to bridge. People swarm over the murky little Flint river with its new barbed wire fences. They come past Chevrolet 4 and they come up the street past Fisher 2.

It seems as though the street can hold no more, but Fisher 1 is just arriving, a procession 5,000 strong. They come, flags at their head, singing. The old dam of fear has burst. They are in the grip of a mighty creative power. They march from the plants to the center of town back to union headquarters. Such a mass of joyful, cheering people has never been seen in Flint before. The streets are lined all the way. Men and women from the cars and marchers shout to the groups of other working people who line the streets, "Join the Union! We are Free!"

The marchers arrive in front of union hall. They gather continuously, more and more, in increasing thousands. The hall itself is jammed. They no longer leave people into the building. Inside and outside, the loud speakers are going. Homer Martin, Wyndham Mortimer, Bob Travis and the other strike leaders address the roaring crowds.

They are no ordinary crowds. This is no ordinary demonstration.

Mighty joy, powerful as a force of nature tears through Flint.

It is the joy of victory, but it is more than the joy of war

Except to Walk Free

ceasing, it is the joy of creation. The workers are creating a new life. The wind of freedom has roared down Flint's streets and the echoes will never die again. The strike has ended! The vailant working people of Flint have begun to forge a new life out of their splendid, historic victory!!

7. THE WAGNER ACT: 2*

1937

On April 12, 1937, the Supreme Court, by a vote of five to four, declared the Wagner Act constitutional. It held that the Constitution's interstate-commerce clause could support the kind of power that the National Labor Relations Board was exercising. Chief Justice Hughes wrote the majority decision (excerpted below).

... The authority of the federal government may not be pushed to such an extreme as to destroy the distinction, which the commerce clause itself establishes, between commerce "among the several States" and the internal concerns of a State. That distinction between what is national and what is local in the activities of commerce is vital to the maintenance of our federal system.

But we are not at liberty to deny effect to specific provisions, which Congress has constitutional power to enact, by superimposing upon them inferences from general legislative declarations of an ambiguous character, even if found in the same statute. The cardinal principle of statutory construction is to save and not to destroy. We have repeatedly held that as between two possible interpretations of a statute by one of which it would be unconstitutional and by the other valid, our plain duty is to adopt that which will save the act. Even to avoid a serious doubt the rule is the same.

* *National Labor Relations Board* v. *Jones and Laughlin Steel Corporation*, 301 U.S. 1 (1937).

Except to Walk Free

We think it clear that the National Labor Relations Act may be construed so as to operate within the sphere of constitutional authority. . . .

Thus, in its present application, the statute goes no further than to safeguard the right of employees to self-organization and to select representatives of their own choosing for collective bargaining or other mutual protection without restraint or coercion by their employer.

That is a fundamental right. Employees have as clear a right to organize and select their representatives for lawful purposes as the respondent has to organize its business and select its own officers and agents. Discrimination and coercion to prevent the free exercise of the right of employees to self-organization and representation is a proper subject for condemnation by competent legislative authority. Long ago we stated the reason for labor organizations. We said that they were organized out of the necessities of the situation; that a single employee was helpless in dealing with an employer; that he was dependent ordinarily on his daily wage for the maintenance of himself and family; that if the employer refused to pay him the wages that he thought fair, he was nevertheless unable to leave the employ and resist arbitrary and unfair treatment; that union was essential to give laborers opportunity to deal on an equality with their employer.

The Act has been criticised as one-sided in its application; that it fails to provide a more comprehensive plan. But we are dealing with the power of Congress, not with a particular policy or with the extent to which policy should go. We have frequently said that the legislative authority, exerted within its proper field, need not embrace all the evils within its reach. The Constitution does not forbid "cautious advance, step by step," in dealing with the evils which are exhibited in activities within the

The C.I.O.

range of legislative power. The question in such cases is whether the legslature, in what it does prescribe, has gone beyond constitutional limits.

Our conclusion is that the order of the Board was within its competency and that the Act is valid as here applied. The judgment of the Circuit Court of Appeals is reversed and the cause is remanded for further proceedings in conformity with this opinion.

8. THE WAGNER ACT: 3*

1937

President Roosevelt's feelings about the Supreme Court's decision upholding the Wagner Act were recorded the next day, April 13, during an "off the record" news conference. It was a typical Roosevelt performance.

Q. MR. PRESIDENT, in your Message to Congress of January sixth you asked the Judiciary to aid in making democracy successful. Have you any comment on the decision of the Supreme Court?

THE PRESIDENT: Not on the record. All I can tell you for the record is that of course these opinions are very long and I have only read them over in a very cursory way last night. I have not had a chance to read them with any care and therefore any comment at this time must be withheld.

Off the record, and really off the record and just in the family, I have been chortling all morning, ever since I picked up the papers. I have been having a perfectly grand time. When I picked up one of the papers, the dear old Herald-Tribune, and saw the editorial entitled, "A Great Decision," I harked back, and I got Steve to do a little digging for me and he found just exactly what I thought he would find. It is a joy. It goes back to—what is the date of that—September, 1935, when a committee of very, very distinguished lawyers calling themselves The National

* Franklin D. Roosevelt, *Public Papers and Addresses* (New York, 1941), vol. VI, pp. 153–54.

The C.I.O.

Lawyers' Committee and operating under an organization known as The American Liberty League—this is all off the record, what are you taking this stuff down for? (*Laughter*)

Q. You may change your mind. (*Laughter*)

THE PRESIDENT: No, I won't change my mind; this is off the record. They got a committee to make a very careful analysis of the Wagner Labor Relations Act and they concluded that it was thoroughly and completely unconstitutional. On September 21, 1935, the Herald-Tribune carried a beautiful editorial called, "Thumbs Down on the Wagner Act," citing with complete approval the unanimous opinion of the lawyers' vigilance committee, saying that it was a splendid opinion, and warning the country as to what would happen if an Act like that could possibly be found constitutional. And now, this morning, they come out with "A Great Decision." Well, I have been having more fun. (*Laughter*)

And I haven't read the Washington Post, and I haven't got the Chicago Tribune yet. (*Laughter*)

Or the Boston Herald. Today is a very, very happy day.

9. VIOLENCE AGAINST LABOR: 1[*]

1937–39

Amid increasing reports of company terror against the union movement, the Senate authorized a comprehensive investigation of the practice, which was in clear violation of civil liberties (free speech, assembly, etc.) not to mention the various provisions of the Wagner Act. The investigation, headed by Senator Robert La Follette, Jr., of Wisconsin (son of the great progressive warrior), lasted three years, during which time it heard some hair-raising testimony. The hearings gave the public an idea of what went on below the surface of industrial life and why conflicts, when they erupted, were often so violent. Following are translations of terms once commonly used in the work of labor surveillance, espionage, and terror.

Fink: One who makes a career of taking employment in struck plants or of acting as a strikebreaker, strike guard, or slugger.

General Op: A labor spy who holds an influential position in a labor union.

Hooking: Entrapping an employee into spying on fellow employees. Usually accomplished by approaching the prospective hooked man under a pretext and engaging him to write reports.

Hooker: Detective agency official who induces workers to become spies.

[*] U. S. Senate Committee on Education and Labor, *Violations of Free Speech and the Rights of Labor*, 75th Congress, 2nd Session, 1938, Senate Report 46, Part 3.

The C.I.O.

Hooked man: An employee engaged in industrial espionage without knowledge that he is reporting to a detective agency or that his reports are going to the employer.

. . .

Inside man: A spy placed in a plant as an employee.

. . .

Missionary: A spy whose work it is to spread antiunion or antistrike propaganda in the general neighborhood of a plant and particularly among the wives of workers. One not employed in the plant.

Noble: A lieutenant of strike operations usually in charge of a detachment of guards, sluggers, and finks.

Operative [also *Op*]: A spy employed by an agency. Usually has a secret designation. An operative may be a hooked man or professional spy.

Outside man: A spy under a cover but not masquerading as an employee in a plant.

Roping: Securing information by striking up acquaintance or friendship with union men.

Rough shadowing: To keep a man under surveillance in such a manner that he knows that he is being followed.

. . .

Slugger: A specialized type of fink used to attack, assault, and beat up strikers or union leaders. Generally armed.

Strikebreaker: One whose trade it is to take employment in struck plants. Distinguishable from "scab" who is a workman. May pretend to work in the plant or act as a guard. A fink.

10. VIOLENCE AGAINST LABOR: 2*

1937–39

At the end of his committee's hearings, in 1939, Senator La Follette presented a summary account of what it had learned over the past three years. Following is a tiny excerpt of that incredible report.

THE COMMITTEE first turned its attention to the dirty business of labor spying, which is described in its report on Industrial Espionage. This practice, which is so abhorrent to the American concept of a free society, was found to be flourishing in every quarter. Organized businesses were taking in millions of dollars for dealing in labor spies. National and local employers' associations regarded labor espionage as a regular part of their services to their members. Great interstate corporations maintained private espionage systems which rivaled the detective agencies in scope and in ruthlessness. The poison of espionage was spreading throughout industry, creating strife, and corroding mutual trust between management and labor.

The leaders in the detective-agency field were summoned to testify. Pinkerton's National Detective Agency, Inc., with offices in 27 cities, was the most powerful dealer in the labor-spy traffic. The firm was grossing well over $2,000,000 a year. Robert A. Pinkerton, president of the agency, who in 1935 held 70 percent of its stock, received in that year $129,500 in dividends. The agency had in-

---

* U. S. Senate Committee on Education and Labor, *Oppressive Labor Practices Act*, 76th Congress, 1st Session, Hearings, pp. 14, 16, 18, 26.

The C.I.O.

fluential connections. From 1930 until the first part of 1936, Carl de Gersdorff, partner of Cravath, de Gersdorff, Swaine & Wood, a prominent Wall Street firm of attorneys, served on the board of directors of the Pinkerton agency. The clients of Pinkerton's figured among the most powerful corporations in the country. Between 1933 and 1936 Pinkerton had 309 industrial clients, many of them giants in their respective fields of industry, such as the General Motors Corporation, Bethlehem Steel Corporation, Pennsylvania Railroad Co., and Baldwin Locomotive Works.

This blue-ribbon agency employed no less than 1,228 industrial spies between January 1, 1933, and April 1937. More significant, however, than the number of spies at work, the huge sums of money spent for their services, and the list of agency clients, were the facts developed concerning the union affiliations and the position of the spies themselves. This information provided a true index of the extent of the power which professional labor spies wield over the American worker. The facts were truly astounding. Pinkerton operates in practically every union in the country, from the Amalgamated Association of Meat Cutters and Butchers of America to the United Mine Workers of America. Every important international union, many smaller and local unions, even company unions—whether affiliated with the American Federation of Labor, the Congress of Industrial Organizations, or independent, whether craft or industrial—have their quota of Pinkerton spies. . . .

The committee summoned the heads of large and responsible corporations, and their personnel officers in order to determine the reasons for the use of labor spies in industry.

In the General Motors Corporation the committee

Except to Walk Free

found an amazing situation. In a year and a half, from January 1934 through July 1936, the corporation spent over $994,000 for labor spies. Fourteen separate spy agencies were employed by the corporation. It used the Pinkerton National Detective Agency; the Corporations Auxiliary Co.; the Railway Audit & Inspection Co.; the Wm. J. Burns International Detective Agency, Inc.; the Cal Crim Detective Bureau, Inc.; the McGrath Detective Agency of Cleveland, Ohio; the spies of the National Metal Trades Association; the National Corporation Service, Inc.; the O'Neil Industrial Service; and others. At times as many as 200 spies were reporting on the activity of its workers in the sixty-odd plants of the corporation. The irresistible logic of espionage reached its final stages when the General Motors Corporation used the Pinkerton agency to spy upon its own Corporations Auxiliary Co. spies. The corporation found itself a victim of its own devices. In order to spy upon its workers and its officials it admitted into its employment and exposed its business secrets to a swarm of unscrupulous men whose trade was corruption and deceit. . . .

A serious threat to civil liberties lies in the use of private police systems in the field of labor relations. Private police have a legitimate function, that of protecting property against theft and acting as watchmen. There can be no justification, however, for an employer to mobilize a private army, paid for by him and obeying his orders, to police the public highways during periods of labor dispute. The public is entitled to the maintenance of law in an orderly fashion. It is a mockery of the law when the employer arms his own troops and usurps the functions of public authorities.

There can be only lawless law enforcement when an employer is permitted to purchase the power of the State

The C.I.O.

through the connivance of a subservient or corrupt public official.

The Republic Steel Corporation maintains a force of uniformed armed police of 300 to 400 men, varying according to labor difficulties. These men are used to follow union organizers in the streets of our largest cities. Members of the Republic police force have been identified as having beaten up union men who were attempting to pass out leaflets in the public highways. The captain of the Republic police force in Cleveland, Ohio, has admitted that he assaulted and beat two men who furnished information to this committee during its inquiry last year. . . .

In investigating the Little Steel Strike of 1937, the subcommittee subpoenaed the Youngstown Sheet & Tube Co. and the Republic Steel Corporation for inventories of munitions kept on hand in their plants. The results were astonishing. The Youngstown Sheet & Tube Co. had 8 machine guns of standard Army tripod type, 369 rifles, 190 shotguns, and 454 revolvers, together with over 6,000 rounds of ball ammunition and 3,950 rounds of shot ammunition. It also had 109 gas guns, with over 3,000 rounds of gas ammunition. The Republic Steel Corporation had proportionately more gas and gas equipment. It was, in fact, the largest purchaser of tear and sickening gas in the United States, purchasing a total of $79,000 worth during the period under investigation. This total far exceeded not only purchases of other companies, but also the purchases of law-enforcement agencies. First among the law-enforcement agencies purchasing gas was the Ohio National Guard, which had bought slightly over $20,000 worth, or almost one-fourth as much as the Republic Steel Corporation. In addition to this gas, the Republic Steel Corporation owned 552 revolvers, 64 rifles, and 245 shotguns, with over 83,000 rounds of ball and shot ammunition.

Except to Walk Free

These industrial arsenals far overshadowed the arms and gas equipment in the hands of local law-enforcement authorities in the communities in which they had plants. The Republic Steel Corporation, with 53,000 employees, purchased more than 10 times as many gas guns and more than 26 times as many gas shells and gas projectiles than the police force of Chicago, with a population of almost 4,000,000 souls. Taking the arsenals of these two companies together, there were over 1,800 firearms, over 300 gas guns, over 160,000 rounds of ammunition, and over 10,000 rounds of gas ammunition. This would be adequate equipment for a small war. . . .

11. A. PHILIP RANDOLPH'S CALL FOR A MARCH*

1941

A. Philip Randolph was the outstanding spokesman for black trade unionists in recent times. He was president of the sleeping-car porters' union of the A.F. of L. and for many years the leading black socialist in the country. By 1941 it had become clear to him that despite their protestations of racial equality organized labor and the New Deal could not be counted on to do very much for black workers—that black workers would have to help themselves. And so in early 1941, as the country girded for a war that was bound to come, Randolph began to organize a march of black people on Washington, this being the only way, he believed, that the Roosevelt administration could be induced to provide minimal rights to black workers. The threat of such a march had its effect. Roosevelt gave in and, in June 1941, signed an executive order establishing a Fair Employment Practices Committee to guarantee equal job opportunities to black workers. Randolph called off the march.

We call upon you to fight for jobs in National Defense.
We call upon you to struggle for the integration of Negroes in the armed forces, such as the Air Corps, Navy, Army and Marine Corps of the Nation.

* *The Black Worker*, May 1941.

Except to Walk Free

We call upon you to demonstrate for the abolition of Jim-Crowism in all Government departments and defense employment.

This is an hour of crisis. It is a crisis of democracy. It is a crisis of minority groups. It is a crisis of Negro Americans.

What is this crisis?

To American Negroes, it is the denial of jobs in Government defense projects. It is racial discrimination in Government departments. It is widespread Jim-Crowism in the armed forces of the Nation.

While billions of the taxpayers' money are being spent for war weapons, Negro workers are being turned away from the gates of factories, mines and mills—being flatly told, "NOTHING DOING." Some employers refuse to give Negroes jobs when they are without "union cards," and some unions refuse Negro workers union cards when they are "without jobs."

What shall we do?

What a dilemma!

What a runaround!

What a disgrace!

What a blow below the belt!

'Though dark, doubtful and discouraging, all is not lost, all is not hopeless. 'Though battered and bruised, we are not beaten, broken or bewildered.

Verily, the Negroes' deepest disappointments and direst defeats, their tragic trials and outrageous oppressions in these dreadful days of destruction and disaster to democracy and freedom, and the rights of minority peoples, and the dignity and independence of the human spirit, is the Negroes' greatest opportunity to rise to the highest heights of struggle for freedom and justice in Government, in

The C.I.O.

industry, in labor unions, education, social service, religion and culture.

With faith and confidence of the Negro people in their own power for self-liberation, Negroes can break down the barriers of discrimination against employment in National Defense. Negroes can kill the deadly serpent of race hatred in the Army, Navy, Air and Marine Corps, and smash through and blast the Government, business and labor-union red tape to win the right to equal opportunity in vocational training and re-training in defense employment.

Most important and vital to all, Negroes, by the mobilization and coordination of their mass power, can cause PRESIDENT ROOSEVELT TO ISSUE AN EXECUTIVE ORDER ABOLISHING DISCRIMINATIONS IN ALL GOVERNMENT DEPARTMENTS, ARMY, NAVY, AIR CORPS AND NATIONAL DEFENSE JOBS.

Of course, the task is not easy. In very truth, it is big, tremendous and difficult.

It will cost money.

It will require sacrifice.

It will tax the Negroes' courage, determination and will to struggle. But we can, must and will triumph.

The Negroes' stake in national defense is big. It consists of jobs, thousands of jobs. It may represent millions, yes, hundreds of millions of dollars in wages. It consists of new industrial opportunities and hope. This is worth fighting for.

But to win our stakes, it will require an "all-out," bold and total effort and demonstration of colossal proportions.

Negroes can build a mammoth machine of mass action with a terrific and tremendous driving and striking power that can shatter and crush the evil fortress of race prejudice and hate, if they will only resolve to do so and never stop, until victory comes.

Except to Walk Free

Dear fellow Negro Americans, be not dismayed in these terrible times. You possess power, great power. Our problem is to harness and hitch it up for action on the broadest, daring and most gigantic scale.

In this period of power politics, nothing counts but pressure, more pressure, and still more pressure, through the tactic and strategy of broad, organized, aggressive mass action behind the vital and important issues of the Negro. To this end, we propose that ten thousand Negroes MARCH ON WASHINGTON FOR JOBS IN NATIONAL DEFENSE AND EQUAL INTEGRATION IN THE FIGHTING FORCES OF THE UNITED STATES.

An "all-out" thundering march on Washington, ending in a monstrous and huge demonstration at Lincoln's Monument will shake up white America.

It will shake up official Washington.

It will give encouragement to our white friends to fight all the harder by our side, with us, for our righteous cause.

It will gain respect for the Negro people.

It will create a new sense of self-respect among Negroes.

But what of national unity?

We believe in national unity which recognizes equal opportunity of black and white citizens to jobs in national defense and the armed forces, and in all other institutions and endeavors in America. We condemn all dictatorships, Fascist, Nazi and Communist. We are loyal, patriotic Americans, all.

But, if American democracy will not defend its defenders; if American democracy will not protect its protectors; if American democracy will not give jobs to its toilers because of race or color; if American democracy will not insure equality of opportunity, freedom and justice to its citizens, black and white, it is a hollow mockery and belies the principles for which it is supposed to stand.

The C.I.O.

To the hard, difficult and trying problem of securing equal participation in national defense, we summon all Negro Americans to march on Washington. We summon Negro Americans to form committees in various cities to recruit and register marchers and raise funds through the sale of buttons and other legitimate means for the expenses of marchers to Washington by buses, train, private automobiles, trucks, and on foot.

We summon Negro Americans to stage marches on their City Halls and Councils in their respective cities and urge them to memorialize the President to issue an executive order to abolish discrimination in the Government and national defense.

However, we sternly counsel against violence and ill-considered and intemperate action and the abuse of power. Mass power, like physical power, when misdirected is more harmful than helpful.

We summon you to mass action that is orderly and lawful, but aggressive and militant, for justice, equality and freedom.

Crispus Attucks marched and died as a martyr for American independence. Nat Turner, Denmark Vesey, Gabriel Prosser, Harriet Tubman and Frederick Douglass fought, bled and died for the emancipation of Negro slaves and the preservation of American democracy.

Abraham Lincoln, in times of the grave emergency of the Civil War, issued the Proclamation of Emancipation for the freedom of Negro slaves and the preservation of American democracy.

Today, we call upon President Roosevelt, a great humanitarian and idealist, to follow in the footsteps of his noble and illustrious predecessor and take the second decisive step in this world and national emergency and free American Negro citizens of the stigma, humiliation and

Except to Walk Free

insult of discrimination and Jim-Crowism in Government departments and national defense.

The Federal Government cannot with clear conscience call upon private industry and labor unions to abolish discrimination based upon race and color as long as it practices discrimination itself against Negro Americans.

V

The New World of Labor 1947–74

The Second World War consolidated and enlarged the spectacular gains made by labor in the 1930s. And when the war ended, in 1945, the union movement was at the summit of its power, its nearly 14 million members—7½ million in the A.F. of L., 4½ million in the C.I.O.,[1] the rest independent (mainly railroad brotherhoods and civil service employees)—constituting a fifth of the total work force and enjoying a legitimacy and prestige it had never before had.

But matters changed very quickly. A spurt of postwar unemployment, coupled with high prices, led to an explosion of strikes in 1946, notably in autos, railroads, and coal. President Harry S Truman, who was just beginning to settle in as Roosevelt's successor, responded harshly, aggressively, using his war powers to seize the mines and threaten to draft the railroad workers (a million strong) into the Army. The unions had sound reason to believe

---

[1] The A.F. of L. expanded greatly during the war years, the building trades in particular. Also, many companies preferred to sign up with the A.F. of L. rather than the more militant C.I.O. It may be interesting to point out that the various A.F. of L. unions were no longer so fastidious about craft jurisdictions—about which workers belonged where. With the C.I.O. looking over their shoulders, they were happy to enroll anyone who came along.

263

Except to Walk Free

that the new President was their enemy. Suddenly, they found themselves facing an uncertain future.

The portents darkened further with the election of the 80th Congress, in 1946. It was the first Republican-dominated Congress since 1928, and it was manifestly conservative, consisting as it did of young ideologues determined to punish the beneficiaries of the New Deal, chief among them labor. In June 1947 the 80th Congress passed the Taft-Hartley Act over Truman's veto. The Act imposed a number of conditions highly unpalatable to organized labor: It required workers in vital industries to "cool off" for sixty days before they could strike; it denied the closed shop, even if employees approved it; it allowed companies to sue unions for breach of contract and other damages; and it demanded that union officials take a non-Communist oath. The unions' worst fears, it seemed, were being realized.

As it turned out, the Taft-Hartley Act proved to be only a minor irritant to them. But this was something they could not have known at the time. Their leaders saw it as an attempt, the start of a sustained effort, to undo the accomplishments of the past decade and restore for big business the open shop of bygone days.

The unions welcomed help wherever they could find it, even from erstwhile antagonists. It was President Truman, in fact, who became their sturdiest pillar of support. He won over the unions completely by his veto of the Taft-Hartley bill and the extraordinary solicitude he showed them in his 1948 presidential campaign. They reciprocated by producing a heavy turnout for him, thereby making possible his astonishing upset victory.

As far as labor in general was concerned, the lines were now clearly drawn between the Democrats and the Repub-

The New World of Labor

licans; the former opposed, the latter favored, the Taft-Hartley Act.

For the A.F. of L., supporting the Democrats implied a slight change of tactics, a slight shift in its allegiances. In the past the A.F. of L. had been neutral or even pro-Republican, and indeed many of its larger unions (carpenters, teamsters, several of the building trades, etc.) were still pro-Republican, the Taft-Hartley law being in no way inimical to them. For the C.I.O., however, supporting the Truman administration involved much more than a political tactic. It was fraught with deep ideological significance, and it permanently affected the life of the organization.

The C.I.O. had always been identified with the Democratic Party—the Democratic Party, that is, of the Roosevelt era, the Democratic Party that had governed the country during the war against fascism. Since its founding in 1935 the C.I.O. had been a united front of Communists, Trotskyists, Democratic Socialists, and militant New Dealers who had subordinated their differences to the task of organizing the unorganized and winning the war. But conditions had changed radically since then. The Soviet Union was now the perceived threat, and the Truman administration was mobilizing public opinion for the long, gloomy Cold War ahead. The Communist-led unions of the C.I.O.—the electrical workers, West Coast longshoremen, fur and leather workers, metal miners, among others—condemned the Administration as the architect of American imperialism, the savior of world capitalism. The rest of the C.I.O., fearful of alienating the government and public opinion, decided to remove the stigma of its origins and demonstrate its patriotism (at a time when it was fashionable to call people's patriotism into question) by expelling the unrepentant Communist unions, by purg-

Except to Walk Free

ing itself clean. The expulsion, carried out in 1948-49 (the height of the Cold War), was purely ideological. No charge of misconduct was made against the offending unions, for they had not violated the rules. To do the deed "legally" the C.I.O. wrote a retroactive loyalty oath into its constitution.[2]

The prime movers in bringing about this moral catharsis, it should be noted, were the most zealous of the liberals, such as Walter Reuther, head of the United Auto Workers. Liberals above all were concerned to distinguish their brand of left politics from the Communist. It was their way of answering the standard conservative accusation that communism differed from liberalism or democratic socialism only in degree, one leading inexorably to the other; that liberals were "soft on communism." The C.I.O., like many another liberal organization that purged itself of real or suspected Communists (e.g., the American Civil Liberties Union, the National Association for the Advancement of Colored People) desperately wanted to prove it was as respectable, as irreproachable, as any 100 per cent American institution, that it too could be counted on to lend zealous support to the struggle against world communism.

The A.F. of L. and the C.I.O. were definitely drawing closer together. Their ancient antagonisms were abating.

---

[2] This is not to exonerate the Communists or depict them as hapless victims. For their part, they were willing to bend trade unions—the whole C.I.O. if possible—to their political ends, however the Soviet Union defined them. Until 1946 they more or less adhered to the popular front; no one supported the war effort more enthusiastically, even to the extent of ruthlessly opposing any wage increases. After 1946 a new line came down: Communists were to resume the class struggle, particularly against the Truman administration, with all the power at their command. This meant working for Truman's defeat in 1948, no matter how adverse the consequences might be for organized labor.

The New World of Labor

Each was assuming more of the qualities and colorations of the other. Even the old jurisdictional conflicts were losing their bite. The larger A.F. of L. unions, once apostles of the craft principle, were tending toward greater centralization along industrial lines. Meanwhile, the C.I.O. unions were acknowledging the special claims, in effect the craft status, of their skilled workers. There was no logical reason, and less and less was there an ideological one, for the two labor giants to remain at odds with each other—indeed, to remain apart from each other.

At last, in 1955, they were reunited under the less than inspired name of the A.F.L.-C.I.O. (American Federation of Labor-Congress of Industrial Organizations) and under a constitution that recognized the full equality and autonomy of each of its affiliated unions. This was a major concession by the A.F. of L., the "mother" organization, which had only reluctantly welcomed back her prodigal children. The C.I.O.'s concession was to accept George Meany as president (Reuther becoming vice-president),[3] even though Meany had throughout his long career (which began in a Bronx plumbers' local and prospered in the New York building trades) exemplified the business-union tradition and general conservatism of Gompers and Green. But Meany was a shrewd and supple man and a masterful bureaucratic infighter, as he was to prove abundantly in the years ahead, and as his rival—the younger, charismatic Walter Reuther—was to learn to his cost.

No sooner had the A.F.L.-C.I.O. come into being than it confronted a crisis arising from charges of racketeering and criminality in several of its unions. There was evidence of pervasive corruption, above all in the Teamsters

[3] The heads of the A.F. of L. and C.I.O., William Green and Philip Murray respectively, had both died in 1952. Meany and Reuther had taken their place.

Except to Walk Free

Union, the largest and probably most important union in the country. The Teamsters president was himself sent to jail for embezzlement. And the man who took his place was the notorious James Hoffa, reputed to have extensive ties with the underworld. How extensive, how much control gangsters exercised, was brought out in widely publicized Senate committee hearings in 1957–59. The recitation of sordid facts from scores of witnesses, among them Hoffa (who never concealed his contempt for the whole proceeding), frightened the public and gave the enemies of trade unionism a new weapon of assault. Yesterday it was communism; now it was gangsterism.

To fend off its critics the A.F.L.-C.I.O., in December 1957, expelled the Teamsters (a million and a half strong and organized from coast to coast) along with two smaller racketeer unions, the Laundry Workers and the Bakery Workers. Expulsion may have satisfied the A.F.L.-C.I.O. that it was improving its image, appeasing a wrathful citizenry; it certainly had no effect on the Teamsters, which never stopped growing. Hoffa, if anything, was more a hero to his rank and file than ever before.[4] And neither were they daunted by the passage, in 1959, of the Landrum-Griffin, or Labor Management Reporting and Disclosure Act, which empowered the government, among other things, to remove from office union leaders who were demonstrably corrupt or elected unfairly, protect dissident members, and prevent blackmail by unions of one another or employers. But the law has been extremely difficult to enforce, even in those very rare instances when the gov-

[4] The Senate hearings did lay the groundwork for Hoffa's fall years later. He managed to alienate two men serving on the committee: Senator John F. Kennedy and the senator's brother and chief counsel for the committee, Robert F. Kennedy. In 1961 John Kennedy became President and Robert Attorney-General. Three years later Hoffa went to jail.

The New World of Labor

ernment has had the will to do so.[5] Racketeer unions so far have had little to fear from the law.

The Eisenhower years (1953–61) marked an interregnum in the history of American labor. It was a period of retrenchment and comparative quietude. With the Korean War ended, relations with the Soviet Union began to improve, and defense outlays were cut back. The country accordingly experienced a series of recessions, each more serious than the preceding one, during which time the rate of unemployment continued to rise, reaching a high of 7½ per cent in 1958—the highest since the Great Depression. As a result, organized labor slowly lost ground, its membership rolls contracting to pre-World War II levels.

The inevitable further result was that the unions drew closer to the Democratic Party than ever before. The A.F.L.-C.I.O. became the party's most assiduous vote getter, its most reliable fund raiser, the centerpiece of its broad coalition of interest groups. And so, in the 1960s, when the Democrats held national power again, it was only natural that the union movement—George Meany in particular—should enjoy a privileged status in the councils of government. Not even in the palmy days of Franklin D. Roosevelt were the unions so cosseted and championed as they were in the administrations of John F. Kennedy and Lyndon B. Johnson. Politically, organized labor had come into its own.

Economically, too. The unions benefited egregiously from the prosperity of the 1960s. Kennedy and Johnson

---

[5] The government intervened in the rigged United Mine Workers election of 1969 only because the leader of the insurgent faction (along with his wife and daughter) were brutally slain. Public indignation forced the Labor Department to oversee the re-election, which the insurgents won handily. It was later established that the old-guard leadership, including Tony Boyle, the Union's ex-president (and John L. Lewis's chosen successor), had ordered the murders.

Except to Walk Free

launched a policy of vast government spending in research and development, aerospace industries, missile and other defense technologies. The military-industrial complex, proliferating beyond all limits, caught organized labor in its iron embrace. Millions of workers, many of them well paid, depended on such expenditures for their livelihood. This may explain why the A.F.L.-C.I.O. displayed so much enthusiasm in behalf of the military-industrial complex, why it persistently called for extravagant subsidies of failing defense companies (e.g., Lockheed) and such ventures as the supersonic transport, and why it loudly applauded the government's ten-year war on the Indochinese people.[6]

Organized labor, at any rate, resumed its expansion during the 1960s. At this writing (1974) it accounts for about 21 million people, a quarter of the labor force. That may not seem like extraordinary progress, the proportion being slightly more than it was in 1945. Yet in absolute numbers—considering the fact that there were 50 million in the labor market then, compared to 85 million today—the progress has been considerable. Especially so since the ratio of blue-collar to white-collar workers was 60:40 then, 35:65 now. Unions, in other words, have lately grown most in the white-collar and service sectors of the economy (teachers, medical personnel, civil servants, et al.), and it is these sectors which supply the potential for future growth—for the future, perhaps, of the labor movement as such.

The expansion and success of the unions in the past

---

[6] There has been, in addition, George Meany's pathological hatred of communism. But even if a more moderate man had been president of the A.F.L.-C.I.O. its policy would have been scarcely different. Very few of its member unions, after all, disagreed with Meany. And when they did it was because Richard Nixon was President and the Indochina war was a Republican war. Meany, of course, backed Nixon to the hilt on the war.

The New World of Labor

decade has defined their character and their place in society. It is safe to say that they have established themselves as an integral part of the industrial system (and increasingly of the "postindustrial" as well). They have brought peace and order. Management depends on them to undertake many of the responsibilities it once held: the recruitment and discipline of workers, the fulfillment of contracts, etc. Management has learned that unions serve a valuable purpose, providing an intermediate, or buffer zone between management and the workers. Strikes occur infrequently, and when they do occur they cause little or no violence and few catastrophic consequences (loss of jobs, destruction of the union, etc.). The 1877 uprising, the Molly Maguires, Homestead, Pullman, Coeur d'Alene and Leadville, Lawrence and Paterson, the Ludlow Massacre, the 1919 steel strike, the Toledo and Minneapolis and San Francisco strikes, the Akron and Flint sit-downs, the Memorial Day Massacre—these belong to the legendary past, the *ur*-history of the labor movement. Collective bargaining has replaced class conflict. The standard of living of unionized workers has, all in all, kept pace with the extraordinary rise in national wealth.[7]

Not that all unions have shared equally in the bounty. A rough equation can be made: The stronger the union and the more prosperous the industry the greater is the share of wealth its workers receive relative to other workers in other industries. One need only contrast the income levels and status of, say, the skilled members of the building trades (powerful unions, affluent industry) to hospital and drug workers (a weak union, a marginal industry). The other unions can be located somewhere between these extremes.

[7] That is, until 1973, when the cost of living began to soar, leaving such wage increases as workers could secure trailing behind.

Except to Walk Free

There is another element in the equation: The greater the share of wealth that the union appropriates—that is, the higher it stands in the working-class hierarchy—the more conservative it tends to be. It is hardly an accident that the building trades and the teamsters have carried on unimpaired the elitist tradition of the old A.F. of L. If they acknowledge any solidarity with the rest of labor it has nowhere been evident. At the same time, some of the ex-C.I.O. unions have retained a semblance of the old-style liberalism, if not militancy. They have resisted the inclination to degenerate into pure and simple business entities. The most notable example of this kind of C.I.O. consciousness has been the United Auto Workers, whose leaders have scrupulously tried to uphold the social-democratic ideal set by the late Walter Reuther.

One last element in the equation: The greater the gains organized labor as a whole has made, the greater its distance from the unorganized mass of people below it. That mass, totaling about a fourth of the country's population, includes the millions who labor at unskilled, dead-end jobs (farm labor, housecleaning, laundry work, etc.) and barely eke out a living; as well as those who for one reason or another—age, disability, chronic illness, the need to care for children—subsist at or below the "poverty line" ($4,500 a year for a family of four, itself a grotesquely low figure, even for one extremely parsimonious, or, rather, ascetic, adult). In an economy whose cost of living keeps rising, this mass of Americans keeps falling farther and farther behind. They simply have no way of defending themselves, because they have no power; that is, no organization. Their only help has come from a liberal, welfare-oriented federal government. When such a government is absent—as it has been since 1969—their fate

The New World of Labor

is to suffer anonymously, for they have no voice, their existence being their sole reproach.

The relatively privileged condition of organized labor (keeping in mind the qualifications) has been reflected in the policies and conduct of its spokesmen. They have appeared to embrace the status quo with the zeal customarily displayed by Rotarians or the Chamber of Commerce. During the 1960s and during much of President Nixon's first administration they seemed to make it their peculiar mission to oppose the forces of reform and insurgency in America. No man, no retired admiral, no politician on the far right, outdid George Meany in upholding the government's Indochina policy, in urging an even more aggressive anti-Communist stance, and, of course, in condemning the burgeoning student protests.[8]

Also, organized labor as a whole played at most a passive role throughout the civil-rights movement of the 1960s. And as the demand for civil rights has cut closer to the bone—as blacks and other minorities began insisting on access to jobs hitherto denied them, especially in construction and the more highly skilled industrial trades, and to positions of seniority and leadership—so the unions have thrown up terrific resistance, employing all their enormous power and influence at every level of government to balk the express intention of the law. Some unions here and there, a few at best, have removed racial restrictions, but only after the courts have forced them to do so.

Then there is the matter of corruption and racketeer-

---

[8] When the New York hardhats savagely beat up the anti-war demonstrators in 1970 they expressed the sentiments of the A.F.L.-C.I.O. leadership. President Nixon was visibly moved by this show of confidence in him, and he later rewarded the labor official who helped organize the riot—Peter Brennan by name—by appointing him Secretary of Labor.

ing. Gangsterism in the Teamsters union persists as tenaciously as ever, and it continues to dominate numerous smaller ones. Corruption is inseparable from the larger, more inclusive issue of union democracy. And on this issue little progress has been made since the earliest days of the A.F. of L. Now, as then, unpopular leaders rarely get defeated in elections (whatever the union constitution may specify); they must be overthrown. Rebellions, however, are, in the nature of things, exceedingly rare, no matter how discontented the rank and file may be. The fact is, union leaders usually govern their appanages until death, and sometimes (through their heirs and assigns) long after. The A.F.L.-C.I.O. Executive Council resembles nothing so much as the College of Cardinals (the upper sixties being the average age of its members), providing the most striking confirmation of the iron law of oligarchy.

No wonder the unions have alienated intellectuals and radicals, their historic allies and helpmeets. Much of the left dismisses unions as collaborators of the capitalist power elites, as latter-day "labor-fakirs." And they dismiss the rank and file as well for allowing themselves to be co-opted and seduced, for yielding up their freedom, their class solidarity, their commitment to egalitarian ideals, for a mess of pottage. Never in modern times have radicals and the labor movement been so far apart—indeed, so rancorously at odds—as at present.

But there is more to it than meets the eye. The New Left's criticisms of unions and workers may be too sweeping and indiscriminate. It also ends up in a cul de sac. If organized labor stands condemned—what then? Where else is the fulcrum of radical reform?

Organized labor, it should be emphasized, is no monolith. It is polycentrist. Despite his pretensions, George

Meany does not speak for all unions, perhaps not even a majority of them. After all, in the 1972 presidential election, when he was professing neutrality (in effect, favoring Nixon), about a third of the A.F.L.-C.I.O. unions were siding with George McGovern. There are unions, led by the U.A.W., that hark back to an earlier epoch: in their liberal politics, their sense of social responsibility, their maintenance of reasonably open and democratic procedures. They embody a hope that may ripen and fructify.

It is a mistake, moreover, to freely generalize about workers one way or the other, either to romanticize them as proletarian heroes or to denigrate them as gulls and yahoos. Workers, even the most privileged among them, have much to be discontented about (none can ever rise beyond modest middle-class income level). If, in the recent past they have directed their animus at blacks and the poor and the students, in the future they may direct it at others. More and more workers, in fact, are young, alienated, and rebellious themselves; more and more of them have come to assume an avant-garde life-style, and are receptive to new ideas.

Blacks and other minorities can also be expected to help regenerate organized labor. The number of blacks belonging to unions has been growing inexorably—it now exceeds two million. And they now constitute a force capable of claiming the rights to which they are entitled; nothing can stop them. Nor should we omit the new hope of unionism, the members of the service and professional trades who are, by and large, better educated and more socially conscious than other workers.

All in all, American workers contain possibilities undreamed by their detractors and their leaders alike. Who can tell? They may yet redeem the nobler inheritance of their past.

1. THE TAFT-HARTLEY ACT*

1947

> The fact that President Truman's veto of the Taft-Hartley bill was overridden by such a large margin (68 to 25 in the Senate, 331 to 83 in the House) indicated how strongly the public felt, how considerable was the backlash against organized labor following the New Deal and the war.

Sec. 101 . . . "Sec. 8 (b) . . . That where there is in effect a collective bargaining contract covering employees in an industry affecting commerce, the duty to bargain collectively shall also mean that no party to such contract shall terminate or modify such contract, unless the party desiring termination or modification—

"(1) serves a written notice upon the other party to the contract of the proposed termination or modification sixty days prior to the expiration date thereof, or in the event such contract contains no expiration date, sixty days prior to the time it is proposed to make such termination or modification;

"(2) offers to meet and confer with the other party for the purpose of negotiating a new contract or a contract containing the proposed modification; . . .

"(4) continues in full force and effect, without resorting to strike or lock-out, all the terms and conditions of the existing contract for a period of sixty days after such notice is given or until the expiration date of such contract, whichever occurs later: . . .

* Public Law 101, 80th Congress.

"(h) No investigation shall be made by the Board of any question affecting commerce concerning the representation of employees, raised by a labor organization under subsection (c) of this section, no petition under section 9 (e) (1) shall be entertained, and no complaint shall be issued pursuant to a charge made by a labor organization under subsection (b) of section 10, unless there is on file with the Board an affidavit executed contemporaneously or within the preceding twelve month period by each officer of such labor organization and the officers of any national or international labor organization of which it is an affiliate or constituent unit that he is not a member of the Communist Party or affiliated with such party, and that he does not believe in, and is not a member of or supports any organization that believes in or teaches, the overthrow of the United States Government by force or by any illegal or unconstitutional methods. The provisions of section 35 A of the Criminal Code shall be applicable in respect to such affidavits. . . ."

Sec. 304. Section 313 of the Federal Corrupt Practices Act, 1925 . . . is amended to read as follows:

"Sec. 313. It is unlawful for . . . any labor organization to make a contribution or expenditure in connection with any election at which Presidential and Vice Presidential electors or a Senator or Representative in, or a Delegate or Resident Commissioner to Congress are to be voted for, or in connection with any primary election or political convention or caucus held to select candidates for any of the foregoing offices, or for any candidate, political committee, or other person to accept or receive any contribution prohibited by this section. . . ."

Sec. 305. It shall be unlawful for any individual employed by the United States or any agency thereof in-

Except to Walk Free

cluding wholly owned Government corporations to participate in any strike. Any individual employed by the United States or by any such agency who strikes shall be discharged immediately from his employment, and shall forfeit his civil service status, if any, and shall not be eligible for reemployment for three years by the United States or any such agency. . . .

2. EXPULSION OF THE COMMUNISTS*

1949

The debate in the 1949 C.I.O. convention (which met in Cleveland) revealed just how angry the non-Communist union leaders were at their Communist brethren, how thoroughly their rhetoric reflected the conflicts of the Cold War taking place outside. Two of the men who argued most vehemently for expulsion—Michael Quill and Joseph Curran (their remarks excerpted below)—had been themselves, until recently, part of the Communist faction. Worth noting, too, is the fact that no non-Communist came forward to oppose the removal of the Communist-led unions.

. . . The Committee recommends that the Constitution of the C.I.O. adopted in Portland, Oregon, on November 25, 1948, be re-adopted by this Convention as of this date, November 1, 1949, with the following changes:
(A) PAGE 10: Article IV concerning Officers and Executive Board is amended by the insertion of a new Section 4 which reads as follows: "Section 4. No individual shall be eligible to serve either as an officer or as a member of the Executive Board who is a member of the Communist Party, any fascist organization, or other totalitarian movement, or who consistently pursues policies and activities directed

* *Congress of Industrial Organizations, Proceedings, Eleventh Constitutional Convention* (Cleveland, 1949), pp. 240, 262–63, 267, 273, 304–6, 325.

Except to Walk Free

toward the achievement of the program or the purposes of the Communist Party, any fascist organization, or other totalitarian movement, rather than the objectives and policies set forth in the constitution of the C.I.O." . . .

*Joseph Selly, President
of the American Communications Association*

Several speakers have referred to the fact that this proposed amendment to the constitution represents a fundamental and basic change in the character of this labor organization, of this Federation. I don't think that point can receive too much emphasis. It is my humble opinion that the adoption of this resolution so completely reverses the fundamental policies of C.I.O. on which it was founded as to make the organization unrecognizable, as to give it a character not only different but the opposite of the character it formerly enjoyed.

And what was the fundamental characteristic of C.I.O. which endeared it to millions of workers throughout this country, which made it possible to conduct effectively an organizing job among all the groups in this country, which made it the hope and made it express the aspirations of the Negro group and other minority groups, the people of my own faith, the Jewish faith, and all other peoples? That characteristic was that C.I.O., unlike the organizations that preceded it, was founded on the principle of the democratic rights of the rank and file of the organizations affiliated to it.

We have spoken much at one convention after another on civil rights resolutions and other resolutions about our devotion to the fundamental American principle of freedom of thought and expression. Let me remind you gentlemen that is pure demogogy unless we agree such freedom of thought and expression, freedom of opinion and differences must be granted to the minority group; and I will go further and say unless we learn the lesson that there must be tolerance not merely of a minority but a minority of unpopular opinions, unless that remains the policy of C.I.O. we will have surrendered one of the most cherished heritages of the American people.

A long time ago the revolutionists set this yardstick to judge the kind of nation we should have today,—and I am referring to Washington and Jefferson and William Lloyd Garrison and Wendell Phillips—those gentlemen, risking their lives for this principle, were subjected to abuse. Garrison was rode through the streets of Boston because he dared to say the Negroes should be free and were equal to the white man. He dared to say that in an atmosphere where it was an unpopular opinion; but the people fortunately ultimately acknowledged the principles of Jefferson and Garrison and Phillips and history affirmed what they stated in the beginning. . . .

All of us, of course, get up and say we are in favor of the enforcement of the Constitution of the United States and of the Bill of Rights. All of us have engaged in many struggles in order to make this a reality, and I urge upon those who support this resolution that they consider carefully what they are doing, because they are here now proposing an amendment to the C.I.O. constitution which they are at the same time arguing is in violation of the Constitution of the United States of America and of the Bill of Rights. We are considering here the enactment of a loyalty oath, a purgatory oath. . . .

Walter Reuther, President of the United Auto Workers

Every time you get into this basic question as to whether or not free people, through their democratic organizations, have a right to protect themselves and their freedoms, these people raise pious, hypocritical slogans, they talk about unity, they talk about autonomy, they talk about the democratic rights of the minority, they raise the civil rights issue, and they do everything they can to becloud the real issues involved in this debate.

Let's brush aside all of this ideological rubbish and get right down to the hard core of the facts in this situation. A trade union is a voluntary association of free men held together by common loyalties, common objectives, common hopes, common aspirations and common ideals. How does a voluntary association of free men function? It draws its strength from the basic loyalty of the people who make up its membership, and its strength grows out of the fact that because of that basic loyalty they also have the kind of discipline that free men must exercise on a voluntary basis if they are going to exist and work together as free men.

But what happens is this: the minority want all of the rights, they want all of the protection, they want all of the benefits that flow from being a part of this voluntary association, but they want none of the obligations and they refuse to accept any of the responsibilities. You cannot have a democratic right within a free, voluntary association unless you are also prepared to accept the democratic obligations and responsibilities which parallel those democratic rights.

The Communist minority in our organization, like the disciplined Communist majority throughout the world, want the rights and privileges without the obligations and responsibilities, and we are saying here and now that those people who claim the rights and privileges must also be prepared to accept the responsibilities and the obligations.

There is room in our movement for an honest difference of opinion. Sincere opposition is a healthy thing in the labor movement. But there is a fundamental difference between honest opposition and sincere difference of opinion and the kind of obstructionism and sabotage carried on by the Communist minority, because the Communist minority is a trade union opposition group who disagree with C.I.O. policies, because they believe that there are other policies that ought to take the place of our current policies. They are not a trade union group. In one sense they are to be pitied more than despised, because they are not free men, they are not free agents working in this movement. Their very souls do not belong to them. They are colonial agents using the trade union movement as a basis of operation in order to carry out the needs of the Soviet Foreign Office. And when you try to understand the basic characteristics of the Communist minority opposition group you have got to begin to differentiate between the kind of a minority opposition group of that kind and a minority opposition group that has a basic, honest trade union opposition in their differences with the official policies of their organization. . . .

Michael Quill, President of the Transport Workers' Union

When Harry Bridges says Communism is not the issue here,—Harry, you are lying like hell and you know you are. And you are not leaving C.I.O. because you could not keep your membership for one month after leaving C.I.O. You see, it was a nice, soft business up until now. As long as they could stay in C.I.O. and peddle the Party medicine, as Walter Reuther said, with the label of C.I.O., it was easy, but when they are forced out and have to take off their outer coat and really show their red underwear, then they will not be able to hold their membership. And that is why they are split. . . .

Joseph Curran, President of the National Maritime Union, chairman of the Resolutions Committee

NOW THEREFORE BE IT RESOLVED THAT:

1. This Convention finds that the Certificate of Affiliation heretofore granted to the United Electrical, Radio and Machine Workers of America has fallen into the control of a group devoted primarily to the principles of the Communist Party and opposed to the constitution and democratic objectives of the C.I.O., and in particular to the following declaration in the Preamble of the Constitution of the C.I.O.:

> "In the achievement of this task we turn to the people because we have faith in them and we oppose all those who would violate this American emphasis of respect for human dignity, all those who would use power to exploit the people in the interest of alien loyalties."

and in conformance with the provisions of Article III, Section 6 of our Constitution, this convention hereby expels the United Electrical, Radio and Machine Workers of America from the Congress of Industrial Organizations and withdraws the said Certificate of Affiliation.

2. This Convention recognizes that overwhelming majority of the membership of the United Electrical, Radio and Machine Workers of America are not members of the Communist Party, and further recognizes the desire of the working men and women in the electrical and allied industries for a free and autonomous union affiliated with the C.I.O. and devoted to the constitutional principles and policies of the C.I.O.

3. This Convention hereby authorizes and directs the Executive Board immediately to issue a Certificate of Affiliation to a suitable organization covering electrical and allied workers which will genuinely represent the desires and interests of the men and women in those industries.

Harry Bridges, President of the West Coast Longshoremen's Union

The resolution, I notice, deals with a series of charges. There are four pages of the resolution in hysterical language setting forth reasons why the Union is so-called Communist dominated, and that its officers are serving as agents of a foreign union. And yet when I look at the charges I don't find one single charge that says the Union has not done a job for its members and has not organized hundreds of thousands of workers in an important basic industry, that the Union has not struggled to advance hours, wages and conditions—not a single economic charge is levied against the Union.

I look and I see that the resolution states that the charges are that they are Communist controlled, conceived and dominated—No. 1, in that the Union opposed the Marshall Plan. No. 2, the Union is against the Armament Pact, and so on down the line, the Atlantic Pact, etc. It goes on to say that the Union has disagreed with the C.I.O. in matters of critical affairs, that the Union disagreed with the C.I.O. in their action to repeal the Taft-Hartley law, that the Union accepted into its ranks the Farm Equipment Workers.

I have here the minutes of the ILWU convention last April and a copy of a telegram sent by the C.I.O. It says here that any action taken with respect to the merger of the Farm Equipment Workers with another Union shall

Except to Walk Free

be by the voluntary action of its membership, and if the membership of the Farm Equipment Workers want to join the UE, I would think that it's their business. However, the resolution speaks for itself in that respect. There is not one single charge that this Union has not organized, has not improved wages and obtained seniority, union security, welfare plans, and other things.

So now we have reached the point where a trade union, because it disagrees on political matters with the National C.I.O. can be expelled. And yet we say we are not a political organization. Who is guilty of not following basic trade union policies and principles? In the Union that I represent, wages, hours, conditions, and the economic program come first. It has no loyalty to any political programs or any political party or any government except the American government. Neither does its membership nor its officers take second place to any union in their Americanism and their patriotism.

Philip Murray, President of the C.I.O.

Some delegates say that they have a right to fight the Marshall Plan. I do not deny anybody the right to fight the Marshall Plan, but I do deny the right of an International Union to use the Marshall Plan for purposes of subverting and destroying and undermining the trade union movement in the United States of America. These so-called apostles of democracy who fight the Marshall Plan and other plans designed by our government and our Congress and our people—and by the way, it is the best government in the whole world, the Government of the United States of America—these apostles of democracy assault the Marshall Plan. And why do they assault it? They assault it because the Marshall Plan inhibits the operation of Soviet expansionism. It places certain restric-

The New World of Labor

tions and barriers upon the spread of totalitarianism throughout the world, and these so-called Left Wingers fight the Marshall Plan because the Soviet government is against the Marshall Plan. They prefer to follow the philosophy of Communism and be the satellites of Communism and be the satellites of Sovietism rather than to be loyal to their own country. Those are facts. They have been demonstrated before our C.I.O. Executive Board repeatedly. What do they care about whether the Marshall Plan is used to feed the hungry, to clothe the naked, and to provide medicine for the sick? They manifest no interest in that, none whatever. They follow the Party Line and they follow it religiously on every issue.

I have asked these so-called apostles of democracy to stand somewhere, sometime upon the floor of a national convention of the C.I.O. and to criticize the Cominform, or criticize Russia's policy of expansionism, to criticize any of the policies of Russia, and these hypocrites run from me. They dare not stand upon their dirty feet and give any expression of opposition to anything that the Soviets are doing. They are inbred with a feeling of hatred against democratic institutions and democratic countries. They lend assistance to every satellite of Communist dictated Russia. They would spread their doctrine of fear and hatred among the people of the United States. If our country were engulfed in another war—and God forbid that it ever should be—they would go underground and undermine the people of the United States of America and this government of ours. . . .

3. A.F.L.-C.I.O. CONSTITUTION*

1955

It might prove instructive to compare this constitution with the original A.F. of L. constitution of 1886, which conveyed a sense of class conflict (see, especially, its preamble) altogether absent from this one.

Preamble

The establishment of this Federation through the merger of the American Federation of Labor and the Congress of Industrial Organizations is an expression of the hopes and aspirations of the working people of America.

We seek the fulfillment of these hopes and aspirations through democratic processes within the framework of our constitution and consistent with our institutions and traditions.

At the collective bargaining table, in the community, in the exercise of the rights and responsibilities of citizenship, we shall responsibly serve the interests of the American people.

We pledge ourselves to the more effective organization of working men and women; to the securing to them of full recognition and enjoyment of the rights to which they are justly entitled; to the achievement of ever higher standards of living and working conditions; to the attainment of security for all the people; to the enjoyment of the leisure which their skills make possible; and to the

* *Report of the First Constitutional Convention of the A.F.L.-C.I.O.*

strengthening and extension of our way of life and the fundamental freedoms which are the basis of our democratic society.

We shall combat resolutely the forces which seek to undermine the democratic institutions of our nation and to enslave the human soul. We shall strive always to win full respect for the dignity of the human individual whom our unions serve. . . .

Article II. Objects and Principles

The objects and principles of this Federation are:

1. To aid workers in securing improved wages, hours and working conditions with due regard for the autonomy, integrity and jurisdiction of affiliated unions.

2. To aid and assist affiliated unions in extending the benefits of mutual assistance and collective bargaining to workers and to promote the organization of the unorganized into unions of their own choosing for their mutual aid, protection and advancement, giving recognition to the principle that both craft and industrial unions are appropriate, equal and necessary as methods of union organization. . . .

4. To encourage all workers without regard to race, creed, color, national origin or ancestry to share equally in the full benefit of union organization.

5. To secure legislation which will safeguard and promote the principle of free collective bargaining, the rights of farmers and consumers, and the security and welfare of all the people and to oppose legislation inimical to these objectives. . . .

8. To preserve and maintain the integrity of each affiliated union in the organization to the end that each affiliate shall respect the established bargaining relationships of every other affiliate and that each affiliate shall

Except to Walk Free

refrain from raiding the established bargaining relationship of any other affiliate and, at the same time, to encourage the elimination of conflicting and duplicating organizations and jurisdictions through the process of voluntary agreement or merger in consultation with the appropriate officials of the Federation, to preserve, subject to the foregoing, the organizing jurisdiction of each affiliate. . . .

10. To protect the labor movement from any and all corrupt influences and from the undermining efforts of communist agencies and all others who are opposed to basic principles of our democracy and free and democratic unionism.

11. To safeguard the democratic character of the labor movement and to protect the autonomy of each affiliated national and international union.

12. While preserving the independence of the labor movement from political control, to encourage workers to register and vote, to exercise their full rights and responsibilities of citizenship, and to perform their rightful part in the political life of the local, state and national communities. . . .

4. UNION RACKETEERING: 1*

1957

The issue of criminality in organized labor raised a great fuss. But overlooked or neglected in the public's treatment of it was the complicity of management. Walter Reuther, speaking before the 1957 U.A.W. convention, had some sharp things to say about this.

During the last few weeks you and I and millions of decent, honest trade unionists all over America have been shocked and have been saddened by the headlines that we have been reading—headlines exposing corruption and racketeering in the leadership of certain unions.

I think that we can all agree that the overwhelming majority of the leadership of the American movement is composed of decent, honest, dedicated people who have made a great contribution involving great personal sacrifice, helping to build a decent American labor movement. But, unfortunately, in certain unions the gangsters and the crooks and the racketeers have moved into positions of power.

We happen to believe that leadership in the American labor movement is a sacred trust. We happen to believe that this is no place for people who want to use the labor movement to make a fast buck. We say to these people, "If you want to make a fast buck, that may be your business, but you better make it outside of the American labor

* *Report of Proceedings of the Sixteenth Constitutional Convention of the United Automobile, Aircraft and Agricultural Implement Workers of America* (Atlantic City, 1957), pp. 4–5.

movement, because we are not going to tolerate gangsters and racketeers inside the American labor movement." . . .

American labor had better roll up its sleeves, it had better get the stiffest broom and brush it can find, and the strongest soap and disinfectant, and it had better take on the job of cleaning its own house from top to bottom and drive out every crook and gangster and racketeer we find, because if we don't clean our own house, then the reactionaries will clean it for us. But they won't use a broom, they'll use an ax, and they'll try to destroy the labor movement in the process.

Now, when the A.F.L.-C.I.O. came into being we knew that this problem was there, and we said, "We have to have both a set of moral principles and we have to have effective machinery for the implementation of those ethical and moral standards." So we created in the constitution of the merged labor movement practical machinery that we call the Ethical Practices Committee. That committee is chaired by Brother Al Hayes, the President of the Machinists Union. The other members are Dave Dubinsky of the Garment Workers; Joe Curran of the Maritime Workers; George Harrison of the Railway Clerks; Jack Potofsky of the Amalgamated Clothing Workers. These five men, along with President Meany, are all men of great personal integrity, and I can say to you and I can say to them, that in doing this job of cleaning out the racketeers and the crooks they can count upon 100 per cent support of the UAW until that job is completed 100 per cent.

We urge the McClellan Committee to expose every crook and every racketeer that they can find in the American labor movement, but we also insist that they expose

The New World of Labor

with equal vigor, corrupt and crooked employers in America. All the corruption is not on labor's side.

Here is *The New York Times* of yesterday in which Mr. Robert Kennedy, who is the chief staff person for the McClellan Committee, said: "It is striking to us how little help business has been giving to the Committee. Often management would rather have the *status quo* and make their payoffs."

These reactionary, corrupt managements would rather pay a bribe to a crooked labor leader than to pay a living wage to the workers represented by that crooked labor leader.

I say to the McClellan Committee, we will give you full support and cooperation. Go after the crooks in the labor movement, but go after the crooks in management's side of the problem, and when you find a crooked labor leader who took a bribe from a crooked employer, put them both in jail for about fifteen years and give them plenty of time to talk it over between themselves. . . .

5. UNION RACKETEERING: 2*

1962

Senator John L. McClellan's Committee on Government Operations had concluded its hearings on corruption in unions in 1959. Its final report had contained a scathing attack on Jimmy Hoffa and his associates in various racketeer-led Teamsters locals. Two years later the committee issued another report on what progress had been made in cleaning up the malpractices that had been exposed (now that an anti-racketeering law was on the books). The findings and conclusions (excerpted below) revealed that nothing had changed, that the racketeers were as firmly in command as ever. What was more, the country seemed to have lost interest in the whole matter.

Findings and Conclusions

I. The recorded conversation of Antonio Corallo, Bernard Stein, and Mack Tane on June 30, 1959, and the transcript thereof, as placed in the subcommittee record, was obtained through a listening device installed by virtue of an official order of a New York State court.

The officer of the New York Police Department who had been charged with the duty of monitoring the listening device on June 30, 1959, testified under oath that the transcript of the recorded conversation placed in the record was that as recorded by him. In addition, a second police officer assigned to the New York County district

* U. S. Senate Committee on Government Operations, 87th Congress, 2nd Session, 1962, Report No. 1784, pp. 37-39.

The New World of Labor

attorney's office identified the voices in the recorded conversation as those of Antonio Corallo, Bernard Stein, and Mack Tane.

II. The recorded conversation strongly indicates and the subcommittee so finds that—

1. Despite his resignation as vice president, powerful New York underworld figure Antonio Corallo continued his ownership of Teamster Local 239 and complete control of the local's elected officials from behind the scenes. Local 239 continued to be a part of Corallo's racket empire.

2. Local 239 officials, specifically Bernard Stein, secretary-treasurer, and Mack Tane, director of organization, have been illegally misappropriating local union funds through the device of dummy organizers on the local's payroll.

At the direction of Corallo they were contemplating further raids on the union treasury through additional dummies in order to pay off extortionist Samuel Goldstein and thereby obtain Goldstein's "voluntary" resignation as president.

3. In anticipation of the select committee's expiration in July of 1959, Stein and Tane, under Corallo's direction and with Teamster General President Hoffa's acquiescence, planned to bring Goldstein back on the union payroll as business agent upon his release from prison in November of 1959. They further planned to permit him to resume the office of presidency within 6 months to a year. . . .

JAMES R. HOFFA

I. Hoffa has denied under oath making the statements attributed to him by Bernard Stein that he did not care if the officials of local 239 were robbing, stealing, or deal-

Except to Walk Free

ing under the table, as long as they were not caught. Whether or not Hoffa made such a statement is unimportant. This subcommittee by force of the overwhelming evidence must conclude that Hoffa, in callous disregard of the welfare of the Teamster membership, in fact does not care whether officials of local 239 or, for that matter, officials of any other segment of the Teamsters Union, are robbing, stealing, dealing under the table, or indulging in any other improper or criminal activities.

Hoffa's action and inaction are incontestable proof of this. Evidence before the select committee is a matter of record and need not be detailed in this report.

In the face of the evidence before this subcommittee that officials of 239 were in fact robbing, stealing, and that they were in fact "dealing under the table" (as exemplified by former President Samuel Goldstein, who was convicted of extortion and bribery, and director of organization, Mack Tane, who extorted payoffs from Wesley Pase to insure labor peace), Hoffa's attitude was one of defiant indifference to the interests of the rank-and-file members of local 239 whose treasury was being exploited and misused by corrupt and dishonest officials.

Hoffa testified that he made no investigation into the manner in which the purported organizers were being paid and, in fact, was satisfied that they were bona fide employees since Mack Tane (who invoked the fifth amendment before the subcommittee and was involved in the Pase payoff) had assured him that this was the case.

Additional evidence demonstrating Hoffa's callous disregard of the welfare of the Teamster membership includes the following:

  1. Refusal of Hoffa to take action against Anthony Provenzano, president of Teamster Local 560, who evidently was "dealing under the table" in receiving

The New World of Labor

payoffs from employers to insure labor peace and who is currently under Federal indictment in that connection.

2. Refusal of Hoffa to take action against Frank Matula, secretary-treasurer of Teamster Local 396, who was involved in west coast garbage rackets, and thereafter actually appointing Matula as international trustee while under a perjury conviction and permitting him to perform his duties as trustee while serving a prison sentence.

As a matter of fact, Hoffa testified that Matula, although convicted and imprisoned, was in his opinion innocent. He thus has taken it upon himself to acquit Matula.

3. Hoffa's appointment of Harry Gross as president of Teamster Local 320, despite the fact that Gross had served 2½ years in a New York penitentiary following a labor extortion conviction in 1942, because he had been "dealing under the table." Furthermore, Hoffa, thereafter, refused to revoke Gross' membership in the Teamsters although Gross had been convicted of income tax violations arising out of a series of labor union shakedowns from 1945 to 1949.

4. Failure to take action against William Presser, Ohio Teamster official, who had been convicted of contempt of the Senate and obstruction of justice.

II. The subcommittee concludes that Hoffa was not only aware of Corallo's continued control of local 239, but also knowingly acquiesced in it. . . .

6. THE A.F.L.-C.I.O. AND BLACKS*

1962

A. Philip Randolph, onetime president of the Brotherhood of Sleeping Car Porters and the leading spokesman for black workers in the United States, was a gadfly to organized labor and came repeatedly into conflict with its hierarchy, notably with George Meany. These remarks on the shortcomings of the union movement (delivered before a House committee), though directed at the South, applied to the North as well. And, indeed, they are as applicable today—twelve years later—as they were then.

. . . Exploiters of black labor are also exploiters of white labor. Exploiters of workers make no distinction with respect to race, color, or religion, except with a view to affecting the division of workers since the object of exploitation of labor is profit. The exploitation of workers provoke[s] resistance. Resistance is strong or weak according as the workers lack of organization, or that their organization is strong or weak. If black and white workers are divided by color bias both will be the victims of economic oppression since both will be weak.

Only a strong labor organization is the answer to labor exploitation. A labor organization can only be strong if it brings within its folds all workers in the trade or craft, class or industry. This is a basic lesson the American

* United States House Committee on Education and Labor, 87th Congress, 2nd Session, Part 2, *Equal Employment Opportunity*, pp. 850–51, 853–55.

The New World of Labor

trade union movement has yet fully to learn. The price organized labor pays for the failure to learn this lesson of the unity of workers is evident by the present plight of labor in the South.

Every single campaign to organize the workers into trade unions in the South, either by the A.F.L. or the C.I.O., or by the united labor movement, the A.F.L.-C.I.O., has been an utter and miserable failure. The failure was not due to the lack of financial resources. It was not due to a lack of organizing personnel. It was not due to the lack of organizational know-how.

Failure was due to fear and frustration; a lack of faith and fortitude when faced with the problem of race—a fierce fact of life in the South. Failure was due to a compromise with racialism as a policy of trade union opportunism. Organized labor had no faith in its own cause. White and black workers in the South had no faith in organized labor. . . .

As I previously stated to the House Committee on Education and Labor, it is an understatement to observe that the elimination of racial discrimination from unions, industry and Government and, especially, from all apprenticeship training programs involves the economic life and death of the black laboring masses. This is so for the following reasons:

(1) The relatively small number of skilled Negro workers in the Nation.

(2) Racial barriers to participation in apprenticeship programs.

(3) The concentration of disproportionately large numbers of Negro workers in the categories of unskilled workers.

(4) The phenomenal pace of the automation revolution which is changing the work force and the work tools,

the result of which is the decrease in demand for the unskilled worker.

Now, relative to the first proposition—namely, the relatively small number of Negro artisans in American industry—it is a matter of common knowledge that there is a disproportionate and alarming decline in the number of Negroes in the skilled trades between 1920 and 1950, especially in the building trades where the Negro was once relatively fairly well represented in the South, and where the total number of mechanics has increased. . . . It is because of this serious situation that the subject of apprenticeship training takes on such timely significance. Obviously, unless newly trained Negro artisans in relatively large numbers enter the work force it will be only a matter of a short time when skilled Negro workers will disappear from the building construction occupations of the country.

What about our second issue, racial barriers to Negro workers' participation in apprenticeship training programs?

While it is a grave indictment of the building trades unions, yet no one denies that less than 1 percent of the apprentices of the building trades are Negroes. Even in New York State, perhaps the most liberal, racially, in the country, only 2 percent of the apprentices are Negroes.

Third, how significant is the concentration of a disproportionately large number of Negro workers in the category of unskilled?

The answer is that one of the major reasons for the grim fact that the rate of unemployment of Negroes is twice, or more, the national rate of white workers is that unskilled workers are not only the first fired and the last hired, but also the first to be liquidated by radical technological advances.

The New World of Labor

Hence, the acquisition of skills by Negro workers in apprenticeship training programs is a sine qua non to their survival and progress in the new industrial world of automation.

Furthermore, because Negro workers are trapped in the "no man's land" of the unskilled, they constitute the hard core of joblessness, which means that these workers remain unemployed during depressions, recessions, booms, inflation and deflation; during cyclical, seasonal, residual, technological, ethnical and economic maladjustments of the economy.

Verily, there is a large segment of black slum proletariat, untrained, largely the product of race bias, caught up among the structured unemployed and unemployable and, probably, untrainable. . . .

7. WALTER REUTHER VS. THE A.F.L.-C.I.O.

1967

During the 1960s, while much of the country turned left, while protests against racial discrimination and the Vietnam War mounted, the A.F.L.-C.I.O. under George Meany more and more resembled the A.F. of L. of the 1920s. Responding sympathetically to the protests, Walter Reuther became increasingly critical of the A.F.L.-C.I.O.'s hidebound conservatism and of Meany's leadership in particular. And so, in 1968, what had been anticipated for some time finally took place: Reuther withdrew his huge union from the A.F.L.-C.I.O. He explains his reasons for doing so in this letter to U.A.W. locals, dated February 8, 1967, preparing them as it were for the inevitable next step. It is as good a statement as any on the shortcomings of the A.F.L.-C.I.O.

The U.A.W.'s disagreements with the A.F.L.-C.I.O. are basic and fundamental. They relate directly to democratic trade union principles and policies and the development and implementation of sound union programs. They relate to the overall, far reaching question: What should be the essential role of labor's cause in our 20th century technological society and how best can the labor movement fulfill its purposes and its responsibilities to its members, their families and to the whole of society.

From the outset it should be made unmistakably clear that this action by the U.A.W. International Executive

The New World of Labor

Board is taken not in anger, but in sadness; not out of personal pique, but as a matter of conscience; not out of any desire for self-aggrandizement or as a maneuver to gain personal advantage, but as a matter of principle. For the American labor movement, if it is to fulfill its destiny and become the vanguard of social progress, must restore its sense of purpose and direction, instill vitality, imagination and initiative in its programs and their accomplishment and be imbued with the dynamic spirit of social responsibility. . . .

The merger of the A.F. of L. and the C.I.O. eleven years ago was born in high hopes of a new thrust, a dynamic forward surge in labor's cause both at home and in the world. The U.A.W. leadership shared the exhilaration of the great promise of a vibrant stirring response to compelling new challenges and to new achievements of progressive thought and progressive action for the labor movement.

The 20th century technological revolution, with its automation, computerization and its fantastic new tools of science and technology, confronts the labor movement and the nation with new and urgent problems, compelling challenges and exciting opportunities. Yet the A.F.L-C.I.O., in policy and program, too often continues to live with the past. It advances few new ideas and lacks the necessary vitality, vision, imagination and social invention to make it equal to the challenging problems of a changing world.

It is sad but nevertheless true that the A.F.L.-C.I.O is becoming increasingly the comfortable, complacent custodian of the status quo.

The continued deterioration of the A.F.L.-C.I.O. is most tragic for there is an urgent need in America for a vital, vibrant, dynamic, socially progressive labor movement. The broad public support that an enlightened and responsible labor movement could inspire would provide important impetus to the creative and constructive forces of social change.

If the drift in the A.F.L.-C.I.O. continues, history will leave it further and further behind and it will be less and less an effective instrument to deal with the problems of our 20th century technological society.

In the eleven years of merger, the officers of the U.A.W. who have participated in A.F.L.-C.I.O. deliberations on the Executive Council, the General Board or in Standing Committees have seen the great promise of the merger go unfulfilled and have become increasingly disturbed by the inaction, by the indifference, by policies reflecting narrow negativism and by the lack of dynamic and inspired leadership in the A.F.L.-C.I.O.

A free labor movement needs strong leadership; but there is a fundamental difference between undemocratic, heavy-handed leadership and strong democratic leadership which encourages the democratic process and which demonstrates both the will and the ability to respect dissent and to forge labor unity out of the diversity essential to a free labor movement.

The chief officer of the A.F.L.-C.I.O. has used a heavy hand in discouraging in-depth discussion of basic policy issues and the objective evaluation of new ideas and new concepts. He has failed or he has refused to display a willingness to share democratic leadership responsibility in the formulation of policies and programs for the A.F.L.-C.I.O., and their effective implementation.

A free labor movement must be the instrument of its members and must reflect their hopes and aspirations and must be able to translate their needs and their will into effective policy and program. Its decisions must draw upon the full play of the democratic processes and arise

The New World of Labor

from the substance and splendor of human diversity. A democratic labor movement cannot be used as though it were the private and personal property of one person. . . .

The U.A.W. decision to have its officers resign from their posts in the A.F.L.-C.I.O. does not mean that the U.A.W. is running away from a fight. To run away from a fight on program, policy and principle would be incompatible with the whole history and tradition of the U.A.W. We are choosing rather to make the fight for sound programs, policies and principles in the broad arena of the whole labor movement and not within the narrow, private and exclusive top structure in the A.F.L.-C.I.O.

In the weeks ahead the U.A.W. will be advancing recommended programs and policies for consideration by the American labor movement which we believe are essential to get the American labor movement off dead center and on the march and to make it equal to the complex and challenging problems we face in a 20th century technological society. The recommendations will cover the following basic areas in which the American labor movement must share responsibility and play a decisive role:

I. Internal Reform and Democratization of the A.F.L.-C.I.O.

This will include proposals to:

A. Broaden the Executive Council of the A.F.L.-C.I.O. to make it more representative and instill new ideas, new vision and new vitality;

B. Establish the Executive Committee as required by the Constitution and make it a meaningful, functioning committee;

C. Provide the General Board the opportunity to share fully in leadership responsibility in shaping major pro-

Except to Walk Free

gram and policy decisions and in insuring their effective implementation;

D. Strengthen the work and responsibility of Standing Committees to enable them to make their maximum constructive contribution to the labor movement;

E. Establish a Public Review Board in the A.F.L.-C.I.O. modeled after the U.A.W. Public Review Board and charged with the responsibility to enforce the A.F.L.-C.I.O. Ethical Practices Code and to defend the democratic rights of members;

F. Strengthen the state and local federations and councils by constitutional provisions that will insure that the local unions, chapters or lodges of A.F.L.-C.I.O. affiliates will assume their proportionate share of the cost to perform the essential functions of state and local bodies of the A.F.L.-C.I.O.

II. *A Massive Comprehensive, Coordinated, Cooperative Organizing Crusade*

A. To organize the millions of unorganized industrial, construction trades, retail and distribution, office, technical, professional, federal government, state and municipal workers, school teachers, etc. to enable them to share the benefits and protection of organization;

B. To organize the millions of agricultural workers and working poor in our cities and rural areas to enable them to achieve the status of first class economic citizens in our free society. . . .

IV. *Labor's Role and Responsibility in the Community*

This will include:

A. The development of programs and policies for labor to play its rightful role and meet its responsibilities in the

The New World of Labor

task of rebuilding our cities and rural areas and making low-cost, high quality housing available through the use of the new tools of science and technology in creating a wholesome living environment worthy of free men;

B. Providing educational opportunities to facilitate maximum growth and development of America's children and youth;

C. Assuring a fuller measure of security and dignity for America's older citizens;

D. Removing for all the American people the economic barriers to access to high quality comprehensive medical and health care;

E. Demonstrating greater courage and compassion in extending equal rights and equal opportunity to every American. . . .

8. GRIGGS V. DUKE POWER*

1971

In 1965 (a year after the Civil Rights Act was passed) the black employees of the Duke Power Company of Draper, North Carolina, claimed that they had been denied their civil rights— that they had been unable to be promoted because they lacked a high school diploma or failed a special aptitude test, though neither the diploma nor the test had anything whatever to do with the jobs they wanted. The suit they brought resulted in a landmark decision on the rights of black and other minority workers. In a unanimous verdict, delivered by Chief Justice Warren Burger, the Supreme Court asserted that tests, diplomas, degrees, and the like would no longer be allowed to determine who was hired and who was assigned to what job if they bore no relation to the work that needed to be done. The decision had sweeping implications, applying as it did to industrial, civil-service, and trade-union practices alike.

Congress provided, in Title VII of the Civil Rights Act of 1964, for class actions for enforcement of provisions of the Act and this proceeding was brought by a group of incumbent Negro employees against Duke Power Company. All the petitioners are employed at the Company's Dan River Steam Station, a power generating facility located at Draper, North Carolina. At the time this action was instituted, the Company had 95

* 401 U.S. 424.

The New World of Labor

employees at the Dan River Station, 14 of whom were Negroes; 13 of these are petitioners here. . . .

The objective of Congress in the enactment of Title VII is plain from the language of the statute. It was to achieve equality of employment opportunities and remove barriers that have operated in the past to favor an identifiable group of white employees over other employees. Under the Act, practices, procedures, or tests neutral on their face, and even neutral in terms of intent, cannot be maintained if they operate to "freeze" the status quo of prior discriminatory employment practices. . . .

Congress did not intend by Title VII, however, to guarantee a job to every person regardless of qualifications. In short, the Act does not command that any person be hired simply because he was formerly the subject of discrimination, or because he is a member of a minority group. Discriminatory preference for any group, minority or majority, is precisely and only what Congress has proscribed. What is required by Congress is the removal of artificial, arbitrary, and unnecessary barriers to employment when the barriers operate invidiously to discriminate on the basis of racial or other impermissible classification.

Congress has now provided that tests or criteria for employment or promotion may not provide equality of opportunity merely in the sense of the fabled offer of milk to the stork and the fox. On the contrary, Congress has now required that the posture and condition of the jobseeker be taken into account. It has—to resort again to the fable provided that the vessel in which the milk is proffered be one all seekers can use. The Act proscribes not only overt discrimination but also practices that are fair in form, but discriminatory in operation. The touchstone is business necessity. If an employment practice which operates to exclude Negroes cannot be shown to be related to job performance, the practice is prohibited.

On the record before us, neither the high school completion requirement nor the general intelligence test is shown to bear a demonstrable relationship to successful performance of the jobs for which it was used. Both were adopted, as the Court of Appeals noted, without meaningful study of their relationship to job-performance ability. . . .

The facts of this case demonstrate the inadequacy of broad and general testing devices as well as the infirmity of using diplomas or degrees as fixed measures of capability. History is filled with examples of men and women who rendered highly effective performance without the conventional badges of accomplishment in terms of certificates, diplomas, or degrees. Diplomas and tests are useful servants, but Congress has mandated the commonsense proposition that they are not to become masters of reality. . . .

Nothing in the Act precludes the use of testing or measuring procedures; obviously they are useful. What Congress has forbidden is giving these devices and mechanisms controlling force unless they are demonstrably a reasonable measure of job performance. Congress has not commanded that the less qualified be preferred over the better qualified simply because of minority origins. Far from disparaging job qualifications as such, Congress has made such qualifications the controlling factor, so that race, religion, nationality, and sex become irrelevant. What Congress has commanded is that any tests used must measure the person for the job and not the person in the abstract.

9. WORK IN AMERICA*

1972

In December 1971 Elliot L. Richardson, Secretary of Health, Education and Welfare, asked a special task force of social scientists, trade unionists, and business executives to examine American "health, education, and welfare from the perspective of . . . work." The task force report (*Work in America*), released a year later, was a surprisingly good one, willing, as it was, to face head-on the critical issues—primarily the issue of what has caused and what can be done to overcome the deepening malaise of American workers in general. All in all, the report is a scathing indictment of the American workplace as authoritarian, oppressive, and demeaning. It blames not the workers but the institutions that dominate their lives.

Attitudes Toward Work

Over the last two decades, one of the most reliable single indicators of job dissatisfaction has been the response to the question: "What type of work would you try to get into if you could start all over again?" Most significantly, of a cross-section of white-collar workers (including professionals), only 43% would voluntarily choose the same work that they were doing, and only 24% of a cross-section of blue-collar workers would choose the same kind of work if given another chance. This

---

* Report of a special task force to the Secretary of Health, Education and Welfare, pp. 13, 14, 28–29, 31, 32, 37, 92–93, 147.

question, some researchers feel, is a particularly sensitive indicator because it causes respondents to take into account the intrinsic factors of the job and the very personal question of self-esteem. Those in jobs found to be least satisfying on other measures seldom would choose their present occupation again.

TABLE

Percentages in Occupational Groups
Who Would Choose Similar Work Again

Professional and Lower White-Collar Occupations	%	Working Class Occupations	%
Urban university professors	93	Skilled printers	52
Mathematicians	91	Paper workers	42
Physicists	89	Skilled auto-workers	41
Biologists	89	Skilled steelworkers	41
Chemists	86	Textile workers	31
Firm lawyers	85	Blue-collar workers, cross-section	24
Lawyers	83	Unskilled steelworkers	21
Journalists (Washington correspondents)	82	Unskilled auto-workers	16
Church university professors	77		
Solo lawyers	75		
White Collar Workers, cross-section	43		

Another fairly accurate measure of job satisfaction is to ask the worker the question: "What would you do

The New World of Labor

with the extra two hours if you had a 26-hour day?" Two out of three college professors and one out of four lawyers say they would use the extra time in a work-related activity. Strikingly, only one out of twenty nonprofessional workers would make use of the extra time in work activity. . . .

Society's View of the Manual Worker

We must also recognize that manual work has become increasingly denigrated by the upper middle-class of this nation. The problems of self-esteem inherent in these changing attitudes are further compounded by the impact of the communications media. For example, the images of blue-collar workers that are presented by the media (including school textbooks) are often negative. Workers are presented as "hardhats" (racists or authoritarians) or as "fat-cats" (lazy plumbers who work only twenty-hour weeks yet earn $400.00 a week). The view of the worker in the mass media is that *he* is the problem, not that he has problems.

Today, there is virtually no accurate dramatic representation—as there was in the 1930's—of men and women in working-class occupations. Instead, we have recently had the movie "Joe" and the television series about Archie Bunker. These stereotypes—ignoring the heterogeneity of blue-collar workers—do little to enhance the dignity of the worker or his job. For example, what does Archie do on the job? Is he ashamed of his job? Is that why he won't talk about it at home? Certainly, if he worked in an office we would see scenes of him at work. The negative view of blue-collar work on the show is reinforced by the fact that Archie's "socially enlightened" son-in-law is a future professional.

Research shows that less than one character in ten on

television is a blue-collar worker, and these few are usually portrayed as crude people with undesirable social traits. Furthermore, portrayals tend to emphasize class stereotypes: lawyers are clever while construction workers are louts. But it is not only the self-image of the worker that is being affected; television is conveying to children superficial and misleading information about work in society. If children do, indeed, learn from television, they will "learn" that professionals lead lives of care-free leisure, interspersed with drama and excitement (never hard work) and that blue-collar workers are racist clods who use bad grammar and produce little of use for society.

The ramifications of the low societal view of the worker are extensive and related to the personal problems of workers: low self-esteem, alcoholism, and withdrawal from community affairs. Our interviews with blue-collar workers revealed an almost overwhelming sense of inferiority: the worker cannot talk proudly to his children about his job, and many workers feel that they must apologize for their status. Thus, the working-class home may be permeated with an atmosphere of failure—even of depressing self-degradation. This problem of esteem and identity is, perhaps, related to the recent rise in ethnic consciousness among the working class. . . .

White Collar Woes

The auto industry is the *locus classicus* of dissatisfying work; the assembly-line, its quintessential embodiment. But what is striking is the extent to which the dissatisfaction of the assembly-line and blue-collar worker is mirrored in white-collar and even managerial positions. The office today, where work is segmented and authoritarian, is often a factory. For a growing number of jobs, there is little

The New World of Labor

to distinguish them but the color of the worker's collar: computer keypunch operations and typing pools share much in common with the automobile assembly-line.

Secretaries, clerks, and bureaucrats were once grateful for having been spared the dehumanization of the factory. White-collar jobs were rare; they had higher status than blue-collar jobs. But today the clerk, and not the operative on the assembly-line, is the typical American worker, and such positions offer little in the way of prestige. Furthermore, the size of the organizations that employ the bulk of office workers has grown, imparting to the clerical worker the same impersonality that the blue-collar worker experiences in the factory. The organization acknowledges the presence of the worker only when he makes a mistake or fails to follow a rule, whether in factory, or bureaucracy, whether under public or private control. . . .

Loyalty to employer was once high among this group of workers who felt that they shared much in common with their bosses—collar color, tasks, place of work. Today, many white-collar workers have lost personal touch with decision makers and, consequently, they feel estranged from the goals of the organizations in which they work. Management has exacerbated this problem by viewing white-collar workers as expendable: Because their productivity is hard to measure and their functions often non-essential, they are seen as the easiest place to "cut fat" during low points in the business cycle. Today, low-level white-collar workers are more likely to be sacrificed for the sake of short-term profitability than are blue-collar workers. . . .

[Young Workers]

Today's youth are expecting a great deal of intrinsic reward from work. Yankelovich found that students rank the opportunity to "Make a contribution," "job challenge," and the chance to find "self-expression" at the top of the list of influences on their career choice. A 1960 survey of over 400,000 high school students was repeated for a representative sample in 1970 and the findings showed a marked shift from the students valuing job security and opportunity for promotion in 1960 to valuing "freedom to make my own decisions" and "work that seems important to me" in 1970.

Many of these student findings were replicated in the Survey of Working Conditions sample of young workers. For example, it seems as true of young workers as it is of students that they expect a great deal of fulfillment from work. But the Survey findings show that young workers are not deriving a great deal of satisfaction from the work they are doing. Less than a quarter of young workers reply "very often" when asked the question, *"How often do you feel you leave work with a good feeling that you have done something particularly well?"*

Age Group	Percentage Answering "Very Often"
Under 20	23
21–29	25
30–44	38
45–64	43
65 and over	53

Other findings document that young workers place more importance on the value of interesting work and their ability to grow on the job than do their elders. They also place less importance than do older workers on such extrinsic factors as security and whether or not they are

The New World of Labor

asked to do excessive amounts of work. But the Survey documents a significant gap between the expectations or values of the young workers and what they actually experience on the job. Young workers rate their jobs lower than do older workers on how well their jobs actually live up to the factors they most sought in work. For example, the young value challenging work highly but say that the work they are doing has a low level of challenge. . . .

[The Role of the Trade Unions]

After a phase of initial hostility, the American Labor movement saw many of the techniques of scientific management as a fundamental revolution in American industry, holding great promise for advancing the economic well-being of the worker. Indeed, both industry and labor have benefited greatly from the fruits of increased productivity derived from industrial efficiency.

In part because of this success, labor has continued to emphasize extrinsic rewards for workers. But the union strategy of only bargaining for extrinsic rewards has begun to show signs of wear. Worker discontent with this traditional role of unions has left many union leaders bewildered and frustrated. Jerry Wurf, President of the Federation of State, County and Municipal Employees (A.F.L.-C.I.O.) says that "the greatest labor leader avocation these days is to gripe about the lack of their members' appreciation for all that they are doing for them." There is considerable evidence that (1) alienated workers are less loyal to their unions than are non-alienated workers and (2) workers in jobs with little intrinsic satisfactions are least favorably inclined toward unions regardless of their age. Young workers who are rebelling against the drudgery of routine jobs are also rebelling

Except to Walk Free

against what they feel is "unresponsive" and "irrelevant" union leadership.

There are several reasons why unions have been slow, even slower than management, to come to grips with the problems created by scientific management. Some union officials feel that they have been misled by managerial changes in the past, and that job redesign is yet another scheme to reduce the size of the workforce through wringing every ounce of productivity out of the worker. Another explanation is offered by Albert Epstein of the Machinists and Aerospace Workers, who says that "if the trade unions have not dealt energetically with this question, it is because they are absorbed with other issues which seemed more important to them." But Epstein adds that "there is nothing inherent in the trade union structure which must necessarily prevent it from taking up the question. . . ."

It is true that unions have limited their concern to questions dealing with protection for all jobs in a company or an industry, and consequently, they have little experience with questions of specific job design. The answer to their problem may lie in developing cooperative efforts to carry out the redesign of work. But the first union question is that of a commitment. As Irving Bluestone of the U.A.W. writes, "Just as management is beginning to ponder the new problems of discontent and frustration in the work force, so must unions join in finding new ways to meet these problems." If new ways are to be charted and accepted, the trade union movement must be among the initiators of new demands for the humanization of work. At the very least, such an initiative would improve their members' evaluations of their unions. And, if dissatisfying jobs lead to high turnover: it is difficult to see how unions can develop any long-term attachment among temporary members. . . .

Conclusion

Albert Camus wrote that "Without work all life goes rotten. But when work is soulless, life stifles and dies." Our analyses of Work in America leads to much the same conclusion: Because work is central to the lives of so many Americans, either the absence of work or employment in meaningless work is creating an increasingly intolerable situation. The human costs of this state of affairs are manifested in worker alienation, alcoholism, drug addiction, and other symptoms of poor mental health. Moreover, much of our tax money is expended in an effort to compensate for problems with at least a part of their genesis in the world of work. A great part of the staggering national bill in the areas of crime and delinquency, mental and physical health, manpower and welfare are generated in our national policies and attitudes towards work. Likewise, industry is paying for its continued attachment to Tayloristic practices through low worker productivity and high rates of sabotage, absenteeism, and turnover. Unions are paying through the faltering loyalty of a young membership that is increasingly concerned about the apparent disinterest of its leadership in problems of job satisfaction. Most important, there are the high costs of lost opportunities to encourage citizen participation: the discontent of women, minorities, blue-collar workers, youth, and older adults would be considerably less were these Americans to have had an active voice in the decisions in the workplace that most directly affect their lives. . . .

Bibliography

This bibliography is intended as a guide for the interested reader. It consists of works that have proved helpful to me in the course of writing this book.

GENERAL STUDIES

Several one-volume histories of labor provide serviceable introductions to the subject: Foster Rhea Dulles, *Labor in America* (New York, 1960 [rev. ed.]); Henry Pelling, *American Labor* (Chicago, 1960); and Joseph Rayback, *A History of American Labor* (New York, 1959)—of which Rayback's is the most thorough and detailed (almost to a fault) and Pelling's the thinnest both in content and bulk. Still useful, too, is Nathan Fine, *Farmer and Labor Parties in the United States 1828–1928* (New York, 1928), and Morris Hillquit, *History of Socialism in the United States* (New York, 1909). The Communist version of American labor is adumbrated by Anthony Bimba, *The History of the American Working Class* (New York, 1927), and by Richard O. Boyer and Herbert Morais, *Labor's Untold Story* (New York, 1955).

Not a history but indispensable for an understanding of American labor is Robert F. Hoxie, *Trade Unionism in the United States* (New York, 1917)—a remarkably keen analysis, as applicable today as when it was first published.

If it is thoroughness the reader wants, he should by all means consult the four-volume work by John R. Commons

Bibliography

and associates, *History of Labor in the United States* (New York, 1896–1932); it is, for those who have the patience, the best study of the subject available. Philip S. Foner, *History of the Labor Movement in the United States*, four volumes (New York, 1947–65), is, on the whole, less reliable. I am not referring to Foner's Marxist point of view, which is in fact a valuable corrective to the anti-radical, pro-A.F. of L. bias of Commons *et al.*

For the documents themselves, the reader might sample a very fine old series (it goes no further than the 1880s, however) to which I am enormously indebted: John R. Commons *et al.*, eds., *A Documentary History of American Industrial Society*, ten volumes (Cleveland, 1910–11). I am also indebted to two one-volume collections for a number of leads and suggestions: Leon F. Litwack, ed., *The American Labor Movement* (Englewood Cliffs, N.J., 1962), and Jerold S. Auerbach, ed., *American Labor: the Twentieth Century* (Indianapolis and New York, 1969).

Three good books deal with the violent side of American labor—with the sustained warfare over the past hundred years between workers on the one hand and capital and the government on the other: Sidney Lens, *The Labor Wars* (New York, 1973); Samuel Yellen, *American Labor Struggles* (New York, 1936); and Louis Adamic, *Dynamite: the Story of Class Violence in America* (New York, 1934).

The history of blacks and labor has still failed to receive the attention it deserves. There are a few competent works: Herbert R. Northrup, *Organized Labor and the Negro* (New York, 1944); Charles H. Wesley, *Negro Labor in the United States* (New York, 1927); Lorenzo J. Greene and Carter G. Woodson, *The Negro Wage Earner* (Washington, 1930); and Sterling D. Spero and Abram L. Harris, *The Black Worker* (New York, 1931). Herbert Hill's monumental study-in-progress, sections of which I have been privileged to see, should be the definitive one on the whole subject of blacks and trade unions. It is eagerly awaited.

Bibliography

PREINDUSTRIAL AMERICA

What was the working man's relation to American democracy in the Jacksonian, or ante-bellum, era? Arthur Schlesinger, Jr., *The Age of Jackson* (Boston, 1946), attempts to deal with the question and is still very much worth reading. Walter Hugins, *Jacksonian Democracy and the Working Class* (New York, 1960), presents a closely reasoned, well-researched analysis of the working men's movement in New York City. Volume two of Commons, *et al.*, *History of Labor in the United States*, exhaustively discusses the movement throughout the country. Herman Schlüter, *Lincoln, Labor and Slavery* (New York, 1913), tries, unconvincingly, to prove that workers opposed the slavocracy despite their differences with the abolitionists; it fails to come to grips with the issue of anti-black sentiment among northern working men. Norman J. Ware, *The Industrial Worker 1840–1860* (Chicago, 1924), is a pioneer study which, however, comes down too hard on radicals and reformers.

TRANSITION

A sympathetic early treatment of the left wing of American labor is still very much worth reading: Richard T. Ely, *The Labor Movement in America* (New York, 1886). Norman J. Ware, *The Labor Movement in the United States 1860–1895* (New York, 1929), picks up where his other book leaves off and shows why the Knights of Labor rose and fell (and is, again, contemptuous of "utopians" and ideologues). The same time is explored in greater depth by Gerald Grob, *Workers and Utopia* (Evanston, Ill., 1961), a highly recommended piece of scholarship and insight. Highly recommended too is David Montgomery, *Beyond Equality: Labor and Radical Republicans, 1862–1872* (New York, 1967). Interesting data on the Knights of Labor (and on much else besides) can be gleaned from the account by its long-time president, Terence V. Powderly, *Thirty Years of Labor* (Columbus, Ohio, 1889). Jonathan Grossman, *Wil-*

liam Sylvis, Pioneer of American Labor (New York, 1945), is disappointing; it adds little to what is already known about Sylvis and the National Labor Union.

The most recent book on the Molly Maguires is Wayne G. Broehl, Jr., *The Molly Maguires* (Cambridge, Mass., 1968), an evenhanded study, but also leaden-footed. More spirited and lively is the Marxist (and clearly tendentious) account by Anthony Bimba, *Molly Maguires* (New York, 1932). See also chapter two of Lens, cited above.

Robert V. Bruce, *1877: Year of Violence* (Indianapolis, 1959), is a solid, engagingly written study of the "Great Strike." This subject, too, deserves much more notice from scholars than it has gotten.

THE A.F. OF L.

Oddly, there is no really good biography of Samuel Gompers. The best apologia of his notable life and career is his own *Seventy Years of Life and Labor* (New York, 1924), two volumes. Bernard Mandel, *Samuel Gompers: A Biography* (Yellow Springs, Ohio, 1963), is a sharp critique indeed, a healthy antidote to the hagiography that has grown up around Gompers. John H. M. Laslett, *Labor and the Left, 1885–1924* (New York, 1970), presents a moderate and evenly balanced critique. There are several informative studies of the A.F. of L. under Gompers' leadership that tell much the same story: Lewis Lorwin and J. A. Flexner, *The American Federation of Labor* (New York, 1923), is a clearly written defense; Philip Taft, *The AFL in the Time of Gompers* (New York, 1957), is a forbidding, ponderously detailed one. Marc Karson, *American Labor Unions and Politics* (Carbondale, Ill., 1958), renders an important service to labor history by uncovering the largely conservative (mainly Catholic) roots among the A.F. of L. rank and file.

Leon Wolff, *Lockout* (New York, 1965)—aptly subtitled "A Study of Violence, Unionism, and the Carnegie Steel Empire"—is the most recent and the most readable history of Homestead. Also on Homestead, see by all means the relevant portions in Alexander Berkman, *Prison Memoirs* (New York, 1913), and in Emma Goldman, *Living My Life* (New York, 1931). The Pullman strike has generated a vast literature not only because it was significant in itself but because it deeply touched, or transformed, the lives of so many people. The following will suffice: Almont Lindsey, *The Pullman Strike* (Chicago, 1942), a judicious and thorough study; Ray Ginger, *Bending Cross* (New York, 1949), the best biography of Debs; and Colston E. Warne, ed., *The Pullman Boycott of 1894* (Boston, 1955), a collection of differing interpretations of the strike and valuable documentary material.

The literature on the I.W.W. is also vast. Several of the standard works were written a long time ago: e.g., John G. Brooks, *American Syndicalism* (New York, 1913), and Paul Brissenden, *The I.W.W.* (New York, 1919). Two recent works are Melvyn Dubofsky, *We Shall Be All* (New York, 1969), a vast and detailed celebration, and Joyce L. Kornbluh, *Rebel Voices, An I.W.W. Anthology* (Ann Arbor, Mich., 1964), a lively reader. William D. Haywood, *The Autobiography of Big Bill Haywood* (New York, 1929), a sadly heroic memoir, is indispensable to anyone wishing to know how the I.W.W. came to exist.

A first-rate book on labor in the 1920s is Irving Bernstein, *The Lean Years* (Boston, 1960). On the A.F. of L. in particular, Taft, cited above, is useful, as are the opening chapters of his companion volume, *The AFL from the Death of Gompers to the Merger* (New York, 1959). A radical analysis of the A.F. of L., one that has lost none of its bite, is David J. Saposs, *Left Wing Unionism* (New York, 1926). A liberal one (by a knowledgeable Englishman) is Vivian Vale, *Labor in American Politics* (New York, 1971). Ronald Radosh, *American Labor and Foreign Policy* (New York, 1969), smites Gompers and the A.F. of L. hip and thigh as collaborators in an imperialist venture. William Z. Foster, master organizer, leader of the 1919 steel strike (and later head of the American Communist Party), describes the whole period in his interesting memoir *Pages from a Worker's Life* (New York, 1939). The latest study of the steel strike, and a very good one, is David Brody, *Labor in Crisis* (New York, 1965).

THE C.I.O.

Irving Bernstein, *Turbulent Years* (Boston, 1970), has again effectively chronicled the history of American workers, this time in the 1930s. The growing sense of crisis that attended the period of industrial violence from 1934 on is clearly limned in Part Six of Arthur Schlesinger, Jr., *The Coming of the New Deal* (Boston, 1959); in Frances Perkins (Secretary of Labor at the time), *The Roosevelt I Knew* (New York, 1946); and in the appropriate chapters of Yellen and Lens, both cited above. The 1934 Minneapolis teamster strike is beautifully presented by Charles R. Walker, *American City, A Rank and File History* (New York, 1937).

The rise of the C.I.O. let loose a deluge of books, only a small number of which can be mentioned here. The A.F. of L. point of view is bodied forth in Philip Taft, *The AFL from the Death of Gompers to the Merger*, cited above. Benjamin Stolberg, *The Story of the CIO* (New York, 1938), is a competent survey. Herbert Harris, *Labor's Civil War* (New York, 1940), is a racy, exhilirating one. Edward Levinson, *Labor on the March* (New York, 1938), is a classic account that, happily, has been reprinted. Mary Heaton Vorse, *Labor's New Millions* (New York, 1939), provides a poignant description of the emergent industrial unions, beginning with the Akron sit-down strike. On the great sit-downs of the auto industry the most authoritative work is Sidney Fine, *Sit-Down, the General Motors Strike of 1936–1937* (Ann Arbor, Mich., 1969). The standard book on the United Auto Workers—its leadership, policies, and ideology in the context of the period as a whole—is Irving Howe and B. J. Widick, *The UAW and Walter Reuther* (New York, 1949). A recondite inquiry into several of the

Bibliography

major unions involved in the struggle is Walter Galenson, *The CIO Challenge to the AFL* (New York, 1960).

Two very fine biographies give us a penetrating insight into the life of the times: Saul Alinsky, *John L. Lewis, An Unauthorized Biography* (New York, 1949), and Matthew Josephson, *Sidney Hillman, Statesman of American Labor* (New York, 1952). Bruce Minton and John Stuart, *Men Who Lead Labor* (New York, 1937), is a good Marxist period piece, a series of sharply etched portraits of heroes (C.I.O.) and villains (A.F. of L.).

On the findings of the La Follette committee, Leo Huberman, *Labor Spy Racket* (New York, 1937), still holds up very well. Jerold Auerbach, *Labor and Liberty* (Indianapolis, 1966), is a detailed, scholarly account of the committee, its work, and its effect on the rise of the C.I.O.

THE NEW WORLD OF LABOR

If one wants to have some idea of economic conditions, especially as they affect labor, the best place to go is to the Statistical Abstract of the United States (Washington, 1973) —that is, to the relevant tables on population, income, and occupations.

A sound, comprehensive history of American labor since World War II, particularly since the formation of the A.F.L.-C.I.O., in 1955, still has to be written. The biographies of the leading figures in the movement also leave much to be desired. There is no first-rate study of Walter Reuther (apart, that is, from the one by Howe and Widick, written in 1948), though two may be safely recommended: Frank Cormier and William J. Eaton, *Reuther* (Englewood Cliffs, N.J., 1970), and Jean Gould and Lorena Hickok, *Walter Reuther: Labor's Rugged Individualist* (New York, 1972). George Meany has found a sympathetic biographer in Joseph C. Goulden, *Meany* (New York, 1972), a compendious piece of work and very informative (in ways scarcely flattering to its hero). Jimmy Hoffa is well portrayed in a frightening chronicle of raw power: Walter Sheridan, *The Fall and Rise of*

Bibliography

Jimmy Hoffa (New York, 1972). And on Hoffa and the Teamsters, definitely see Robert F. Kennedy, *The Enemy Within* (New York, 1960), and Clark Mollenhoff, *Tentacles of Power* (Cleveland, 1965).

The McClellan committee hearings called forth a farrago of books on the whole issue of union democracy, some of them quite fine. Paul Jacobs, *The State of the Unions* (New York, 1963), gives a cogent analysis of business and racketeer unions (typified by the Teamsters). B. J. Widick, *Labor Today* (Boston, 1964), is a splendidly incisive report on the main problems afflicting modern trade unions; and the last chapter ("Labor Leadership Today") bears close attention. Burton Hall, ed., *Autocracy and Insurgency in Organized Labor* (New Brunswick, N.J., 1972), delivers hard-hitting assaults on various corrupt unions while supporting attempts by rank-and-file groups to claim their rights and establish viable democracies. Special mention here should be made of a study that has just come out and that I have read all too hastily: Stanley Aronowitz, *False Promises* (New York, 1974). This much I can say: It is, all in all, the best Marxist critique of organized labor in America I have encountered.

The relations between labor and blacks (those inside as well as outside unions) in recent times are explored in a series of valuable essays by authorities in their fields, trenchantly introduced by the editor: Julius Jacobson, *The Negro and the American Labor Movement* (New York, 1968). A melancholy account of black and white workers in Detroit—a microcosm of America at large—is B. J. Widick, *Detroit, City of Race and Class Violence* (New York, 1973); according to Widick, only class solidarity of the sort that accompanied the rise of the C.I.O. (or, rather, the United Auto Workers) can overcome the festering animosities of our times.

Blue-collar workers have been rediscovered, and the literature on them now abounds. Patricia Cayo Sexton and Brendan Sexton, *Blue Collars and Hard-Hats* (New York, 1971),

Bibliography

sets the record straight on a number of myths that have sprung up of late—among them, that workers are racist, prowar, conservative, affluent, etc.—and envisages the possibility of a renewed, labor-led liberal coalition. This is the theme that underlies a good collection of disparate essays: Irving Howe, ed., *The World of the Blue-Collar Worker* (New York, 1972). More general and wide-ranging (and quite pedantic, too) is Sar Levitan, ed., *Blue-Collar Workers* (New York, 1971). Worth consulting are three studies that deal primarily with the personal, cultural, and community lives of workers: Richard Sennett and Jonathan Cobb, *The Hidden Injuries of Class* (New York, 1972); Arthur B. Shostak, *Blue Collar Life* (New York, 1969); and Kenneth Lasson, *The Workers* (New York, 1971)—this last prepared by Ralph Nader's Center for the Study of Responsive Law.

And to be recommended, finally is the H.E.W. study (a portion of which I included in the text above) *Work in America* (Cambridge, Mass., 1973). It has the singular merit of taking the whole of the workers' lives into account and of discovering there a profound and widespread source of discontent.

INDEX

Abolitionists, 21, 32, 63, 65, 67–68, 69–71, 107–10, 322
A.F.L.-C.I.O. (American Federation of Labor-Congress of Industrial Organizations), 267–75; and blacks, 298–301; constitution of, 288–90; Executive Council of, 274; and labor criminality, 267–69, 273–74, 291–93, 294–96; Report of the First Constitutional Convention, 288–90; Reuther and the U.A.W. vs., 302–7
Agrarianism, 17, 20, 24–27, 60–62, 76, 79
Akron (Ohio), rubber workers' sit-down strike (1936) in, 229–38, 271
Amalgamated Clothing Workers, 214
American Colonization Society, 64
American Federationist, 168
American Federation of Labor (A.F. of L.), 137–49, 150–52, 153–56, 185–86, 230, 253, 257, 263, 264–65, 272, 324, 325; and blacks, 143, 168–70, 196–98, 298–301; and C.I.O., 210, 211, 212–19, 222–24, 225–24, 266–75, 288–90; Gompers-Hillquit debate, 178–83; Gompers on principles governing, 150–52; and Knights of Labor, 137–38, 140; preamble to constitution of, 153–56, 288; and Socialist Labor Party, 141–42 and Socialist Party of America, 178–83; and steel strike (1919), 199–207
American Federation of Labor History, Encyclopedia, Reference Book, 171
American Railway Union, Pullman strike by, 141, 157–59, 160–62
Anarchists, 3, 85, 164
Anarchocommunists, 80–81, 84, 85, 122–26; manifesto of, 122–26

Annals of the Great Strikes of the United States (Dacus), 111n
Anthony, Susan B., 76
Anthracite-coal strike (1875), 78
Apprentice system, 91
Arbitration, 120. *See also* Collective bargaining
Aristocracy, 1, 5, 32–37, 39, 43, 54, 61, 62
Artisans, 1–5ff., 18–21, 32–37, 74, 81–87, 139; Knights of Labor and, 81–87
Associationist movement, 17, 41, 55–56, 75, 107–10
Attucks, Crispus, 261
Auto-Lite strike, 212, 271
Auto workers, 213, 217–18, 228, 263, 266, 314–15 (*see also* United Auto Workers); GM labor espionage and, 253–54; sit-down strikes by, 239–40, 241–44, 326

Bakery Workers Union, 268
Baltimore (Md.), railroad strike in (1877), 111–18
Baltimore and Ohio Railroad, 113–18
Banks (banking system), 16, 22, 26, 94, 109–10, 121
Bellamy, Edward, 81
Belmont, August, 143, 175
Blacks (black workers), 6, 19, 21, 63–66, 67–68, 69–71, 273, 275, 280, 322, 328 (*see also* Abolitionists; Racism; Slavery); A.F. of L. and, 143, 168–70, 196–98; A.F.L.-C.I.O. and, 298–301; civil-rights movement and, 273, 308–10; Civil War and, 69–71; Douglass on work and, 63–66; Du Bois on unions and, 196–98; *Griggs v. Duke Power* and, 308–10; labor movement (unions) and, 75, 97–98, 143, 168–70,

331

Index

196–98, 298–301, 322, 328; Negro National Labor Union, 97–98; Randolph's call for a march on Washington by (1941), 257–62; slaveholders and, 67–68 (*see also* Slavery)

Blue-collar workers, 270, 328–29; and job attitudes, 312, 314–15; view in mass media of, 313–14

Bluestone, Irving, 318

Bolshevik Revolution, 147, 225

Bolton, William J., 114

Bootmakers' Society of Boston, 52–54

Boston Mechanics' and Laborers Association, 57–59

Bourgeoisie. *See* Entrepreneurs; Middle class; Tradesmen

Braddock (Pa.), and steel strike, 200, 206

Brennan, Peter, 273n

Brewery Workers Union, 144

Bridges, Harry, 212, 218, 283, 285

British Trades Union Congress, 137, 151

Building trades, 147, 271, 272

Burger, Warren, 308

Camus, Albert, 319

Cannon, James, 212

Capitalism (industrial capitalism), 3, 4, 6, 42, 62, 73, 79–80, 81, 86–91, 94–96, 99–103, 107–10, 122–26, 178–83, 209–19; Debs on, 174–77; Gompers on, 173, 178–83; Gompers-Hillquit debate on, 178–83; and labor espionage, 250–51, 252–56; market economy and (*see* Market economy); new world of labor (1947–74) and, 263–75ff.; reform movements and (*see* Reform movements); socialist movement and (*see* Socialism); and strikes (*see* Strikes); and unions (*see* Unions); and violence against labor, 250–51, 252–56

Carnegie, Andrew, 175

Carnegie Steel Company, 141

Cartels, 210–11

Chicago Haymarket Massacre, 84–85

Children, 19, 120–21, 204–5; child labor, 19, 120–21, 137, 140, 141; and education, 1, 16, 22–23, 28–29

Chinese immigrants, and labor movement, 3, 28–29, 75n, 98, 143

Christian Socialists, 81

Church, the, 123; and state, 26

C.I.O. (Congress of Industrial Organizations), 209–19, 222–24, 253, 263, 265–75, 326–27, 328; and A.F. of L., 210, 211, 212–19, 222–24, 225–28, 266–75, 288–90 (*see also* A.F.L.-C.I.O.); and blacks, 298–301; expulsion of Communists from (1949), 279–87; "Minority Report of the Resolutions Committee on Organization Policies," 222–24; and sit-down strikes, 229–38, 239–40, 241–44; start and history of, 209–19

Civic Federation, 143, 175

Civil Rights Act, 308–10

Civil-rights movement, 273, 308–10

Civil service employees, 263

Civil War (and postwar) era, 2, 21, 69–71, 73–75ff.

Clayton Act, 146

Cleveland, Grover, 143

Closed shops, 17, 240, 264

Coal miners, 228, 263 (*see also* United Mine Workers); and Ludlow Massacre, 189–93; and yellow-dog contracts, 194–95

Cold War, 265, 266, 269, 278–87

Collective bargaining, 201, 211, 216, 240, 271; Wagner Act and, 216, 217, 220–21, 245–47, 248–49, 250

Colorado Fuel and Iron Company, 189–93

Commission on Industrial Relations (U. S. Senate), 184n, 189n

Committee for Industrial Organization, 216–17. *See also* C.I.O.

Commons, John R. 22n, 28n, 30n, 38n, 41n, 57n, 60n, 92n, 99n, 104n, 321, 322

Commonwealth v. *Hunt*, 53–54

Communism (Communists), 148, 151–52, 218, 265–66, 270n (*see also* Anarcho-communists); expulsion from C.I.O. of, 279–81

Communist (Workers) Party, 148, 210

Communitarianism, 55–56, 57–59

Company unions, 148, 202, 212, 216, 225

Congress, U. S., 95, 96, 246, 248, 250, 252, 264, 309. *See also* Government, U. S.; specific commissions, committees, individuals, legislation, reports

Congressional Globe, U. S. Senate, 67n

Conspiracy laws and trials, 19, 47–54

Constitution, U. S., 45, 246, 281

332

Index

Construction-industry workers, 273, 314
Convict labor, 137
Coolidge, Calvin, 148
Co-operative movement, 2, 20, 57, 75, 83, 94, 102, 107–10, 125, 164
Corallo, Antonio, 295–96, 297
Corruption, labor, 267–69, 273–74
Cotton, labor and, 28, 69
Craft versus mass-production (industrial) unionism, 213–19, 222–24, 225–28, 267
Crime (criminality), union, 267–69, 273–74, 291–93, 294–96
"Crime of Poverty" (Henry George speech, April 1885), 127–30
Crisis, The, 196–97
Curran, Joseph, 279, 284–85, 292

Dacus, Joseph A., 111
Debs, Eugene V., 141, 145, 146, 160, 178–79, 215; and Pullman strike, 157–59, 160; on socialism, 174–77
Debts (indebtedness), labor and, 1, 16, 26
De Gersdorff, Carl, 253
De Leon, Daniel, 141–42, 144–45, 163–67; defense of S.L.P.'s revolutionary approach to trade unionism by, 163–67
Democracy (democratic movement), blacks and, 257–62, 288–90; labor and, 1–14, 16, 80, 109, 305, 323; working men's parties and, 16–17ff.
Democratic Party, 17, 264–65, 269
Democratic Socialists, 265, 266
Depressions, economic, 77–79, 140, 209
Dignity, labor and work and, 1, 16, 87, 102, 313–14
Dobbs, Farrell, 212
Documentary History of American Industrial Society, A, 22n, 28n, 30n, 38n, 41n, 57n, 60n, 92n, 99n, 104n, 322
Double Edge of Labor's Sword, 178
Douglass, Frederick, 63–66
Dubinsky, David, 214, 292
Du Bois, W. E. B., 196–98; on blacks and the A.F. of L., 196–98
Duke Power Company, Griggs v., 308–10
Dunne brothers, 212

East St. Louis race riots (1917), 196, 197
Education (schools), labor and, 1, 16, 17, 22–23, 28–29, 36, 90, 120, 123, 124, 125, 218; and blacks, 65, 98
Eisenhower administration, 269
Ely, Richard, 122n, 323
Emigration. *See* Immigrants
Employment, 127. *See also* Unemployment
Entrepreneurs, 1–2, 8–9, 18–21, 139. *See also* Middle class, Tradesmen
Epstein, Albert, 318
Espionage Act (1917), 146–47
Evans, George H., 60–62
"Expulsion of the Communists" (C.I.O. debate, 1949), 279–87

Fabians, 81
Factory labor (factories, mills), 2, 18, 28–29, 38–40, 74, 121; A.F. of L. and reforms, 137, 140; women and children and, 38–40
Fair Employment Practices Committee, 257
Farmers (farming), 3, 36, 39, 60–62, 79, 85, 128, 130, 145, 272. *See also* Agrarianism
Faulkner, Henry. *See People v. Faulkner*
Federal Corrupt Practices Act, 277, 294
Federation of Organized Trades and Labor Unions of the United States and Canada (F.O.T.L.U.), 137–38
Firestone rubber workers, sit-down strike (1936) by, 229–38
"First International on the Civil War, The," 69–71
First World War, 146–47
Fitzpatrick, John, 202
Flint (Mich.), GM sit-down strike at, 239–40, 241–44, 271
Foner, Philip S., 322
Ford Motor Company, 213, 218
Foster, William Z., 202–3, 205–6, 325
Fourierist movement, 55
Frederick Douglass' Paper, 63n
Free Soil Party, 60
Frey, John P., 225

Garment workers, and unions, 214
Garrison, William Lloyd, 32–37, 281
Gary, Ind., 199
General Motors Corporation, 213, 217, 253–54; sit-down strike (1937); 239–40, 241–44
George, Henry, 79, 80, 127–30; and single-tax movement, 79, 129–30,

333

Index

166–67; speech to Knights of Labor by, 127–30
German-American workers, 3, 5, 79–80, 98, 122
Goldstein, Samuel, 295, 296
Gompers, Samuel, 139, 141–42, 143, 144, 146, 147, 148, 171, 175, 196, 202, 215, 324, 325; debate with Hillquit, 178–83; on principles governing the A.F. of L., 150–52; on socialism, 171–73, 178–83
Goodyear Tire and Rubber Company, 230, 237
Gould, Jay, 84
Government, U. S., 9, 94, 95, 96, 123, 178–83, 184–88 (*see also* Congress, U. S.; specific agencies, bodies, individuals, legislation); alliance with business, 78; and land rights and distribution, 24–27; and Ludlow Massacre, 189–93; and new world of labor (1947–74), 263–75; and Pullman strike, 157–59, 160–62; Randolph's call for a march on Washington (1941) and, 257–62; and Taft-Hartley Act, 276–78; and violence against labor, 250–51, 252–56; and Wagner Act, 216, 217, 220–21, 245–47, 248–49; *Work in America* task force report and, 311–19; and workers (1935–41), 209–12, 216, 218, 220–21
"Great Uprising, The," 111–18
Green, William, 148–49, 211, 216–17, 231, 267n
Greenback Labor Party, 78–79, 83
Greenback movement, 78–79
Griggs v. *Duke Power*, 308–10
Gronlund, Laurence, 81
Gross, Harry, 297

Hammond, James H., 67–68
Hanna, Mark, 143
Harding, Warren G., 148
Harrison, George, 292
Hayes, Al, 292
Maymarket Massacre, 84–85
Haywood, William D. ("Big Bill"), 146–47, 184–88, 215; testimony to the Industrial Relations Board on the I.W.W. by, 184–88
Health, Education, and Welfare Department, *Work in America* study by, 311–19, 329
Hillman, Sidney, 214, 327
Hillquit, Morris, and debate with Gompers, 178–83
Hitchman Coal and Coke Co. v. *Mitchell*, 194–95

Hoffa, James (Jimmy), 268, 294, 295–97, 327–28
Homestead (Pa.), steelworkers' strike at, 141, 271, 325
Homestead Act (1862), 60
Hoover, Herbert, 148, 209, 210
Hours of work, 1, 16, 28–29, 39–40, 82, 86, 96, 121, 133, 135, 191, 201, 211, 313; A.F. of L. and, 140, 151
House Committee on Education and Labor, 298–301
Howells, William Dean, 81
Hughes, Charles Evans, 245
Hutcheson, "Big Bill," 216

Immigrants (immigration), 2–3, 5, 20, 21, 45, 77, 143. *See also* specific people
Indochina, 270, 273. *See also* Vietnam War
Industrialism, 3, 5–6, 8, 23–24, 77–81ff. *See also* Capitalism (industrial capitalism)
Industrial Relations Commission, 178–83, 184–88, 189–93
Industrial Valley (McKenney), 229
Industrial Workers of the World (I.W.W.), 145–47, 179, 184–88, 325; Haywood's testimony to the Industrial Relations Board on, 184–88
International Ladies Garment Workers Union (I.L.G.W.U.), 214
International Socialist Review, 174
International Workingmen's Association (I.W.A.), 69–71, 79–80, 104–6, 139; North American Central Committee, 104–6, 139
Irish-American workers, 2, 20, 21, 98
Iron-boilers, and "wage slavery," 20
Italy, 225, 226

Jackson, Andrew, 76, 83, 323
Japanese-American workers, 143
Jefferson, Thomas, 76, 83, 125, 281
Jewish immigrants, 214
Jim-Crowism, 257–62
Job dissatisfaction, *Work in America* task force report on, 311–19
Johnson, Lyndon B., 269–70
Johnstown (Pa.), steel strike and, 205
Jones, Mother, 203–4
Journeymen, and conspiracy cases, 47–54

334

Index

Kapital, Das, 171
Kennedy, John F., 268n, 269–70
Kennedy, Robert F., 268n, 293
Knights of Labor, 81–85, 99–103, 119–21, 165, 323; and A.F. of L., 137–38, 140; General Assembly of, 82; Henry George speech to, 127–30; initiation and ritual of, 99–103; preamble to constitution of, 119–21
Knights of St. Crispin, 107–10

Labor (labor movement, workers), 1ff. *(see also* Unions and union movement); A.F. of L. and (1883–1929), 137–49, 150–52, 153–56; and agrarianism, 17, 20, 24–27, 60–62, 76, 79; anarchocommunists and, 80–81, 84–85, 122–26; and blacks, 63–66, 67–68, 69–71 *(see also* Blacks); C.I.O. and *(see* C.I.O.); Civil War (and postwar) era, 73–85, 86–91, 92–96, 97–98, 99ff.; and class consciousness, 73–85, 139–47; and communitarianism, 55–56, 57–59; and conspiracy laws and cases, 47–54; and democracy, 1–14, 15–21; and education *(see* Education); Garrison and, 32–37; Gompers-Hillquit debate on, 178–83; Henry George and, 127–30, 166–67; I.W.A. and, 79–80, 104–6, 139; Knights of Labor and *(see* Knights of Labor); Ludlow Massacre, 189–93; National Labor Union and, 75–77, 78, 82, 86, 91, 92–96, 97–98; National Trades' Union and, 41–42, 43–46; new world of (1947–74), 263–65ff.; and politics, 23–24 *(see also* Politics); and reform movements *(see* Reform movements); specific movements); and slavery, 67–68, 69–71; and socialist movement, 79–85 *(see also* Socialism); and strikes *(see* Strikes); violence by companies against, 250–51, 252–56; and women, 38–40 *(see also* Women); and worker attitudes and discontent, 311–19; workingmen's parties and, 15–21; and yellow-dog contracts, 194–95
Labor Board, FDR and, 211
Labor Movement in America (Ely), 122n
La Follette, Robert, Jr., 250. *See also* Senate Committee on Education and Labor, U. S.
Land rights and distribution, workers and, 17, 20, 24–27, 60–62, 76, 79, 83, 120, 123 *(see also* Agrarianism); Henry George and, 127–30
Landrum-Griffin Act (Labor Management Reporting and Disclosure Act), 268
Laundry Workers Union, 268
Lawson, John R., 189–93
Lewis, John L., 214–17, 218, 222, 327; and Akron (Ohio) sit-down strike, 229–32
Liberals, 266
Liberator, 32, 34
Liberia, black workers and, 169
Lick, James, 129–30
Lincoln, Abraham, 21, 69–71, 261
Litchfield, Paul, 231
Little Steel Strike (1937), 255
Living standards, 20, 272–73
Lloyd, Henry Demarest, 81
Local trade unions, 75
Lockouts, 3, 135, 148, 155; Taft-Hartley Act and, 276–78
Longshoremen's Union, 212, 265, 285
Lotteries, 22
Ludlow Massacre (1915), 189–93, 271

McClellan (John L.) committee hearings, 292–93, 294–97, 328
McCormick Harvester, and Haymarket Massacre, 84–85
McGovern, George, 275
McKenney, Ruth, 229
Man, The, 38n
Manual workers, society's view of, 313–14
Market economy, 18–21, 73, 74–75, 86–91. *See also* Capitalism
Marshall Plan, 286–87
Marx, Karl, 69, 79–80, 140, 163, 171–72
Marxists, 3, 4, 80–81; A.F. of L. and, 139–40
Mass media, view of manual workers by, 313–14
Mass-production (industrial) versus craft unionism, 213–19, 222–24, 225–28, 267
Matula, Frank, 297
Maurer, James, 205
Meany, George, 267, 269, 270n, 273, 274–75, 292, 298, 302, 327
Mechanics, and labor movement, 1–5ff., 18–21, 32–37, 44, 73, 120
Mechanics' Free Press, 28n
Melville, Herman, 52
Men and Steel (Vorse), 199–207

335

Index

Middle class, 8–9, 14, 122–26. *See also* Entrepreneurs; Tradesmen
Military-industrial complex, 270
Military service, mandatory, 16
Mill, James, 30
Miners, 2, 8, 10, 74, 78, 144, 147, 183, 187, 189–93, 194–95, 230 (*see also* specific kinds, unions); Ludlow Massacre, 189–93; yellow-dog contracts and, 194–95
Minneapolis (Minn.), truck drivers strike in, 212, 271
"Minority Report of the Resolutions Committee on Organization Policies" (A.F. of L. convention, 1935), 222–24
Mitchell, John, 174, 194–95
Molly Maguires, 78, 271, 324
Money (money policies), 75, 78, 83, 87, 94, 120, 121; greenback movement, 78–79, 83
Monopoly, 55, 57, 58, 133; land, 129 (*see also* Land rights and distribution; Property; Wealth)
Morgan, J. P., 184
Murray, Philip, 267n; and expulsion of Communists from the C.I.O., 286–87
Mussolini, Benito, 225–26
Muste, A. J., 210, 212

Nashoba, Tenn., 30
National Industrial Recovery Act (1933), 211–22, 216
National Laborer, 43n
National Labor Relations (Wagner) Act, 216, 217, 220–21, 245–47, 248–49, 250; Supreme Court decision on, 245–47, 248–49
National Labor Relations Board v. *Jones and Laughlin Steel Corporation*, 245n
National Labor Union (N.L.U.), 75–77, 78, 82, 86–91, 92–96, 97–98; constitution and "Declaration of Principles," 92–96
National Reform Party, 76–77, 83
National Trades' Union, 18, 19, 41–42, 82, 131–32, 133–34, 137, 138; constitution (1835 convention), 41–42; report (1836 convention), 43–46; and working women, 38–40
National Unemployment League, 210, 212
"Negro: His Relation to Southern Industry, The" (Winn), 168
Negroes. *See* Blacks
Negro National Labor Union, 97–99

New Deal, 210–12, 216, 218, 257, 264, 265, 276
New Era, The, 97n
New Harmony (Ind.) experiments, 30
New Left, 274
"New Life Begins for Auto Workers" (Vorse), 241n
New York Central Railroad, 109
New York City Working Men's Party, 16–17; and agrarianism, 24–27; "Committee of Fifty," 24–27
New York *Courier and Enquirer*, 47n
New York *Free Enquirer*, 22n, 30n
Nixon, Richard M., 270, 273, 275
Noble Order of the Knights of Labor, Local Assembly One, 82, 99–103

Oppressive Labor Practices Act, 252n
Organized labor (1947–74), 263–75ff. (*see also* Labor); A.F.L.-C.I.O. constitution, 288–90; criminality in, 267–69, 273–74, 291–93, 294–96; and expulsion of the Communists, 279–87; and Taft-Hartley Act (*see* Taft-Hartley Act); and worker discontent, 311–19
Our Land and Land Policy (George), 121n
Owen, Robert, 17, 30
Owen, Robert Dale, 17, 30

Parsons, Albert, 85
Pennsylvania Central Railroad, 109
People v. *Faulkner*, 47–51
"People at War, The" (Wright), 30–31
Perkins, George, 143
Phalanx, The, 55
Philadelphia and Reading Railroad, 114–18
Phillips, Wendell, 107–10, 281
Pinkerton, Robert A., 252
Pinkerton National Detective Agency, 252–53, 254
Police, company, 254–56
Politics (political activity), labor movement and, 1, 2, 6–7, 17, 22–23, 39, 109–10, 124, 174–77 (*see also* Voting; specific individuals, issues, parties); A.F. of L. and, 138, 146, 147–48; blacks and, 257–62; C.I.O. and, 209–10; Civil War era, 73, 78–79, 80; Debs on, 174–77; Knights of Labor and, 120; National Labor Union and, 92–93;

Index

new world of labor (1947–74) and, 263–75ff.; working men's parties and, 15–21
Populist movement, 79n
Potofsky, Jacob (Jack), 292
Poverty, 19, 24–27, 209–10, 272; Henry George on "crime" of, 127–30
Powderly, Terence V., 119n, 323
Presser, William, 297
Proceedings of the General Assembly of the Knights of Labor, 131n, 133n
Progress and Poverty (George), 79, 127
Proletariat, 2, 122–26, 137–49. *See also* Labor (labor movement, workers)
Property (property rights), labor and, 24–27, 60–62 (*see also* Capitalism; Land rights and distribution; Money; Wealth): anarchocommunists and, 122–26; Henry George on, 127–30
Provenzano, Anthony, 296–97
Public schools. *See* Education (schools)
Pullman, George M., 157–59
Pullman Palace Car Company strike, 141, 157–59, 160–62, 271, 325

Quill, Michael, 279, 283–84

Racism, labor movement and, 5–6, 14, 21, 63–66, 75, 97–98, 168–70, 196–98, 273 (*see also* Blacks); A.F. of L. and, 143, 298–301; A.F.L.-C.I.O. and, 298–301; civil-rights movement and, 273, 308–10; Randolph on A.F.L.-C.I.O. and, 298–301; Randolph's call for a march on Washington (1941) and, 257–62
Racketeering, union, 267–69
Radicals, 16, 17, 215, 274; (*see also* Revolution; specific individuals, issues, movements, parties); A.F. of L. and, 140, 141–42, 143–47
Railroads (railroad workers), 2, 18, 74, 109, 120, 128, 210, 263; strikes, 78, 111–18, 141, 157–59, 160–62
Randolph, A. Philip: on A.F.L.-C.I.O. and the blacks, 298–301; call for a march on Washington (1941) by, 257–62
Reeder, Frank, 114
Reform movements, 8, 14, 15–21, 22–23, 24–27 (*see also* specific individuals, issues, kinds, organizations, parties); A.F. of L. and (1883–1929), 137–49, 150–52, 153–56; and agrarianism (*see* Agrarianism); and blacks (*see* Blacks); C.I.O. and, 209–19, 222–24; Civil War and postwar era, unions and, 73–85, 86–91, 92–96, 97–98, 99–103, 104–6, 107–10, 111–18, 119–21, 122–26, 127–30, 131–32, 133–34; communitarianism and, 55–56, 57–59; Garrison on, 32–37; Henry George and, 127–30; Knights of Labor and (*see* Knights of Labor); new world of labor (1947–74) and, 263–75ff.; Reuther vs. A.F.L.-C.I.O. and, 302–7; socialist movement and (*see* Socialism; specific individuals, parties); worker discontent and, 311–19
Reform or Revolution (De Leon), 163n
Religious revivalism, 20
Report of Proceedings of the Fifty-fifth Annual Convention of the American Federation of Labor, 222n, 225n
Report of Proceedings of the First Annual Convention of the American Federation of Labor, 153n
Republican Party, 21, 60, 148, 264–65, 207n
Republic Steel Corporation, 255–56
Reuther, Walter, 218, 266, 267, 272; vs. the A.F.L.-C.I.O., 302–7; on criminality in organized labor, 291–93; and expulsion of Communists from the C.I.O., 281–83
Reuther brothers, 218
Revolution (revolutionaries), 3, 4, 10, 15, 25, 79–85, 163, 215 (*see also* Anarchists; Anarchocommunists; Radicals; Socialism; specific individuals, issues, movements, parties); A.F. of L. and, 140–47; anarchocommunists and, 80–81, 84–85, 122–26; I.W.W. and, 145–47; and land distribution, 62, 67; socialist movement and, 79ff. (*see also* Socialism; specific parties)
Richardson, Elliot L., 311
Rights of Man to Property, The (Skidmore), 24
Riots (violence), labor movement and. *See* Violence (riots)
Rockefeller, John D., Jr., 184, 189, 190–92, 193
Roosevelt, Franklin Delano, 210, 211,

Index

216, 239, 257, 259, 261, 265, 269; and Wagner Act, 248–49
Rubber workers, sit-down strike (1936) by, 229–38
Russia. *See* Soviet Union (Russia)

St. Louis *Republican*, 111
San Francisco (Calif.), longshoremen's strike in, 212, 271
Schools. *See* Education (schools)
Scott, Tom, 109
Second World War, 263
Selly, Joseph, 280–81
Senate Committee on Education and Labor, U. S., 150–52, 250–51, 252–56
Senate (McClellan) Committee on Government Operations, U. S., 268, 292–93, 294–97, 328
Shaw, Lemuel, 52
Single tax, Henry George and, 79, 129–30, 166–67
Sit-down strikes, 217, 326; General Motors and, 239–40, 241–44, 326; rubber workers (Akron), 229–38
Skidmore, Thomas, 24
"Slaveholders and the Working Men," 67–68
Slavery, 20–21, 35, 67–68, 69–71, 261, 323
Slavocracy, 81, 107–10, 267–68, 328
Sloan, Alfred P., 239–41
Slusser, Cliff, 230
Social Democratic Party, 160
Socialism (socialist movement), 7–8, 79–85, 86–96, 97–98, 99–103, 104–6, 107–10, 111–18, 119–21, 122–26, 144, 146, 148, 151–52, 163–67, 171–73, 185–86, 209–10, 212, 214, 218, 265, 266 (*see also* specific individuals, issues, parties); A.F. of L. and, 139–40, 141–42, 144–47, 151–52; Debs on, 174–77; Gompers on, 171–73, 178–83; Gompers-Hillquit debate on, 178–83; I.W.W. and, 145–47, 149, 184–88
Socialist Labor Party (S.L.P.), 7, 80, 81, 141–42, 163–67, 171–73, 174–77, 180, 185–86; and A.F. of L., 141–42, 144–47, 148, 163, 165–67, 180
Socialist Party of America, 6–7, 81, 144, 146, 148, 171–73, 174–77, 178–83, 185–86, 210; A.F. of L. and, 178–83; Gompers-Hillquit debate, 178–83
Socialist Trade and Labor Alliance, 163, 165

Social reforms. *See* Reform movements; specific individuals, kinds, movements, parties
Soil. *See* Land rights and distribution
Soviet Union (Russia), 148, 225, 226, 265, 266, 269, 286–87; Bolshevik Revolution, 147, 225
Spying (espionage), companies and, 212, 250–51, 252–56
"Statement by General Motors Corporation," 239
Statistical Abstract of the United States, 327
Steelworkers (steel industry), 147, 217, 218, 227–28; labor espionage and, 253, 255–56; strikes, 199–207, 271, 324–25
Stein, Bernard, 294–95
Stephens, Uriah S., 81–82, 99, 165
Strikes, 1, 2, 6, 9, 19, 55, 56, 77–78, 88, 111–18, 120, 135, 145, 157–59, 160–62, 199–207, 211–12, 215, 263, 271 (*see also* specific companies, individuals, places, unions); A.F. of L. and, 141, 144, 150, 155–56; company violence and, 250–51, 252–56 (*see also* Violence); conspiracy laws and trials, 47–51; Knights of Labor and, 83–85; Ludlow Massacre and, 189–93; sit-down, 217, 229–38, 239–40, 241–44; Taft-Hartley Act and, 264, 276–78; Wagner Act and, 216, 217, 220–21, 245–47, 248–49, 250
Students (young workers), and job discontent and attitudes, 315–17, 319
Supply and demand, labor and, 44–45, 73–74, 75
Supreme Court decisions: *Griggs v. Duke Power*, 308–10; *Hitchman Coal and Coke Co. v. Mitchell*, 194–95; and Wagner Act, 216–17, 220, 245–47, 248–49
Sylvis, William H., 86–91

Taft, William H., 143
Taft-Hartley Act, 264–65, 276–78; text of, 276–78
Tailors, journeymen, and conspiracy cases, 47–51
Tane, Mack, 294–95, 296
Taxation, Henry George and, 79, 128–29, 166–67
Teamsters Union, 268, 272, 274, 294–97
Television, view of workers on, 313–14

338

Index

Thirty Years of Labor (Powderly), 119n
Toledo (Ohio), Auto-Lite strike in, 212, 271
Tradesmen, 3, 85. *See also* Entrepreneurs; Middle class
Trade unions. *See* Unions and union movement; specific industries, unions
Trade Union Unity League, 210
Trotskyists, 9, 212, 218, 265
Truck drivers' strike, 212
True Workingman, 60n
Truman, Harry S, 263–64, 265, 266n, 276

Unemployment, 79, 127, 209–10, 263–64, 269; racism and, 298–301 (*see also* Racism); violence and (*see under* Violence)
Union Society of Journeymen Tailors, 47–51
Unions and union movement, xvii–xviii, 1–14, 15–21, 81–85 (*see also* Labor; specific aspects, individuals, issues, unions); A.F. of L. and, 137–49, 150–52, 153–56, 168–70; A.F.L.-C.I.O. and, 267–75; and blacks (*see* Blacks); C.I.O. and (1935–41), 209–10, 222–24; Civil War and postwar era, 69–71, 73ff., 104–6, 107–10, 111–18, 119–21, 122–26; communitarianism and, 55–56, 57–59; company violence and, 250–51, 252–56 (*see also* Violence); conspiracy laws and cases, 47–51; craft versus mass-production (industrial) principle and, 213–19, 222–24, 225–28; criminality in, 267–69, 273–74, 291–93, 294–96; expulsion of Communists from (1949), 279–87; I.W.W. and, 145–47, 179, 184–88; Knights of Labor and, 179–83; National Trades' Union and, 41–42, 43–46; new world of labor (1947–74) and, 263–75ff.; socialist movement and (*see* Socialism; specific issues, parties); and strikes (*see* Strikes); and worker discontent and attitudes, 311–19; and yellow-dog contracts, 194–95
United Automobile, Aircraft and Agricultural Implement Workers of America, 291n
United Auto Workers (U.A.W.), 213, 217–18, 266, 272, 275, 281, 291–93, 302–7, 328; and General Motors sit-down strike, 239–40, 241–44
United Electrical, Radio and Machine Workers of America, 284
United Mine Workers of America (U.M.W.), 144, 148, 185, 214–16, 229; and Ludlow Massacre, 189–93; and yellow-dog contracts, 194–95
United States Steel Company, 200, 205, 217
United States Strike Commission, *Report on the Chicago Strike of June-July 1894*, 157n, 160n
U.R.W.A., 230
Utopianism, 20

Vietnam War, 302. *See also* Indochina
Violations of Free Speech and Rights of Labor, 250n
Violence (riots): against labor by companies, 250–51, 252–56; racial (East St. Louis), 196, 197; and strikes, 111–18, 189–93, 199–207, 212 (*see also* Strikes); and unemployment, 77–79, 81–85, 111–18
Vorse, Mary Heaton, on the General Motors sit-down strike (1937), 241–46; on the steel strike (1919), 199–207
"Vote Yourself a Farm" (Evans), 60–62
Voting (ballot, elections), labor and, 78–79, 80, 98, 176–77 (*see also* Politics); blacks and, 68; and land distribution, 60–62; unions and, 268

Wages (wage system), 16, 20, 45, 55–56, 57–58, 73, 74–75, 86, 88, 89, 90, 120, 191, 201, 211, 271n, 272, 275; A.F. of L. and, 147, 148; Henry George on, 127–30; Knights of Labor and, 133–34, 135; sit-down strikes and, 229–38, 239–40, 241–44
Wagner Act. *See* National Labor Relations (Wagner) Act
Washington (D.C.), Randolph's call for a march by blacks on (1941), 257–62
Wealth, 24–27, 32–37, 107–10, 119–21, 271
West, Robert, 32
Western Federation of Miners, 144
White-collar workers, 270, 275; and

Index

job dissatisfaction and attitudes, 312, 314–15
Wickes, Thomas H., 157
Wilson, Woodrow, 146, 189
Winn, Will H., 168
Women (women workers), 13, 14, 18, 38–40, 76, 133–34, 177; discontent, 319; rights, 13, 14; wages, 148
Workers' Alliance, 210
Workers' Ex-Servicemen's League, 210
Work in America (H.E.W. task force report), 311–19
Working class. *See* Labor
"Working Class Politics" (Debs), 174–77
Working Man's Advocate, 24n, 57n
"Working Men and Agrarianism," 24–27
"Working Men and Politics," 22–23
"Working Men and the Public Schools," 28–29

"Working Men and Women," 38–40
Working men's parties, 15–21; and agrarianism, 24–27; Frances Wright and, 30–31; Garrison on, 32–37; National Trades' Union and (*see* National Trades' Union); and politics, 22–23; and public schools, 28–29; women and, 38–40
World war. *See* First World War; Second World War
Wright, Frances ("Fanny"), 16–17, 30–31
Wurf, Jerry, 317

Yankelovich, Daniel, 315–16
Yellow-dog contracts, 148, 194–95
Youngstown Sheet and Tube Company, 255
Youth (young workers), and job discontent and attitudes, 315–17, 319